PHILADELPHIA GAY NEWS

SEASONS

of the

HEART

SEASONS

of the

HEART

Men and Women Talk about
Love, Sex, and Romance after 60

Zenith Henkin Gross

63   June 2, 2018
August 10, 2018   2,276

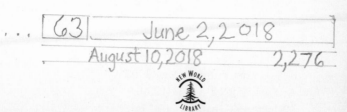

NEW WORLD LIBRARY
NOVATO, CALIFORNIA

New World Library
14 Pamaron Way
Novato, California 94949

Copyright © 2000 by Zenith Henkin Gross
Edited by Gina Misiroglu
Author photo by Michael Ian
Cover design by Mary Ann Calser
Text design and typography by Mary Ann Casler

All rights reserved. This book may not be reproduced in whole or in part,
or transmitted in any form, without written permission from the publisher,
except by a reviewer who may quote brief passages in a review; nor may
any part of this book be reproduced, stored in a retrieval system, or transmitted in any form or by any means electronic, mechanical,
photocopying, recording, or other, without written
permission from the publisher.

Pages 249 and 250 are an extension of the copyright page.

Library of Congress Cataloging-in-Publication Data
Gross, Zenith Henkin.
Seasons of the heart : men and women talk about love, sex, and romance
after 60 / by Zenith Henkin Gross.
p. cm.
Includes bibliographical references.
ISBN 1-57731-108-6 (alk. paper)
1. Aged — United States — Sexual behavior — Case studies. 2. Love in
old age. I Title.

HQ55.G76 2000
306.7'084'6—dc21   99-086971

First Printing, May 2000
ISBN 1-57731-108-6
Printed in Canada on acid-free paper
Distributed to the trade by Publishers Group West

10 9 8 7 6 5 4 3 2 1

LA-2001-17-7

In Sid's Memory
For Bud — and for the special people
whose love centers my life:
Katherine, Peter, Larry, Rose, Ken,
Melinda, and Spencer, Sonya, and Langdon

Contents

Preface   ix

Introduction   1

Chapter 3

Chapter 4

Chapter 5

Chapter 6

Preface

When I turned sixty, I remember thinking, "this is really different."
I have the feeling we don't know much about old age.

— Ursula K. Le Guin, author

Americans need a new old age. And not just Americans. We need a new culture of aging around the world. In Japan, life expectancy is eighty; in Canada, seventy-nine; in the United States, seventy-seven. People who are 100 years and older make up the fastest-growing segment of the population in many developed countries. In the twentieth century, we added thirty years to U.S. life spans; who knows what the next century will bring in extended life?

But, as Le Guin said, we know very little about these added

years, which arrived almost unnoticed in the life of humanity, just as age sometimes arrives as a surprise in the life of the individual.

"Older," said American financier Bernard Baruch, "is fifteen years ahead of my chronological age right now." (He lived to be ninety-five.)

We know much more about the first few years of life — when variations among normal infants are actually smaller than the wide variations in health and strength among the elderly — than we do about the "third age," which is often shrouded in myth, stereotype, denial, and badly outdated ideas and attitudes.

The complex realities of a new old age demand we take a fresh look at all the elements that might make for growth, for what is now being called, by geriatricians and religious leaders, "conscious aging." Those elements include health, material sustenance, connection to others, and community supports in recreation, leisure, and learning.

Key among these elements is a simple, but profound, one: Love.

One of the strongest supports in the storms of life has always been the adult love relationships that exist between married spouses, gay or straight lovers, romantic friends, or close companions.

But it is a sad reality that our age-fearful society would deny love, sex, and romance to people because of their age.

It is a cruel tenet of conventional wisdom, often widely accepted and believed by elders themselves, that love in all its forms — passionate, mellow, friendly — is reserved for the young, fit, and beautiful.

When one is no longer in any of these categories, one's love life is over, or should be, because such feelings are now deemed pathetic, inappropriate, or embarrassing. People older than sixty are supposed to be "beyond all that."

This social prejudice is not true of all cultures, but is largely true in the youth-obsessed United States. It was not a problem in our great-grandparents' day — people generally didn't live that long.

The facts that can overturn these prejudices are now in hand, compiled by researchers in a variety of disciplines including medicine, gerontology, developmental psychology, social work, and psychiatry.

A growing body of evidence shows that sexual impulses and desires last to the end of life, and the need for tender touch, intimate words, and sensuous caresses remains to the last breath.

"If I had a sex partner, I would be first in line for Viagra," said a 101-year-old man interviewed about the new anti-impotence drug. "Yes," said the leading character in a Ruth Prawer Jhabvala short story, "I, an old woman, a grandmother many times over — I hunger and burn! And for whom? For an old man."

In fact, for the last quarter century, a community of researchers — quite hidden from popular view — has been trying to tap society on the shoulder and say, "Pss-t, look, really look at these older people; they are infinitely more varied than you think and they are living in ways far different from your conventional beliefs about them."

Pioneers in this group include Robert N. Butler, M.D., the Pulitzer Prize–winning author of *Why Survive? Being Old in America* and chairman of the first medical school geriatrics department in America, and Richard J. Cross, M.D., medical educator and professor emeritus of human sexuality at the Robert Wood Johnson Medical School, New Jersey. These men have been talking and writing for more than two decades about the reality that older people remain capable of love relationships in many forms to the very end. Twenty years ago, Dean Ornish, M.D., of California, originated a program of exercise and diet for heart patients that he said reversed coronary disease, but after several years, he became aware that something else was vital to his patients' well-being. His later book is titled *Love and Survival.*

And in the 1980s, another unusually humane and perceptive point of view was expressed by Susan Rice, Ph.D., of the social work department at California State University at Long Beach. Dr. Rice wrote that intensely important issues of intimacy and sexuality for older women need to be more closely addressed. "We must normalize sex for the elderly," she wrote, and have more "creative strategies" for becoming sensitive to their needs.

But Drs. Butler, Cross, Rice, and their colleagues were talking to a public deaf to their pleas for dealing with the coming longevity revolution. "There's a new kind of energy that comes from late life, a new freedom. Unfortunately, few in our society understand that," said Maggie Kuhn, founder of the Gray Panthers and trailblazing advocate for older Americans.

Our society, instead, has settled comfortably into a corporate-driven economy that sees profits only in the eighteen to forty-nine age group, as explained by a TV executive (who will remain anonymous). He said, when interviewed on the "problem" of an aging viewership, "people over fifty are not valuable" to advertisers.

We can see some of this changing slowly, but we can also see that ancient stereotypes die hard, and now, unfortunately, there are new stereotypes joining the old ones.

Now people sixty and older must deal with two stereotypes. They are seen either as ill, ugly, sexless, useless, and dependent (only 5 percent of people over sixty need institutional care) or as extraordinary specimens, superathletes, hang gliding at eighty-five, climbing mountains at ninety, and routinely running and swimming in marathons in their seventies.

In addition, the new stereotype calls for them to have only two interests in life: their health and their finances. Vital as health and money are to livable later years, they are not the only concerns of older people, who still anguish over their children's problems, enjoy old and new friendships, and have other human ties besides those to doctors and bankers. In reality, of course, most people past sixty lead immensely diverse and multidimensional lives on a continuum that runs from total frailty to total athletic stardom.

While conventional attitudes hold that older people experience nothing but loss and decline, recent contemporary research shows just the opposite. Older people learn how to regulate their emotions and deal with life's problems better than younger people, and so experience a certain measure of real serenity. People's emotional lives get richer, deeper, and better controlled, according to Professor Robert W. Levenson, director of the Institute of Personality and Social Research at the University of California, Berkeley, whose studies have shown certain emotional abilities — to understand poignancy, to be able to reminisce productively — can usually only be achieved in later years.

The MacArthur Foundation Research Network on Successful Mid-Life Development has found that happiness actually increases in a person's sixties and seventies over what it was in earlier years. The life satisfaction people express when they become grandparents, put their work struggles behind them, and have some time for their marriage is often quite marked.

These scientific findings were confirmed by the informal responses I encountered in my own interviews with a much smaller number of respondents. When I, as an older woman and an experienced journalist, decided to investigate the new country of love and aging, I found that one of the strongest predictors of how well people withstand all the blows of later life is how connected they are to people, to animals, to nature, and to interests of all kinds.

When I began to enter the world of aging lovers, I consulted the writings of others before me and found they fall primarily into two modes: a chirpy optimism and opaque sunniness like that found in fairy tales or a mood so elegiac, or so dark and tragic, that there was no room to enjoy the time left, or to rest and survey the view from further up the mountain, a view that reflects both sadness and joy.

How I structured my investigation of the real love lives of real people is outlined in the introduction that follows, but I can share one observation here:

In the hundreds of conversations I had with women and men from sixty to ninety-three, I found the strength, the gallantry, the matter-of-fact courage and stoicism, the humor, and the ordinary goodness of people inspiring and poignant. All of life and love does, indeed, seem "to grow dearer near the dark," as poet Archibald Macleish wrote in his poem, "The Old Gray Couple."

Many people I met are determined to proceed "without nightfall upon the spirit," as eighty-three-year-old Quaker leader Mary C. Morrison put it. They will do this in spite of illness, loss, and poverty (many members of both minority and majority elder communities are experts on poverty). Not even an uncaring and negligent society could succeed in turning most of my interview subjects into victims. Some were victims, yes, but the life force beat strongly in a senior center where older Chicanas earn money crocheting, in a homeless shelter where an aged black street musician played piano for noontime free meals, and in college classrooms where older middle- and upper-class people met to write memoirs and rescue history. Some, at all levels of society, were victimized by forces beyond their control (as are many young people), but the ones I talked with planned to soldier on as long as possible. In William Faulkner's eloquent words, they not only endure, they prevail. They seem to be establishing the right of older people to an affectional life up to the end as a new sort of "human right."

It is a privilege to share their stories — tender, raunchy, funny, interesting, and sad, too — and to outline the ways they have constructed their identities — their very souls — as older people experiencing love in all its guises.

Introduction

Past, Present, and Future

Time is like an enterprising manager, always bent on staging some new and surprising production, without knowing very well what it will be.
— George Santayana

When my husband died, I did not think of suicide. I did not, in fact, think of anything much at all. My mind was a frozen, black void with a gray scrim around the edges, through which I dimly saw the figures of our beloved children, and occasionally the shadows of passing friends.

Most who have lost a longtime life partner have been in an emotional earthquake. Familiar landmarks crash down in piles of debris, and the survivor crawls out of the rubble to see what

1

looks like the landscape of the moon — gray, dead, pitted with craters. Even those who had long since ceased to love their companions find it hard to regain their footing in a world now so changed.

In the first intense period of grieving, the last thing most people can think about is how to reconstruct their lives or where they fit in this new world. The fact that they share this period of shock and disorientation with hundreds of thousands of others has no real meaning to them. I certainly did not know or care that women of my age are widowed three times more often than our male contemporaries or that half of all women over sixty-five in the United States are widows.

None of these facts meant anything to me; I only knew that the man I thought I would grow old with on Golden Pond was gone after forty-three years of passionate, loving marriage. However, I felt — amid the incoherent jumble of emotions — that there was still something I was obligated to do, and that was to not make life any more difficult for my three children and their spouses than the sorrow of losing a beloved parent had already done.

This wish not to cause them any more heartache was the duty that kept me alive and in some semblance of function, for I did not want to rupture their lives further by making them come and balance my checkbook or figure out what was wrong with the car. Grief work seemed so unendurably hard that I sought, and found, life-giving help in working with a clinical psychologist from the medical center where my husband had been cared for; she specialized in working with cancer survivor families. Seeing her was the first step toward moving beyond the paralyzing shock and deep depression. Another important step was being with affectionate couples who were longtime friends, and who somehow, brave in their own grief over losing my husband, were able to confront the empty chair at a restaurant table for four with caring patience.

I slowly began to stumble along some personal path to survival, helped by the understanding and support of my children and friends. That survival was to be a solitary one; never in my wildest plans did I ever think of sharing my life again.

I was grateful that good friends never allowed me to drop off their social radars, a fate that, I learned later, befalls many widows. Hearing how unusual it was to be included with couples, and looking back on it now, it seems odd that a man who has lost his wife and is single again is seen as a free spirit, daring and adventurous, and much sought after, while a widow or a divorcée is seen as a lost soul, crying pitifully in the wilderness for rescue.

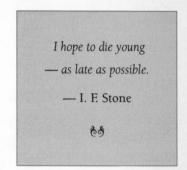

I hope to die young

— as late as possible.

— I. F. Stone

I was not crying in the wilderness; I was trying to focus on work and on the bittersweet news of the expected first grandchild. That would be the new little soul that my husband always assumed he would hold in his arms some day; his death at sixty-three made that image a vanished dream. I was left alone to become "Grandma" without the "Grandpa" of our middle-aged family fantasies.

It was shortly after this grandson's birth, that I was astonished to find that not only had I not destroyed myself in grief or anger, but that I was vividly alive.

Dancing after Hours

For me, the new path I trod with a new love in my sixties and seventies was an astonishing surprise — sweet and wonderful in many ways, scary and risky in others, like most of life and love.

There are as many ways of beginning on this path as there are couples; first meetings can take place in a great many different ways and settings, but one thing is constant: happiness in love or romantic friendships can alight on your shoulder when your gaze is off in another direction completely, as happened in my new life.

It was in a very ordinary way that my current life companion, Richard, and I re-met after having been longtime casual acquaintances. Richard and his late wife had been known to us for many years at a little New England summer colony where we both had cottages. We did that kind of easy socializing typical of people who seldom see each other except during "the season."

Richard was better friends with my husband over those many years than with me because he lived next door to one of my husband's fishing friends, and the three men would spend soft summer dusks cleaning fish and discussing the state of the world, sharing cold beer and politics on his neighbor's porch.

When Richard lost his wife, he did what many men (and not so many women) do in these cases; he quickly sold the summer cottage and moved back to California where he had once worked and where his three children were making their lives and families. He knew nothing of my husband's death until five years afterward when, on a sentimental journey back to "the summer place," he learned from his former neighbor of our family's loss. He asked to pay a condolence call, and we became reacquainted after the losses, tragedies, and absences we both had endured. I was nearly sixty-six then and he was nearly seventy.

Was it love at first sight for both of these bereaved spouses, presumed to be lonely and desperate for companionship?

Not at all.

Neither of us was "lonely" as that is usually understood. We were both intensely sad about the absence of the special people who had been at the center of our lives. But each of us had children, grandchildren, and friends, as well as siblings and other family members who included us on trips and holiday visits.

What did — slowly — bring us together was the dawning realization that each of us was the only person the other had encountered who, at roughly the same age and stage in life, understood what we had lost and what that loss had done to us.

Another strong bond was our summertime tie to the Island

where we both had so many happy years, where my children had grown up working in the seaside restaurants and shops, and where his son had spent his honeymoon. Before I re-met Richard, none of the men I had dated in the intervening years seemed to have the slightest understanding of my heart's link to that special place that held the youth of my children and where my husband now slept in the beautiful little rural cemetery. Only Richard, whose wife was also buried there, seemed to understand. People thought that was a morbid coincidence, but we found it comforting and helpful in sharing feelings and memories.

It took a number of meetings — long walks and quiet dinners, sometimes at my home, sometimes with mutual friends, occasionally just the two of us in the corner of a restaurant — before I saw, not through a mist of tears and memories, but through the clear spectacles of *now*, that Richard was an especially nice friend. He was intelligent, charming, supremely witty, and able to comprehend *my* life in a way that only age peers can do. We had other bonds — both of us had been journalists and book authors. His field was humor writing (one of life's best defenses against pain) and he had published two comic novels as part of a long writing career. He dubbed us "the last defenders of the alphabet" and we united as fellow soldiers in the battle against what we feared (perhaps wrongly) might be an electronic war on books.

He, too, seemed to be beginning to see me for the first time, not as he had always seen me before in my role as wife, mother, and Island hostess, but as a woman alone, trying to put back together the pieces of my life and reconnect with all the important people I cared about — children, close friends, and my own mother, now in her nineties, who needed my attention.

Learning the Music Again

Whether you are male or female, love blossoms differently when we are older.

We are so amazed to be laughing again, to be seeing life

with that freshness of the other's vision, to (timidly at first) think of ourselves as part of a couple, that some of the other elements of rapture do not come into play at once. For older lovers, finding the seasons in color again — after the blackness of death and emptiness of the world — is astounding enough at first.

But, of course, sex and romance do come into the picture when a level of easy comfort and certainty are reached. What helps friends become lovers is that they *know* each other in a reassuring way, if only later in a passionately sexual way. And it surprises young people to learn that older couples, when they newly meet, or re-meet as we did, have to think about what sexual life in the beginning of the twenty-first century is really like. The question now is the same for lovers of all ages: Do we know who this person is?

Now we are in an era that includes AIDS, secret drug use, and many threats to what, as younger lovers, we used to think of as blissfully exuberant, ecstatic lovemaking with few deadly consequences. Recent reports from medical authorities show that AIDS is on the rise among older people. Latest figures show that those over fifty account for about 10 percent of all new cases in this country each year.

A new candor marked not only my life with a new partner, but has marked nearly all the men and women whose lives I touched for this book. With some amusement, a seventy-six-year-old Arizona man told me that his Valentine gift to a new woman companion was his HIV-negative lab report. She reciprocated with a negative one of her own.

I was surprised at how many people told me they handled these new late-life challenges by sharing with new partners their sexual histories and past intimacies. This was surprising because this was the generation that had been raised to be reticent, even secretive, about sex in general, and certainly about their personal lives.

When Richard and I joined our lives, admittedly in an unconventional way for our generation, we knew something about each other, but still had to catch up on our lives in the years we were out of touch.

The emergence of love and sex that slowly took place had its own share of hurdles to overcome; there are beloved ghosts present when widows and widowers come together, and it took me a long time to cease feeling "unfaithful" to my late husband, while Richard struggled with guilt about mistakes in his late wife's medical care that he felt he had failed to perceive in time.

Living with these realities, love grew more slowly, steadily, and deeply than is typical for wildly optimistic, generally fearless young people. Our progress toward the bedroom door was more like adult marathon race walkers than the wobbly running in all directions of young lovers. Other older lovers, under the lash of time, may move more quickly than we did.

"I don't just seize the day — I seize the hour," said one vivacious seventy-nine-year-old woman interviewed in a retirement community in California.

Although our intimate time is as important and exciting to us as to couples half our age, Richard and I have decided, because of the pulls of our children and grandchildren in widely separated cities on two coasts and because of the financial and legal complications of a marriage contract, to have a "commuting" unmarried romance in which we each stay in our comfortable homes with our established family-friends network and go back and forth to each other as much as possible.

We try to share as much of each other's lives and families as we can, and believe that our commitment to each other is no longer about family-and-home building as when we were young, but rather to help each other age as gracefully and with as much joy, health, and dignity as possible.

Not all couples wish for this kind of relatively unstructured relationship; many find a return to daily domestic life exactly what they want, and they hasten to contract a legal marriage as soon as possible, both to comply with convention and to meet their own personal needs. Richard's and my story is only one of tens of thousands, and we are aware that not all such arrangements succeed; quite a few end in disappointment, even anger, some in sorrow and new losses that are hard to bear with less time left.

However, in the chapters to follow, you will find hopeful stories that are both the same as ours and different in many ways. There will be stories of those who have been together for the whole journey, as well as those with new loves who have been willing to risk loss again. Stories of love and longing belong to every age and there will be some with a truth you sense with your heart, and some others that will blaze brand new trails for you to consider as you enter this new terrain of older love.

Mapping the New High Country

This book is about love in the lives of older women and men, seen against the backdrop of rushing time that moves them beyond the busy middle years to new experiences and adventures as they age.

It is about Brenda L., seventy-six, who is married for the third time after being widowed twice and who says her third marriage is the only one that has been profoundly happy and sexually fulfilling.

It is about Miriam G., sixty-seven, who will be celebrating her forty-fifth wedding anniversary soon and still believes her husband is the sweetest, nicest man she has ever met. She says he is also her satisfying lover and best friend.

It is about Carol B., who had an unhappy youthful marriage in which she suffered torment and abuse, and who thought herself lucky to escape with her life. She managed single parenthood and a job successfully for many years. Now at sixty-two, she is living a new life with a beloved partner, a man of

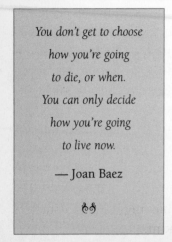

You don't get to choose how you're going to die, or when. You can only decide how you're going to live now.

— Joan Baez

seventy-one, who, she says, "has shown me what love and joy can be. I never get over my surprise that this has happened to me after so many years!"

The book is also about Joyce T., who after a long conventional marriage that produced several children and grandchildren, came out as a lesbian, and now, at sixty-four, is living with a woman companion of sixty-eight, in a monogamous relationship that is both a shield against the slings and arrows of discrimination and a comfort, as their seventies loom on the horizon. Three of Joyce's children and all of her four grandchildren accept the new love; her ex-husband and one son do not.

And then there is Lillian R., who at seventy-two, lost her husband of fifty years, and now, three years later, still is filled with anger, loneliness, and ambivalence about friendship or romance with men friends.

Most of the women I interviewed for this book, even when they were coping with physical problems of varying degrees of seriousness, did not want to be deprived of a vision of themselves as alert, alive, and in the world. They don't want to be pushed into "post" categories. They are post-menopausal, but certainly not post-sexual. They may be post-raising-kids, but they are not post-family; indeed, many of them still bear family responsibilities. They may be post-three-inch-heels, but they are not post-beauty.

In spite of the fact that men generally no longer make eye contact with them on the street, hard hats don't whistle at them, and waiters ignore them when dining alone, most older women are insisting on letting the world know they are ready for the pleasure of a kiss or a caress that comes from someone other than their dearest children or friends.

To answer famed psychoanalyst Sigmund Freud's question, "What do women want?": these women want to be recognized as possible romantic partners in a situation where warmth, kindness, and wit across a candlelit table might be as attractive as being the toast of the beach in a bikini.

Just as the way we are getting older is changing, so the experiences that men and women report in this most intimate arena of life are changing.

Why Women First?

This book is written about women first and their partners — both gay and straight — because late love is more problematical for women than for men, although getting older in youth-crazed America is hard on both genders.

The late writer Diana Trilling, the widow of author Lionel Trilling, when alone in her eighties and nearly blind, said, "Everyone knows that any man who wants a wife can have one, younger than himself if that is what he looks for. No man, whatever his age, need be alone...loneliness, that is for widows." This may be so not only because of the overabundance of single women in these age groups, but also because of the double shadows of ageism and sexism that have followed women from adolescence to old age.

A seventy-year-old man can wear "arm candy" — a woman half his age, and society does not blink an eye; in fact, he gets overt approval from other men. But a woman of seventy having dinner with a thirty-five- or forty-year-old man is assumed to be his mother, since a younger man could not possibly be romantically interested in a woman that much older. (This despite the fact that Gray Panther founder Maggie Kuhn said, when she was in her eighties, that "a lovely thing" in her earlier life was that she once had a lover forty years younger than herself.) The younger man–older woman scenario is changing, but at an excruciatingly slow pace.

Fay Weldon, the British novelist and short story writer, who is married to a man eighteen years her junior, put it this way: "Because I'm past sixty doesn't mean that I am past the period of wanting romance in my life. There is no contradiction between being mature and being romantic." Slightly tongue-in-cheek, she pointed out the advantages of being with a younger man: "He's an improvement over men who were not raised to believe that women were human."

Ageism, which Kuhn defined as "the notion that people become inferior because they have lived a specified number of years," is allied with rampant sexism in the lives of older women.

This double whammy comes down particularly hard on physical appearance. Women sustain an assault on their self-worth, when they are no longer young, slim, and pretty, that is almost unbelievable. Since many women themselves have accepted that love, romance, and sex are only for the youthfully spandexed, they frequently put themselves on the shelf before anyone can do it to them.

But I found in exploring the love lives of older women and their partners that a lively revolt against this stereotype is underway and that women are living many varieties of love — from wildly sexual to warmly sedate — to the end of life and behind society's back. From one end of the U.S. (and Canada, too) to the other — in retirement communities, in high-rise condos, in modest cottages — older women and their partners are joyously breaking down the stereotypes and myths.

Because I have been a journalist for more than forty years and had already published a book on family relations, I set out to try to find out how elders are changing the stereotypes of aging love, doing away with the sexless, mindless images, and shattering the myths that older lovers are "above all that."

My own experience of late-life loss and new love made it possible for me, at seventy-four, to talk easily with the candid and articulate women and men who were willing to share their personal lives with me. Of course, not everyone turned out to be comfortable talking of intimate matters. Some said they would like to be interviewed, but when the subject veered to actual personal stories, they withdrew from the project.

Many who were willing to talk at some length were honest about the disappointments and failures of late romance, when, in many cases, the task of meshing past lives just proved too difficult, or incompatibilities were as real as when younger couples can't make it work. In some cases, the risks of ill health or money worries exacted higher prices in emotional energy than they could pay. And believe it or not, sexual and emotional predators roam among the elderly as well as among younger people.

But as I listened to these elders, I came to believe that my own and my companion's rich and complex story is not unique, or even rare. I came to believe that many older women, right into their nineties, want, need, and will manage to have either love or romantic friendships in all their infinite variety — erotic, playful, companionable, sweetly mellow — in just the same ways their love styles varied when young.

A Word about the Men

Although, as we have seen, women encounter aging in painful collisions with the fantasies of an ever-youthful America, the calendar is not kind to older men, either, and they face some special problems in the new world of late-life love relationships. In the chapters to follow, male readers may recognize themselves in that world of loneliness and rootlessness that an older man who is widowed or divorced inhabits — often to his restless dismay.

While it is true that older men are at a premium because of the superabundance of single older women, they often have not cultivated the network of friendships and social contacts that women put together throughout their lives. Older men frequently have left friendships, community activities, and child raising to their wives, while concentrating almost completely on their work lives and perhaps, if lucky, a few hobbies or sports interests. This is especially true of the men now in their seventies and beyond who were brought up in the era of "separate spheres" for the genders — where husbands made the living and wives handled most of the human relations, so that even their ties to their children need renewed attention.

So, while I wrote first about women and the heavy burdens of ageism and sexism they carry, this book is also about men like Philip S., now seventy-nine, who believed his wife of forty-eight years was his irreplaceable "golden girl," but yet was so despairingly lonely after her death, that he answered a "personals" ad in a newspaper with the happiest of results. He now lives, unmarried, with a charming widow who had advertised herself as "an outdoor person in the summer and an indoor reader by the fire in the winter."

It's about Doug F., who wanted only to remarry as quickly as possible after his divorce, and yet because all the social contacts had been made by his wife, was bewildered about plunging into the new world of dating as he neared eighty. "I was AWOL during the sexual revolution," said this wry, candid World War II veteran. He was pushed and prodded by his children to go to his college reunion and similar events, and began to be a faithful "Uncle Doug" at weddings and first communions of nieces and nephews and their children. Doug met Dolly, a twice-widowed seventy-year-old, at a mutual friend's second, late-life wedding and they have been happily married for two years.

Ernie T., sixty-nine, although quick to begin socializing after his wife's death, did not enjoy Doug's success with a new partner. He had two or three brief relationships after becoming a widower, but none seemed to work out. At the time of his interview, he had, at least temporarily, decided against seeking a new long-term commitment and was dating only occasionally.

Victor S. was widowed at eighty and has astonished his family by taking excellent care of himself, including looking after his home, his personal needs, and his health. He is rightly considered by his children and grandchildren to be unusual among men of his generation in his skill with household chores. Victor is a fine cook and invites friends for dinner regularly. He is not especially interested, at this time, in seeking a new relationship. His coping skills are especially surprising because his late wife was a top-notch homemaker in the earlier mode of her generation, who did virtually all the cooking and household tasks during their fifty-one years together.

Men as partners, singles, lovers, husbands, and pals will tell their stories, too, in the pages to follow.

Conducting the Inquiry

My interview group was made up of 230 women and 112 men, between the ages of sixty and ninety-three, mostly white, mostly middle-class, with a small percentage of women of color and Asian and Hispanic women and men. This core group was augmented by briefer, less personal discussions with another sixty men and women about general thoughts on aging and love, not necessarily about the details of their own experiences, but what they saw in society as a whole.

It is important to stress that these groups are not in any way scientific, representative samples of the American population as the new millennium unfolds; they were chosen by what statisticians call "a sample of convenience," which simply means that I began my outreach by going to the obvious places: senior centers, class reunions of high school and college graduates who marked fortieth and fiftieth year meetings, retirement communities featuring centralized social gatherings where many older couples could be visited in a short time, adult education classes in a variety of settings, and even athletic events featuring senior participants. My interviews represent "snapshots" of people at a given moment in their lives in a particular setting.

Of course, my own circle of friends, family members, and colleagues were eager to help and I found that having them provide introductions and leads to elders they knew or had heard about meant a widening set of ripples in the pond.

During the five years I worked on the book, not all interviews were face-to-face; some were done through letters, Internet chat rooms, long-distance telephone interviews, and the use of diaries and memoirs that some women were willing to share as we sat together, or communicated by fax and phone. Because it took so long and the geography covered was widely spaced — from California to Florida and in major cities and suburbs on both coasts and in the Midwest — the lives of some respondents changed as we were working together. Some who were interviewed for the chapter on long-running marriages became widows or widowers in the interval; others who had been alone after widowhood or divorce, embarked on new relationships; and some of the men encountered sharp changes in their patterns — retirement, divorce, or health problems — but continued to be interested in my inquiries and some wanted to stay in contact about their own experiences.

All my respondents were guaranteed anonymity if they wished it, so some names, locations, and occupations are changed, though the stories are true and largely in their own words. Where the name is a pseudonym, I use only an invented first name and an initial; those who did not mind the use of their real names are given their actual names in full.

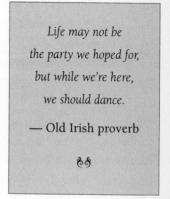

Life may not be

the party we hoped for,

but while we're here,

we should dance.

— Old Irish proverb

Cultural barriers are high in many minority communities when it comes to sharing intimate, personal information with strangers. I found that establishing trust and understanding with women from Hispanic, Asian, and African American communities was not difficult in woman-to-woman ordinary sociability terms, but reaching into deeply personal domains was a daunting and not very easily accomplished task. Trustworthiness and sensitivity take a long time for an interviewer to establish and I was always, under the best of circumstances, a brief visitor in these lives. However, some satisfying interviews with minority community women (no men) were arranged and are included here, with many disguises of identity as requested.

These are buttressed by secondary sources listed in the Resources section. These resources steered me toward better understanding what was common to aging love in many different cultures and what was different. (In a small rural Japanese village years ago, women who reached their sixty-first birth-days put on crimson petticoats as a sign of their continuing flir-tatious vitality — not in the United States!)

After I entered into many interior dialogues with such rich sources, I also counted up my own odyssey: hundreds of miles of travel, yards of tape recordings, pages and pages of notes, and many dozens of hours with men and women whose mov-ing stories became part of my own life. What can be learned from these new friends?

If you listen closely to individual voices, you can hear stereotypes shattering and myths crumbling. You can see the outlines of a new kind of aging love and consciousness on a distant, but quite distinct, horizon.

In pages to come, we will learn to detect and deflect the stereotypes, not to accept them; to mount the imaginary barri-cades against those who would keep us myth-bound as we age; and to rewrite the loving, sexy, romantic scenarios society would censor against us.

In chapter 1, we'll see how two couples wrote their own scripts and learned new lessons in love.

Chapter I

Not the End of Song
Love When the World Says "No" and Elders Say "Yes"

I'm in love again…and darn glad of it — good news!
— Cole Porter, "I'm in Love Again"

Mother, how *could* you?" asks an exasperated daughter who thinks her eighty-three-year-old widowed mother is too — well, too *old* — to consider remarriage.

"Bill, I don't know how to say this, exactly, but just between us, don't you think you're a little — well, you know — sort of *past all that?*" asks an anxious friend when his seventy-eight-year-old golfing buddy, long a widower, confides he's planning to move in with a vivacious seventy-three-year-old divorcée.

These maddening stereotypes and atrophied slices of conventional wisdom about love between mature adults are hard to deal with for the generation past sixty. However, men and women now well into grandparenting age are fighting these punitive myths in ways that provide models not only for their peers, but for their middle-aged children and younger friends who will be coming along behind them.

Listen to Gussie and Clyde, the real-life heroine and hero of screenwriter Aaron Latham's tender memoir, *The Ballad of Gussie and Clyde.* He reported on the real story of his father's late life marriage after the death of his mother.

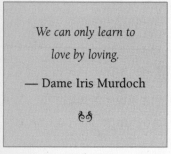

We can only learn to love by loving.

— Dame Iris Murdoch

After a brief courtship, this exchange takes place: "'Gussie, I love you,' Clyde said. She was shocked. She hadn't expected him to say it. She hadn't expected him to feel it. He was eighty-four years old. She was eighty-one.... 'I love you, too,' Gussie said, startling herself."

How in the world did Gussie and Clyde come to such happiness despite the conventional belief that romantic love should have been left behind many years ago when they each lost their spouses?

Partly they got there through the universal need of human beings to be as deeply connected as they can — which is true for older lovers as well as young ones. The sleepless nights, the giddy euphoria — they're all symptoms of love *at all ages* and *in all cultures,* according to anthropologist Helen Fisher, Ph.D., author of *The Anatomy of Love,* who has studied love across many cultures.

Partly Gussie and Clyde got to their bliss by being courageous and open to the beauty and possibility of life, even though, as they progressed, they encountered serious health problems, which they continued to face together, bravely still holding hands.

And in practical terms, they got their little slice of Texas paradise by being ready to try new adventures, new travel, and new friends.

Their meeting was a mixture of the old and the new.

They had known each other as children in a small, close-knit Texas town, Latham tells us, but their life paths had diverged sharply for more than half a century. Gussie had married, moved far away, raised a family, and been widowed many miles from Spur, Texas. But then Clyde's family decided to make his eightieth birthday party a real reunion of family and old-time friends and sent invitations to the "Willis girls" — Gussie and her sisters. When they weren't able to attend because of illness in the family (Gussie saved her invitation, though!), Clyde called Gussie to find out how they all were.

The rest, as they say, is history.

Similarly, this same courage and daring exists among dozens of couples, courage and daring equal to that of youthful lovers and then some — often with more at stake because of the shortness of the time left.

Time — that bittersweet force that can make love deeper, richer, and more expressive than it was in youth or even middle age — is one of the biggest differences between older and younger lovers.

With that thief, time, in the background, there are many couples who can tell us at first hand what a new lease on life really means for the past-sixties and how they fought the prejudices against them in their late season of passion. Here are the stories of two of them.

Surprised by Joy: The Story of Barbara and Dave

The courage to take risks, the poignant passage of time, and the great pleasures of late love, as demonstrated by Gussie and Clyde in their small town milieu, are also exemplified by a big city couple, Barbara and Dave T.

Barbara is a seventy-two-year-old dynamo, the second wife of Dave, a seventy-eight-year-old widower and retired attorney.

She is the whirlwind that drives the couple as they make a new life in their new setting. Dave, the survivor of a difficult first marriage, cannot believe the vitality and fun that Barbara (known from the cradle as "Bobbie" and always "the cutest girl in the class") has brought into his life.

When they sit in the sunny breakfast room of their Arizona ranch house, reminiscing about their lives, Dave says, in charming and artless surprise at his good fortune, "I still can't get used to having someone love me that much and 'do' for me so wonderfully."

Bobbie is a small, trim brunette from an Italian-American family and is an irresistible, wisecracking, outgoing Big Mama — not in size, but in heart. She did not always love wisely, as her tempestuous history reveals, but she loved well and frequently, and now, in her seventies, is at last with a man whom she calls "this treasure," her fourth husband. The contentment that she and Dave, a big, gruff teddy bear of a man of Armenian Jewish background, have found in their late love is clear even to a casual observer. It illustrates a point Dr. Fisher makes in her book, that a component of all successful love affairs is the feeling of "attachment," which she describes as "that sense of calm and peace and security that you have with someone."

For Bobbie, that attachment follows a stormy history, including three marriages and many love affairs, that left her so emotionally exhausted that being single for several years seemed like liberation, even with three children to support from different husbands.

In addition to the newfound freedom of singlehood, she credits some midlife psychotherapy for helping untangle the threads of an emotional life dominated by what her parents felt was "proper" and by "what people will say." These pressures are not unusual for women of her generation or even for some contemporary women. Bobbie, however, was unusual in seeking therapy, because in the years she matured, therapy was considered appropriate only for those who were truly insane or frivolously faddish.

While Bobbie was tumultuously pursuing her maturity, Dave was living through a long marital failure that so froze his emotional life that he became a workaholic, immersing himself in his legal work as though it were a lifeline thrown to a drowning man. He nursed his first wife through a long illness with an impeccable sense of duty and responsibility, but far from the depth of love he would come to know in his late seventies. When his wife died, he had no interest in dating or searching for a new relationship. He, like Bobbie, was weary and fearful of new demands for intimacy.

How did these two battle-scarred veterans open themselves to the possibilities of romance, sex, and love?

Two key factors are at work: one is the way society has changed and the other is the way Bobbie and Dave were willing to shift their mind-set from myths and stereotypes that said they were too old and too tired for new love to an attitude of openness and possibility.

The changes in society that might make Bobbie and Dave be seen as viable romantic partners are summarized by Robert Butler, M.D., author of *Why Survive? Being Old in America,* who urges older people to seek the "new lease on life" that late love brings, but also to recognize that relationships between men and women are changing from what they were in Bobbie and Dave's youthful days.

"These late relationships," says Dr. Butler, "are taking place in a new, changed society, so the relations between men and women will become much more equitable and honest and fair."

Another societal change that works strongly in favor of Bobbie and Dave is the healthy, vigorous way people age today, as evidenced by the fact that no one thinks it unusual that these two seventy-somethings met on the ski slopes and shared their mutual passion for skiing from the beginning of their romance. They call themselves "sports addicts," a term certainly unknown to their parents, born at the end of the nineteenth century and fearful then that too much exercise would "make ladies sweat."

Two years after that meeting they married, and retired to Arizona to a life in which Bobbie's skills and talents are recognized in the new way described by Dr. Butler.

Dave is delighted to respect his wife as the CEO of their retirement years. She is the one who has organized their interest in sports and opened them to a world of new friends and new activities. With another couple, they recently treated themselves to the fulfillment of a long-held wish; to play the St. Andrews course in Scotland, where golf is said to have originated, and to travel a bit in Europe.

"I would never have had the energy or the know-how to put it all together at a price that didn't break the bank," says Dave proudly.

This kind of equality with a husband who is widely respected in his profession is a new experience for Bobbie.

Though she had considerable talent as an artist, she was never encouraged, as a young woman coming of age in 1930s, to consider the possibility of art — or much of anything else — as a career. Even when she turned herself, without standard educational credentials, into a splendid art teacher, gaining recognition in the small private school where she taught, the wider world noticed only her failed marriages and turbulent love affairs.

Both Bobbie and Dave confess to mistakes in their pasts that make them all the more surprised to have found a safe harbor and so much joy at this stage. Dave's self-imposed isolation, typical of widowers adrift after the death of active partners, and Bobbie's record of divorces and failed affairs were formidable hurdles to overcome, but overcome them they did!

The terror of the bar association, Dave, like many men successful in worldly pursuits, is tongue-tied about intimate matters and he has to hold Bobbie's hand and gulp a few times before he can say "I think men are handicapped when it comes to late love because they've devoted so much of their lives to work. They just didn't build up the networks of friendship and support that I think women have."

"When I met Bobbie," he confides, "I realized suddenly that I let my work and my wife's last long illness cut me off from everybody except other lawyers in my firm, and my kids. It was only because my children pushed me, that I joined the ski trip where we met. I'd always gone as someone else's guest because I thought I never had time for a lodge membership. I think men have a hard time facing being alone. It's tough on your kids, too, to see you moping after the loss of a spouse, even one you didn't get along with."

Dave thinks that is why many men rush into new marriages or new relationships after death or divorce; he believes there's a lot of truth in the old proverb that "widows mourn, widowers replace." Of course, not all widowers are as lucky as Dave. Many make disastrous mistakes in the rush to "replace."

That may account for the statistics that show the divorce rate among older men after a quick remarriage is even higher than the already high national rate.

Bobbie's confessions are saltier than Dave's, and mostly have to do with the love affairs she remembers with a wicked gleam in her eye that somewhat belies the sorrow she says she feels about having both received and administered a lot of heartaches in the years before Dave.

"There was one guy," she recounts with just a tinge of fondness still remaining, "who was the most amazing lover — he did not look at all like your basic idea of a romantic leading man. He was big and sloppy and never well-groomed, not particularly handsome, and he could be moody at times, too. But he was just loaded with sex appeal and was wonderful with my kids…." Her voice trails off in a haze of memory.

What happened?

"Oh," she says, sitting up straight and replying crisply, "I found out that if I thought he was so exciting, a bunch of other women did too! When I learned he was carrying on two or three other affairs at the same time, that was the end of *that*."

Through it all, Bobbie retains an earthy wisdom and humor, and an emotional energy, that qualifies her to give some suggestions about how other women might find the safe harbor and the surprising joy that she and Dave now know.

It is hard to reproduce the wit and patter — half TV talk show, half sage elder — that sprinkles Bobbie's conversation, but here, distilled, are some of her recommendations for those men and women who may be ready for new relationships:

- Be happy within yourself and do not expect another person to confer happiness on you. A new romance can enhance your pleasure in life, but can't plant it within you if you haven't got it to start with.

- Don't *ever* give up on your sexuality and sensuality! Don't be embarrassed to admit you want a love life that includes sex at whatever age. Lust is a good thing! And consider many options when you think about lovemaking so you don't get hung up on conventional intercourse as the only way to express love or receive and give pleasure. Viagra is great (Bobbie and Dave think) but the real answer is loving intimacy.

- Keep communications open and work steadily at improving understanding between partners. Let your special person know clearly what your emotional and physical needs and wishes and dreams are.

By following these tips, Bobbie and Dave feel they have gained a measure of contentment — secure in each other's understanding and delighted with each other's physicality — unknown to them in earlier relationships, including Dave's thirty-year-marriage. All he says, paraphrasing playwright Anton Chekhov, about that unhappy period is: "If you want to know what loneliness is, try an unsuccessful marriage." His courage to try again and the success of his new love let all the air out of the balloons that float, invisible but present, above the heads of older people, painted with signs that say "it's not for you any more."

Though Bobbie and Dave believe they have created their own Eden, they are candid about the snakes that lurk. One problem is that relations with his children are cool and her own children seem somewhat bemused by the radical changes in her life these days.

His children are markedly distressed and seem to resent the interloper on what they regard as their mother's turf, a not uncommon response, according to Adele M. Holman, Ph.D., a family therapist in New Jersey and author of *Family Assessment,* a guide for mental health professionals and educators.

She points out that, in some cases, even children who have busy lives of their own and who are, on the surface, glad that parents have found companionship feel somewhat displaced and uncertain. Even adult daughters who have heavy responsibilities in their own homes often don't like surrendering their father's care to a strange woman.

"And," says Dr. Holman, "a son who finds another man in his mother's bed is certainly living out some Shakespearean stories we all know. From Hamlet to Freud, it isn't an easy experience."

(In chapter 2, "Troubles and Triumphs: The Baggage We Bring," we explore the relationships with adult children and similar issues older couples face in attempting to mesh past lives.)

After Dave leaves the room, Bobbie confesses one of the few things she thinks is wrong with her present life: "He'll be eighty soon," she says, staring out the window. The silence is eloquent and poignant. Besides these moods of light and dark, there are other mismatches as well. Dave likes to talk shop with other attorneys (while Bobbie yawns), and she would like to travel more (while Dave likes to stay put). But they have established that easy banter and teasing that so many other

> *Love is the emblem of eternity, it confounds all notions of time, effaces all memory of beginning, all fear of an end.*
>
> — Madame de Staël
>
> ఠఠ

couples seem to use to work out disagreements and then they head off for another ski trip.

"We always have a good time" is now their joint mantra.

Bringing the Invisible into the Light

As we have seen, Bobbie and Dave, in their seventies, take full advantage of society's changed approach to health and vigor for elders, and also do a lot of hard work on their own to shatter stereotypes and show themselves to the world as newlywed lovers.

But what about people older than Bobbie and Dave — that portion of the population that is moving into their eighties and nineties, more like Gussie and Clyde — who make up the fastest growing segment of the U.S. population? It is estimated that by the middle of the twenty-first century more than 800,000 Americans will be over 100.

So many people are reaching their eighties and nineties, that we must look at late love in *those* lives, too, because it is this portion of the elder population that most often faces the vicious and intense "ageism" that Maggie Kuhn, the Gray Panther leader, railed against, saying over and over in every forum she could reach for a quarter of a century, "Old age is not a disease and a disaster — it is a triumph! The losses, the illness, the failure — we're still here!" (She died at eighty-nine.)

The larger society victimizes older men and women by rendering them invisible; they just aren't *seen* by younger people in all their multidimensioned reality, and if seen at all, are noticed as lovable old coots, sitting on the porch and knitting or whittling while the world roars past. Younger and even middle-aged people don't *expect* to see them because they believe they are all either in age-segregated retirement communities or nursing homes.

I don't know whether that image was revised when seventy-seven-year-old astronaut John Glenn spent some of *his* old age whirling around the Earth in space orbit, but my hunch is that the myths surrounding elders are so ingrained that he was written off as so exceptional and unusual as to have little relevance to the aging population in general, despite Glenn's own statement that "old people have ambitions and dreams just like everybody else."

This invisibility — this big black hole in popular culture into which many different kinds of older adults have disappeared — is clear in virtually all media, beginning with television where the popular mystery star, Angela Lansbury, now seventy-three, found her highly successful show, *Murder, She Wrote,* canceled because of the most rampant ageism-sexism combination. This goes back, of course, to TV's belief that only people between eighteen and forty-nine spend money! It wasn't so much Lansbury's own age, as it was that the viewers she attracted "skewed old," in the deathless language of TV advertising.

This in spite of a recent newspaper business story that bore the headline "New On-Line Traders: Older, Wiser, and Richer," telling how people well over sixty are becoming savvy Internet investors and how they are bringing both money and stability to this fast-growing corner of the investment market.

Novelist E. Annie Proulx, says the dialogue in her books reflects the fact that she just "hangs out and eavesdrops on people." "I'm at an age where I can be invisible," she says. "Nobody notices older women. It's assumed they are just there.... I can sit in a diner and there will be people in the booth next to me, and because I'm a woman of a certain age, they'll say *anything,* as if no one were there. People will say absolutely outrageous, incredible things." Proulx was sixty-one years old when she gave that interview on the occasion of winning the Pulitzer Prize.

In the movies, "Hollywood paints older women as alone and bitter, selfish or smothering, funny if they have sex, pathetic if they don't," according to movie critic Ann Roiphe, reviewing some movies in which "Monstrous Moms" are key figures.

As in all aspects of aging, women become invisible more rapidly and at younger ages than men, but aging men are not exempt from the punishments of youth-mad America either.

Eleanor Hamilton, Ph.D., of California, a retired psychologist and sex therapist, now eighty-seven herself, points out that widowers, if they have not led a very resilient or extroverted life and are set in their ways, are often paralyzed by loss, cling to the old routines, and stay home, fearful of new challenges, while society looks the other way. The older man can become "more and more depressed, more and more vulnerable to illness" until he, too, becomes invisible to society, Dr. Hamilton warns.

One of the hardest fighters against these shadows created by a society in which individual strength is so valued, dependency so abhorred, and mortality so feared, is Thomas Perls, M.D., a geriatrician at Beth Israel Deaconess Medical Center in Boston, who is leading a Harvard University study of 100-year-olds.

Says Dr. Perls, "Eighty-five is young!" He has studied 160 centenarians since 1993 and he says all have lived until ninety-three or ninety-four in good health. These folks may be invisible to society at large, but they are out in the bright sunlight to all who know and work with them.

"That really turns the whole idea of aging on its head," Dr. Perls said. "Most people," he continued, "have the thought 'who would want to live that long?... it just means having all the diseases.' But it's the opposite. To get to such an age you have to be healthy the majority of your life."

Dr. Perls and other gerontologists agree that while Americans want to live longer, they are anxious — realistically — about long periods of dependency and frailty. However, Dr. Perls's research, and that of John W. Rowe, M.D., president of the Mt. Sinai Hospital and School of Medicine in New York, and others in the field, seems to indicate that there is a modest reduction in the amount of time people spend in poor health during their final years. In other words, a briefer period in which they are invisible!

In spite of the reality Dr. Perls's studies reveal, and even in spite of many Americans' direct personal experience with the new way of aging of their own parents — who pursue travel, education, and community activism with such avidity their children can't get them on the phone — bless E-mail! — social prejudice against aging lovers remains strong and painfully cruel.

When the society pages of a Connecticut newspaper carried the wedding story of a couple in their eighties, a young college student parking the guests' cars at the ceremony was heard to mutter, "it's disgusting."

The *New York Daily News* in 1997 reported the story of a couple, aged seventy-nine and eighty, who had been childhood sweethearts, married other people, were widowed, found each other again, and at long last, were married to each other.

Television reporters interviewed not only the couple, but a young barmaid at their hotel. She thought they were "sweet," but, she wondered, "what — you know," giggling, "what can they actually *do?*"

The answer: A lot!

The question betrays the typical youthful and middle-aged confusion about both sex and aging and renders invisible once more the very real sensuous realities of touch, kiss, and embrace among the elderly that continue to defy all myths and stereotypes.

Much more typical of the *real,* as opposed to the media-constructed, romantic and sexual lives of elders is the couple we will call Alex and Sarah R., who demonstrate how people in their nineties can successfully struggle against the forces that would make them invisible. Instead, they have found a way into the brightness of sunlight and the glow of candlelight.

Banishing the Shadows: The Story of Sarah and Alex

Sarah is ninety-two and Alex is ninety. Their lives were stamped with the conventions and norms of their generation, a generation for whom divorce was strictly forbidden and in which parental or religious authorities played a very large role in choosing marriage partners.

As a result, Sarah and Alex's present happiness is almost like a fairy tale in which the prince and princess overcome terrible obstacles before reaching the Magic Kingdom. But this white-haired Cinderella and her Prince Charming achieved joy only after lifetimes of sorrow, betrayal, and loss during long, miserably unhappy marriages that they dared not end, and that injured the children of each. The death of her husband freed Sarah, and Alex's life was so unhappy with his first wife that he finally found the strength to go against all the codes of his generation and seek a divorce.

Consequently, these lovers did not find each other until they were in their sixties, but have lived a blessed romance since. Sarah and Alex must be among the most genetically favored creatures in the world, but I am guessing that they resemble what will become routine in our youngest generation as they reach their elder years.

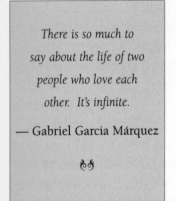

There is so much to say about the life of two people who love each other. It's infinite.

— Gabriel Garcia Márquez

Sarah is relatively healthy, totally self-sufficient in daily activities, and living a married romance with Alex, a straight-backed, slight, white-haired charmer who speaks quietly in a mellow baritone and shines with pleasure when he speaks to or about his wife of thirty years. They live in a modest bungalow in a retirement village in New Mexico.

Sarah is a poised and lovely woman of great refinement, with a sweet and pretty face that was once that of a real beauty and is still most attractive with bright blue eyes, ageless high cheekbones, and well-tended white hair. The plentiful wrinkles and laugh lines do not detract from her enchanting smile.

She and Alex are certainly aged, and they move slowly, but do not suggest the unattractiveness and decline that is the stereotype of advanced years. Surely there are many in their nineties who do not share this combination of good luck and genes, but here, at least, we do have the poster couple whom baby boomers — concerned about what is coming down the road — could adopt as a model.

Whatever changes old age has brought about, for Sarah this is a time of dear contentment that follows a long life of poverty and struggle in a blue-collar town in Michigan, a thirty-seven-year first marriage from hell, and crushing disappointments in relations with her own parents.

For Alex, the love he shares with Sarah is something he could never have even fantasized about as he struggled to end the thirty-year first marriage that nearly destroyed him.

He explains: "Divorce in my generation was just a very hard thing to think of…there was a certain code of honor that other men my age had; it may sound very old-fashioned today, but in my day, it was sort of the old saying 'you made your bed, now lie in it,' and that was what you were supposed to do."

Sarah describes a similar hobbling of convention when she tells how, despite intense misery in her marriage to a cold, unloving husband, she turned away a kind and generous suitor who was willing to be with her in the context of an affair or any other arrangement she wished.

"This was just something I couldn't do — no matter how unhappy my marriage was," she says simply, thinking back to the days before World War I when she was a very young woman just emerging from her adolescence and absorbing the social programming of home, church, and neighborhood.

Unlike Bobbie and Dave, who lived in the same apartment complex, Sarah and Alex were total strangers when they met, but their chance meeting is a classic example of the dictum — almost the eleventh commandment — "Thou shalt go where thy interests lie." Everyone who deals with older people — social workers, counselors, doctors — all urge them not necessarily to go looking for partners per se, but to follow the interests they have always pursued, or start new ones — and new friendships will flow from those interests.

And, of course, many older people whose codes of conduct resemble Sarah and Alex's, have traditional bases of affiliation — the church, synagogue, or mosque; hobby clubs and senior centers — where today there are active programs designed to ease the social changes that have occurred over the past century.

Sarah and Alex met because each had a lifelong interest and involvement in music. To support herself as a young woman too poor to attend music school, the naturally talented Sarah gave voice lessons to children in her little factory town, learning at an early age the consolation and joys of music. It was only after she was widowed and could afford music studies, that her talent blossomed and she could attend concerts and music festivals at home and abroad.

Alex, though his profession was as a research scientist for a pharmaceutical company, had always studied music and played as a gifted amateur in a string quartet.

At the most difficult juncture of his divorce proceedings, friends dragged him away to the Salzburg Music Festival in Austria. It was there, in a crowd waiting to present their tickets for a concert that he and Sarah began chatting in the manner of people waiting in lines all over the world. Of course, when they look back on it now, they feel it was predestined by the gods that they would be standing in the same line, going to the same concert on the same day, thousands of miles from their respective homes.

For them, the commandment "Thou shalt follow thy interests" could not have been more appropriate, as neither had gone to the music festival in any "search" mode. Sarah was tasting heady freedom from years of misery and Alex was preoccupied with ending an unbearable situation. But the slow growth of affection, and later romantic passion, was inspired by music and that music remains a profoundly shared joy to this day.

Each continues with other interests, too. Sarah does gardening with the help of a young neighbor, and Alex maintains his lifelong interest in politics and current events.

And what about sex now, in their tenth decade?

"Different, but okay, I guess," says Alex noncommittally.

Alone with me, Sarah says, "Oh, if only he wouldn't worry so — it's fine — and beautiful for me and I believe when he stops worrying, it's fine for him, too."

She confides that health problems for both of them — arthritis and asthma for her, prostate and kidney problems for him — have altered but not destroyed the pleasures of touch, caress, and gratifying sensation that they provide for each other.

Alex became impotent after a series of surgeries, and for a period was depressed and worried. Adhering to the traditional notion that erection and penetration are the only "manly" ways to make love, he believed he was no longer a "real" man.

Sarah, who blossomed sexually for the first time in her life within their emotionally secure marriage, was able, through patience and love, to convince him that the caresses and adaptations they made provided her with much pleasure.

As he felt Sarah responding to his touch and kiss, to caresses of many kinds, he began to relax a little about the male preference for conventional intercourse, learning to stop comparing himself to the man he was at age sixteen, and looked at the many available pleasures of sleeping in each other's arms in the time left to them.

Sarah was asked how long it took for him to overcome these fears, and her answer was "quite a number of months," but she explains, "We have such a good time together in every way that he just couldn't stay depressed. We know how lucky we are to have this much health at our age, so we don't fuss about not being teenagers any more."

What is soulful for both of them is their closeness, their intimacy, and their success at telling each other everything. She describes this picture:

"Doing the dishes is his job, and when he's at the sink, I come up behind him sometimes and embrace him from head to toe. It's very nice." Her smile is knowing and blithe.

"You know," Sarah adds, "my early memories of conventional sex aren't happy ones, and I don't long for those days back again. What we have now is so much better in every way."

Alex and Sarah are interested in the anti-impotence pill, Viagra, but wary about introducing "yet another pill" into the array of drugs they now take; they will probably discuss this with Alex's doctor at some point. They are not at all sure that Alex really needs to change the new patterns of pleasure giving and lovemaking that he and Sarah find so satisfying now.

When commenting on Viagra, doctors have urged men to pay more attention to the quality, rather than the quantity, of sexual experiences and reminded them that women are interested in romance and real communion, not athletic performance.

Although reaching a profound level of emotional intimacy is not a problem for Alex and Sarah, they do have some problems caused by aging. Sarah is not as active in the garden as she was, and her voice, of course, shows its age, but this does not dampen her enjoyment of their joint world of music.

Alex turned ninety recently, and received an outpouring of attention and love from friends and family that was so intense it almost overwhelmed this lucky pair. Their children urged relatives and friends to write letters, send photos, and record memories to be included in a special album.

One great-niece, newly thirty-five, wrote about Sarah and Alex's late blooming romance and about all their activities and interests.

She ended by writing: "In other words, dear Aunt Sarah and Uncle Alex, you have totally screwed up all my notions about what it means to grow old!"

These two couples — Dave and Bobbie on the ski slopes and Alex and Sarah listening to music together — show us ways in which mature people can defy cultural taboos to find love in the process of "conscious aging." The lessons they have to teach are important and worthy of our examination.

Risks and Rewards

The wisdom that older lovers impart — especially to women — begins with courage, for it is well known that there are many more older women than older men, and that the disparity grows as one ascends the age ladder. Still there are thousands of singles of *both* genders who have been discouraged and cheated by a variety of *shouldn'ts* ("It's not nice, at your age"), *can'ts* ("As an older man, I should expect sex to fade; it's only natural"), and *fears* ("Older women interested in sex and love are seen as pathetic and embarrassing; I won't risk that — at least leave me some dignity").

Glancing once more at our two couples, we see how they turned these attitudes around so that both new lovers and long-marrieds can share in the renewal of life, hope, and joy that late relationships can confer.

These are their life lessons:

Lesson 1: Spring Yourselves Free of the Beauty Trap.

Realize and believe that the smarts, the pizzazz, and the experience life has given you are valuable and attractive. Any observer can see, for example, that the standard image of feminine allure — young, slim, ravishingly pretty — has been completely overcome by both Bobbie and Sarah; the beauty myth is just not on their radar. This does not mean in the slightest that they have "given up" and do not care about their appearance — both have great self-respect and wear appropriate clothing and modest makeup, whether on the golf course or at a concert.

Bobbie caught the physical fitness train as it went whizzing past and is quite fit, aerobically speaking, but she has gained weight over the years, her waistline is not what it was in her twenties, and her legs no longer elicit the whistles they did when she was in her forties. But she feels well, looks poised and attractive, and her husband thinks she is the sexiest thing going.

Sarah exercises, even with her arthritis, her white hair is nicely done, and soft makeup enhances her brilliant blue eyes. Women (both straight and gay) who are trying to deprogram themselves of the belief that they must remain young looking forever because that is what a partner wants, need to look at Dave and Alex. Both chose women in their own age range and made choices based on deep emotional needs for sympathetic understanding and kindness. They demonstrate the wisdom of

Margaret Fowler, editor of *Love in Bloom,* an anthology of stories of old age. She writes, "For older lovers, failures of the body are more acceptable than failures of the soul." This is especially meaningful precisely because many older women do not share the degree of health and vitality that our two models have, and many have serious health problems that do not, however, diminish their gifts of spirit and empathy.

In giving up the ancient stereotypes about love being only for the slim, trim, and surgically altered, women have some surprising allies.

At nearly seventy, Clint Eastwood is still considered a magnetic movie star. When interviewed about why he chose nearly-fifty Meryl Streep as his co-star in *The Bridges of Madison County,* he said, "The pressure on women to stay young is unfair. Men are taught the forties are great, the fifties are great. Women are taught, 'I'm past thirty, what do I do now?'" Eastwood added what many older men have come to discover, "There's something about a woman who knows something that is more interesting."

Similarly, CBS newscaster Dan Rather, who has seen his share of pretty TV faces come and go in his sixty-nine years, wrote a special ad for the movie *Mother,* complaining that sixty-four-year-old Debbie Reynolds should have had an Oscar nomination for the "wonderfully real" performance she gave. "American movie audiences are mostly unacquainted with women over sixty," he wrote. "Reynolds has given us a glimpse of the possibilities that are in acting, in moviemaking, in *life,* for anybody who takes a chance no matter what his or her age."

For men, the issue of physical appearance as they age is a complex one. While they also suffer some of the same slings and arrows from the cult of American youth, they are permitted a bit more leeway. The TV anchorman with gray or white hair is seen as a serious, grave voice of authority; the TV anchorwoman with gray hair is not seen at all. Men generally have not faced an intense lifelong pressure to "look pretty." Little girl beauty pageants, teenage struggles with slimming but deadly eating disorders, middle age liposuction and, finally, drastic cosmetic surgery as the seventh and eighth decades loom — none of these have marked the life course of most men until recently, when face-lifts for men have become more frequent.

While men often are allowed to make up for balding pates and paunchy middles with money and power (that's beginning to work for some women, too, as they are discovering the brave new world of professional achievement), men must still worry about age discrimination in the workplace where younger, cheaper workers can replace them after a career's worth of service. The increase in cosmetic surgery for men, plus special hair dyes and new masculine fragrances that go far beyond the witch hazel aftershave lotion of their dads, show that men, too, are caught in the beauty trap sprung by a relentlessly youth-oriented society. The average man cannot afford a "trophy wife" (the twenty-five-year-old mate of a sixty-five-year-old powerful, wealthy, and influential man) to make him feel young and virile; he has to settle for a male cologne called "Egoist"; thus does the beauty myth punish both genders!

Lesson 2: Change Your Mind Set!

Approaches to love and companionship, attitudes about romance and sex, habits of mind and heart — these were all formed half a century ago for most older people and in a different time and place, with different national mores and customs.

All those strict gender roles ("Nice girls don't") are blurred now; the usual ways to be a couple that we knew in the 1930s and 1940s are different now. People live together comfortably without marriage, women unashamedly telephone men first, husband sharing is not as unknown (or at least as undiscussed) as it was sixty years ago, and grandmothers have learned from their grandchildren that marriage with everyone who strikes your sexual fancy is not strictly necessary.

"Older people," says Benjamin Schlesinger, Ph.D., professor

of gerontology and social work at the University of Toronto (Canada), "must fight as hard as they can, finding new resources inside themselves, to accept their lifelong right to sexuality and their need to adapt to different seeking, dating, and mating patterns as they age."

"The task today," writes Dr. Schlesinger, "is to break through the myths, taboos, and misconceptions to give recognition to the reality, the beauty, the problems and pains of sex in the later years so we can ... help our senior citizens exercise their legitimate rights as sexual beings."

To break out of one's old blinders of habit and culture is a key step to new relationships as we age. Many of the couples I interviewed had come together across religious, ethnic, and even occasionally across racial lines. They had bridged huge differences in culture, education, and background. Some met new partners when their old neighborhoods changed and people of different ethnic and racial backgrounds moved in.

Lesson 3: Jump In, the Water's Fine!

There are exciting new ways for older adults to meet that are light years away from the small world of home, church, and school that contained most of the meeting places for romantic couples in our parents' day.

The Sunday school picnic has given way to the Internet chat room; the decorous personal introduction from friends and family has given way to "personals" ads in newspapers and magazines, and the annual trip to visit relatives in the next town has been replaced by bike trips in Italy — all ways older adults meet and court as the twenty-first century begins.

The "personals" columns are an especially vivid example of a contemporary meeting place, since they exemplify a way of becoming acquainted that not only did not exist fifty years ago, but that many older adults today thought they would never consider — and yet they *are* considering them, in increasing numbers. These ads — usually placed in carefully selected publications that act as efficient "screening" devices —

allow people of similar interests to meet in safe public settings and are now routinely accepted.

Moreover, the age ranges specified in the "personals" ads are constantly rising and many times, age "seventy-plus" is listed as the desirable age in a sought-after partner. (There is a lot of joking about how everybody lies about their ages in these ads, but everyone makes allowances for that.)

Miss Lonelyhearts Meets the World Wide Web

Another area into which elders are jumping with a big splash is the Internet.

When your widowed grandparents met new mates at church socials earlier this century, the Internet did not exist, but now it is an astonishing global meeting place — rife with bulletin boards, the SeniorNet, on-line magazines for elder interests, and easily retrieved information on any subject in the world. The presence of E-mail, that peculiar hybrid of Victorian letter writing and twenty-first-century casual rapping, means that people in widely varying time zones can know their messages will be picked up when convenient. In fact, the number of couples of all ages who are meeting, courting, and quite often marrying through E-mail relationships grows daily and has been the subject of lengthy analyses in everything from scholarly tomes to perky news features in print and on TV.

In an article titled "But Did You Get Her E-mail Address?" Katie Hafner, a reporter covering cyberspace for the *New York Times,* points out that once the telephone became a convenient way to communicate, "the intensity of conducting a love affair by letter tapered off." But now, she adds, "with E-mail, people in relationships are once again formulating their feelings and desires by writing them down." This development — the getting-to-know-you kind of letter writing on the Internet — is simply an updated version of what Dr. Eleanor Hamilton (see Introduction), the California psychologist, sex therapist, and popular columnist for the *Point Reyes Light* newspaper, has long advocated in her column.

One of her heartwarming tips to seniors who are in the first stages of a romance is to exchange long love letters. "Write about your hopes and dreams, your wishes and fantasies. Let the other person know what you like and enjoy, what your goals are, what intimacy means to you," writes Dr. Hamilton.

"The written word," she writes, "requires a thought process not based on hormones, but on the mind's concerns." Will it be the same on E-mail? This generation of elders will join young people in finding out! Hafner calls it "the revival of the epistolary romance." Interestingly enough, E-mail acquaintances seem to be happening in exactly the same pattern we have seen in the real world: sometimes the elder E-mailers are longtime friends getting back in touch after a long absence and many life experiences, sometimes they are new acquaintances perhaps meeting in cyberspace for the first time as they pursue common interests in sports, politics, art, or anything else under the sun. (A partial list of Web sites offering information of special interest to elders is located at the back of this book; a complete list is too vast!)

Another contemporary way of making new friends, which was as totally unknown to previous generations as the idea of visiting Mars, is today's adventurous travel right here on Earth. This too, takes many forms, including Outward Bound whitewater rafting trips, walking or biking tours for old college English majors through England's Lake District, and professionally guided archaeological digs for amateurs — the range of possibilities grows constantly. Single elders find these not only exciting places for possible romance, but, at the very least, they also offer stimulating new friendships and interests. And, as today's traveling baby boomers age, the number of special tours for those no longer interested in mountain climbing or snorkeling in unknown seas is growing rapidly. Ecotourism for increasingly concerned older environmentalists is another new travel option.

Elderhostel study groups are still another worldwide network, offering foreign study, specialized courses in the U.S., and many other educational opportunities since 1975 and creating many new interests and friendships, as well. Some 323,000 elders took Elderhostel programs in 1996 alone.

The tried and true ways of meeting — singles groups at the neighborhood church or temple, introductions through mutual friends, attendance at high school and college reunions — all continue to provide surprising amounts of magic for the heart, even if they may not provide a new romance. Martin L., an American expatriate living in Paris, wrote in a Christmas letter to friends that one of the highlights of the year had been going back to the U.S. to attend his fifty-fifth high school reunion in a small town in Indiana. Even though some of his best-remembered friends were gone, the ones he did see were a delight, and, to his surprise, everyone there enjoyed catching up and renewing old ties so much that they all vowed to try to stay in touch and be connected through whatever late life brought to them — both joys and sorrows.

Just as new ways of meeting are sometimes very different from those earlier patterns that older adults grew up with, so the very relationships that may result are quite different from the engaged-married-live-together-forever lockstep of their parents. All kinds of new forms of togetherness have emerged in today's fluid, mobile society, and elders have only to look around attentively to see some of them. One notable new pattern for older lovers is the romantic friendship, a new feature in the relationship landscape of most conventional Americans, though not unknown in other cultures around the world.

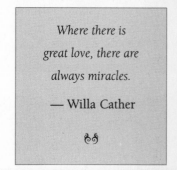

Where there is great love, there are always miracles.

— Willa Cather

Amitie Amoureuse: The Romantic Friendship

As always, the French have a word for it: *amitie amoureuse* is what they call that quite contemporary situation in which a couple — either gay or straight — are not married and do not even live together all the time, but are, nevertheless, unmistakably a *couple*. They may maintain separate residences, but often share deeply in each other's family lives with children and grandchildren; they may live in the same town or city, or perhaps live a thousand miles apart and have a commuting romance. Sex may be an important part of the union, or it may be fleeting and intermittent or absent altogether.

An eighty-year-old man, John S., who lives a ten-minute drive from the home of his seventy-four-year-old "significant other," Nancy T., says "our 'romantic friendship' gives both of us a lot of space and time to ourselves, but offers intimate pleasures and comforts as we all get older and our circle of friends inevitably diminishes."

Romantic friendships are especially attractive to the women in such partnerships because, frequently widowed, they may want a breather from daily rounds of homemaking. Women past sixty often have a history of such intense family caretaking over such a long period of time, sometimes punctuated by exhausting nursing duties, that a fast spin back to twenty-four-hour domesticity is not as appealing as it is to many men in their age group who are used to twenty-four-hour on-the-job wives.

Whether previous caretaking responsibilities are the issue or not, many women simply want the time for interests, talents, and hobbies they never had time to pursue before. Here, too, it's difficult for many men to quite accept that a prospective partner might wish to stay free for her painting classes or travel or yoga workouts and might not want to be available for company on a daily, hourly basis.

But in spite of the old hangovers from earlier relationships (men wanting to be cared for in a domestic setting, etc.), men and women are increasingly establishing loving friendships that are fun, exciting, romantic, and sexy — but don't mean necessarily a wedding ring or yet another new domicile to furnish.

"Romantic friendships," explained one seventy-eight-year-old man, Tom W., "are somewhere between sexual ecstasy and best pals, between having the earth move, and putting on old sneakers to take a walk together."

Looking at today's greatly changed and expanded world, it seems clear that for women who reject the notion that plump grandmothers have nothing to say about adventure, romance, sex, or different new lives and for men who can break free of the narrow world their work often imposed on them the outlook for new seasons of love and passion to the very end of life is brighter than we've been gloomily brainwashed to believe.

In the next chapter, "Troubles and Triumphs: The Baggage We Bring," men and women cope with the very real issues of meshing earlier lives and dealing with each other's children, finances, and health as they walk together into the uncharted territory of later life. And, in the chapters to follow, there is good news about how new knowledge (Viagra is only the beginning), new attitudes, and new understandings are changing this most intimate part of lives.

TRAILBLAZER

Nelson Mandela

"If you were a man who had grown up in a tiny village in rural South Africa, spent twenty-seven years in jail for your political beliefs, and succeeded in changing the course of history, what would you ask for your eightieth birthday? A bride?"

That question was asked by the *New York Times* in July 1998 when it covered the wedding of then president Nelson Mandela, of South Africa and Graça Machel, the widow of the former president of Mozambique, Samora Machel. President Mandela and Mrs. Machel were sweethearts for two years, holding hands on state visits around the globe, but the handsome suitor had to overcome Mrs. Machel's reluctance to give up her role as chief representative of her late husband's political legacy before they could wed. Observers believe that President Mandela finally convinced her that she would be able to keep her late husband's name, continue her work as an attorney and an international campaigner for children's rights, and maintain her status as one of the most influential people in her home country, continuing the struggle for democracy there.

Friends and aides noted the high spirits President Mandela exhibited in the days before the wedding, while steadfastly refusing to tell reporters anything — neither confirming nor denying the wedding rumors. But, in a moment of rare high jinks for the normally reserved and dignified leader (he is, after all, a real prince of his tribe in South Africa), he called Mrs. Machel while a reporter from a Soweto newspaper was in his office and told her about the headlines concerning the impending marriage.

"Eh, Mamma," he said to her, "there is a front-page

story here saying you are going to have wedding bells on Saturday with this old man — but I cannot talk now because the reporter will write anything I say."

They were wed at his residence in a Johannesburg suburb where clergy from four major faiths — Protestant, Jewish, Muslim, and Hindu — gave their blessings.

Earlier, Archbishop Desmond Tutu, the Nobel Peace Prize winner from South Africa, had publicly, but lightheartedly, chastised them for being together without marriage, teasing them that they were setting a bad example for the grandchildren.

The wedding, which took place on his eightieth birthday, set off a nationwide celebration; it marked the third marriage for Mandela and the second for his bride. Each has children by earlier marriages. Even the guards at the prison where Mandela was held for decades sent best wishes. The bridegroom said he was happier than he believed possible.

Chapter 2

Troubles and Triumphs
The Baggage We Bring

The past isn't dead. It isn't even past.

— William Faulkner

Miriam B.'s stomach knotted and her throat went dry as she looked into the faces of her three grown daughters and her adult son and their spouses as they all sat around the dining table in the family homestead at an Easter gathering.

In a wild moment of panic, she thought, *No, I can't go through with this*, but then the seventy-two-year-old widow took a deep breath and said, "There's something important I have to tell you." The exuberant conversations and the floating laughter stopped and eight faces turned expectantly toward her. She had been alone for five years since their father's death, but they were unprepared for her next statement.

"I've…I've met a very interesting man who seems to be interested in me, too, and…and…well, I believe we are going to be important to each other in a new life. I don't expect to be married again, but I think you should know that this man and I, well, we're going to be together, I think," she said.

There was a stunned silence for a few seconds and then her three daughters and her daughter-in-law leapt to their feet, ran around the table, and in an excited rush of exclamations hugged and kissed her and one said, "Oh, Mom, we are *so* happy for you! You're going to have a new life — we *wanted* you to have this life!"

But her son sat stone still and looked as though he had been hit on the head with a baseball bat. He said nothing for a few moments while his wife watched him anxiously, and then he said, clearing his throat and attempting to sound calm, "Just who is this person, Mom?" "This person" turned out to be a family acquaintance, recently widowed himself, but that did not immediately salve the son's sense of shock and disapproval.

What's going on here? A simple gender difference about love and romance? A bit of an Oedipal struggle of son and new male father figure? An older woman who didn't know quite how to break such life-changing news to her grown kids?

It's all that and many, many more complex issues that are packed into the baggage that late-life lovers bring into their new relationships. In this chapter we will see how late-life lovers meet, court, and triumph over a mind-boggling array of problems, ranging from resistant children to lawyers who insist on a prenuptial agreement, from doctors who say their health problems are too scary to consider a new relationship to friends or other family members who are still mourning the lost spouse or companion and who drag their feet discouragingly when new relationships appear on the horizon.

The happy endings we saw in chapter 1 *do happen often,* but sometimes the task of meshing past lives is just too big, too hard, or too tangled for success, and late-life lovers find they lack the resilience and emotional stamina to confront all the challenges.

Sometimes it's as simple as dramatically different expectations.

"I wanted her to cook and keep house like my wife used to, but she wanted to go out every night to dinner or order in Chinese. I got tired of Chinese," explains one widower in his eighties. Luckily for them, the China syndrome became clear before they moved in together and the relationship ended without much damage to either party.

"His late wife had been a very elegant lady and he was constantly criticizing my clothes and my hair and makeup. I knew it wouldn't work. I was sad about it, because in many ways we were very compatible, especially sexually, but I just wasn't ever going to be the corporate wife, perfectly groomed, presiding over perfect dinner tables," says photographer Sarah N., sixty-nine, about her failed romance with a sixty-four-year-old businessman.

"I'm sort of a quiet guy who likes to take life seriously and thoughtfully," reports Harry M., seventy-eight, "and it took me a long while to start going out again after Ruthie's death. I was very attracted to Tina (a sixty-nine-year-old widow), because she was vivacious and lively, and very pretty, too. But the pace! She was just too frenetic for me! She entertained a tremendous amount, we visited people — it seemed we were always packing or unpacking — all over the world, and there were no social or cultural activities she ever wanted to miss. It was a bit much." Harry and Tina parted amicably after a short romance (Tina, too, felt Harry couldn't handle her schedule in a satisfying way) and Harry is now happily remarried to a pleasant woman two years older than himself, who is devoted to her books, her garden, and her classical music collection, as well as to her children and grandchildren.

Sarah, Harry, and the anti-Chinese food widower are now in what the French call *le troisieme age* — the third age, the one that follows youth and middle age. In that part of life, hundreds of thousands of couples all over the world — not just in the U.S. — *do* make a new relationship work and move toward completely new experiences. How do they build that new structure and what obstacles do they overcome?

Miles to Go before They Sleep: John and Betty

The sweet chaos of making a new late life — which includes climbing over, above, and around objections from adult children and sometimes other relatives and friends; dealing with money issues; and squarely facing looming health problems as they age — is exemplified in the tale recounted by John and Betty.

> It is easier to have hope when one is very old. One sees that over the course of time, people have managed to overcome countless difficulties with amazing resourcefulness.
>
> — Maggie Kuhn

John T., seventy-one, is contemplating a third marriage after losing two wives to death, and he and his fiancée, sixty-three-year-old Betty R., are ruefully admitting to themselves that the array of financial problems facing them could daunt even fearless young couples.

John is retired from a middle-management job in an engineering firm that did not pay him a Hollywood salary, but that, in the economic postwar boom days, did provide a good pension and health benefits (something he isn't so sure his children will have in the future) and he, like many returning World War II veterans, rode the real estate inflation boom of the 1960s and 1970s in Boston to accumulate a comfortable retirement nest egg. His marriage to his first wife was also typical of the returning veterans: partners in hard work and savings, she sadly did not live to enjoy the comforts of a secure retirement. His second wife died shortly after they were married and, with her own income, was not a factor in his financial life.

Betty, the partner he has chosen for the rest of his journey, was left a widow in her late thirties with three small children, remarried, and later divorced. She has been alone now for many years and finds that the emotional, sexual, and intellectual world of her relationship with John has brought her joys and fulfillment she could never have imagined for the last part of her life. In the years alone, she started and built up a successful business running a temporary employment agency and was financially independent when she met John at a mutual friend's home.

The deep attachment and pleasures they find together are clear to any observer, but before they legally marry, they must decide not only the usual question of the children's roles in their mutual assets, but face a number of problems specific to their life histories. One of Betty's three children is autistic and, now an adult, has been maintained in an expensive private residential care home. This is not a question of inheritance, but of a large ongoing expense that will last for the rest of John and Betty's lives, and perhaps afterwards, as well.

John's two children are married with their own families, but he is helping one of them build a summer home with a modest amount of financial help. If and when they marry, should Betty share in giving away that portion of their mutual assets? In addition, both Betty and John have mortgages on their primary homes and Betty has a small mortgage on a lakeside cottage her husband built in the few years before his tragically premature death. The property is emotionally meaningful to Betty and her children — should the mortgage be part of debt John assumes jointly with her when they marry?

Sitting across from them in a candlelit neighborhood restaurant a few blocks from Betty's home, I can see by the way they nestle close together, hold hands occasionally, and look into each other's faces with warmth and laughter as we talk, that these two people have found a special loving companionship to grace their later years — but what of the problems they face?

Unlike those long ago days when John and Betty were new-lyweds in their first marriages — armed only with sky-high exuberance and a coffee table made of orange crates and bricks — they now are veterans of homes and children, owners of two sets of coffee makers and toaster ovens, and a couple of cars more than they need.

And the complications of their lives don't end with household goods and vehicles; John is worried about stepparenting a handicapped child and Betty is worried about how her soon-to-be stepson, who has had first dibs on his father's assets since widowerhood, will greet a family member bearing the imposing title of "new wife."

And always, older remarried couples face the danger that friends will feel abandoned when one spouse or the other — or perhaps both — begins a new life not necessarily within the same social circle. Betty, for example, had been widowed and divorced so quickly at a relatively young age, and was alone for so many years before she and John became engaged, that her close, loyal, and loving circle of longtime friends was taken aback to realize that she would soon have heavy claims on her scarce amount of nonwork time.

"Remarriage for older persons is a complex event because both [the husband and wife] have a long, prior family history," points out Professor Timothy H. Brubaker of Miami University in Oxford, Ohio, an expert on later life families.

Two other family life researchers, M. S. Moss and S. Z. Moss, writing in the *Journal of Gerontological Social Work* in the early 1980s, raise vividly the picture of new late-life marriages being influenced by memories of the earlier marriages. "Unlike first marriages in which the couple is seen as a twosome, the new marriage is viewed through the prism of the first marriage," say Moss and Moss.

But it's also important to point out, says Professor Brubaker, that family history is important to retain and it could *enhance* the new relationship.

Whether John will be able to become a caring stepparent to Betty's autistic son may, indeed, be positively influenced by the caring responsibility he's already shown in managing the illness and deaths of his earlier wives. Betty, because she finds meaning in the cottage her late husband built so many years ago, may be a good participant in helping John's son build his own summer home. They both seem ready to view their beckoning future through the lens of the past, but also to make that a source of strength to build on in a whole new world of love and experience.

Unpacking the Bags and Ironing Out the Wrinkles

John and Betty, and many, many more like them, have to confront issues that are both common to all late-life lovers and specific to their own situation. Betty's handicapped child is a factor not usually present in a new relationship; John's laid-back approach to helping his son all along the way to maturity may not be typical of many older men.

But regardless of the specifics, there are some questions that seem to apply *universally*; that is, most couples forging new love relationships in later life seem to encounter one or more of these basic issues:

- Money and property issues; how to divide and conquer. There are legal instruments, such as prenuptial agreements, that can help here.
- Decisions on where and how to live — retirement lifestyle in an age-segregated community, active involvement in a busy city life, choices dictated by health concerns — all must be considered.
- Resistance from children and other relatives and friends.

Expert counsel on all these are available to couples like John and Betty from a virtual army of matrimonial lawyers, divorce mediators, geriatric social workers, and other professionals who can help.

These are among the issues any late-life lovers might encounter, but there *are* possible solutions ahead for those with complex track records in the marital marathon.

Merited or Inherited: Money Matters

Money sits like a scheming spider at the center of a web of issues that seem to touch the lives of older people whichever way they turn when they want to remake their lives with new loves.

"Maybe money can't buy happiness, but it sure keeps the kids in touch," said actress Lucille Ball. That truth reflects the reality that this generation of parents and grandparents has reached a level of affluence unknown in earlier times.

Today's long-lived elders are probably the most financially secure generation ever, not forgetting that millions of older Americans still live from one Social Security check to the next, with little health insurance or savings. But the generation that fought World War II, which NBC newscaster and author Tom Brokaw calls "The Greatest Generation," *has* managed to pile up assets — homes, savings, pensions — undreamed of by their parents, who often emigrated penniless to this country or faced wars and depressions unknown to today's young people. Between the world wars, for example, home ownership was *not* the norm — it was a distant dream for a nation of renters. Now 67 percent of Americans own their homes.

The latest figures available from the Federal Reserve Board, culled from a 1995 survey, show that households headed by people between sixty-five and seventy-four had a median net worth of $104,100 — the highest of any age group cited in the study. So, when older men and women attempt to join their lives — either in conventional legal marriages or simply by living together — the questions arise thick and fast, especially in a national culture that reveres money as much as it reveres youth.

How shall each partner ensure their separate children will receive an equitable inheritance, while providing for the new spouse as well? And what about late-life divorce, always a possible sad companion to late-life marriage? There aren't so many years left in which to earn back assets that must by law be divided among older divorcing spouses. These and similar questions can be real deal breakers for older (and sometimes wiser) couples who want to join their lives in some fashion as they age.

The Prenuptial Agreement: Distrust or Common Sense?

The prenuptial agreement in which the management of the couple's assets and debts is clearly spelled out means that everybody, including the adult children, knows what to expect. Mike McCurley, president of the American Academy of Matrimonial Lawyers, points out in the *Wall Street Journal* that "at one time the only people who did prenups fit the [stereotype] of the rich old man marrying the fox. That is no longer true at all." "Now," he says, "many older couples… are remarrying and more of them are demanding security and predictability in the law."

However, prenuptial agreements are not for everybody, although Betty and John say they will probably try to work one out. Many new relationships founder on this rock because if one partner requests it, the other partner may feel that the request indicates lack of trust or even lack of a firm commitment.

"It [prenuptial agreement] does seem a little like hedging your bets," says Betty, "but I guess in our case — well, everything is so complicated!" John says he thinks it probably would help all the children to have one, but he won't press it if it makes Betty unhappy.

This web of concerns includes not only pensions and savings, as well as debts, but property, too. Mixing adult children and money-property issues can be such a legal tangle that many Johns and Bettys opt to stay out of a legal marriage and just live together without mutually worked out wills and other contracts.

"It's the [legal] marriage that worries the kids the most,"

says Lili Singer, coordinator of the bereavement program for Westchester Jewish Community Services in Hartsdale, New York, during an interview with financial writer Elizabeth Seay that was published in a *Wall Street Journal* article. "A woman's kids aren't going to like the situation if their father paid for the house and it's going to go to someone who met her when she was sixty-five years old," says Singer.

But sometimes legal provisions seem unduly harsh and paranoid when viewed in the light of the many aging folks with character and gumption who put a human face on these complications.

Fanny G. married Max R. when both were in their late seventies and she sturdily announced to all their children that going down to Florida with Max for what turned out to be their last few years was quite enough for her and that she wanted nothing that Max's first wife had worked so hard to put together. "The house, the goods, they all belong to his children," she said firmly. "If he dies before me, my own children will take care of me." (She had four adult children.) That is exactly what happened when Max died after five good years of sunshine and Fanny's marvelous cooking. Max's own children were so touched by Fanny's clear grip on her priorities, that they, unasked, also contributed to her maintenance in her aged last years, along with her own children.

Not all newly remarried wives are like Fanny and some have no children of their own to look to for assistance, so clear plans outlined in wills, in agreements about cost sharing, and in negotiations about where the couple will live, have to be — and *can* be — handled in such a way that they express love and caring, rather than suspicion and tentativeness.

"Your Place or Mine?" Couples and the Sense of Place

Any marriage counselor can tell you that money is always more than money — it symbolizes love and fantasy, is a means to repair frayed relations with children or other family members, and carries a host of other emotional and practical meanings, as well as reflecting beliefs and values, which we have seen acted out in the lives of the couples described above.

But another element in past lives that older lovers must try to join seamlessly is a sense of belonging to a special place.

As we have seen, Betty and her children are deeply attached to the house on the lake that her first husband built and the questions of how they should pay for the house and how John will feel spending part of each year there when every step reveals the loving handiwork of Betty's late husband are issues that need some thought and work, as both partners realize.

A shared sense of a special place can be a great bond, as it was in my case (see Introduction). Luckily for me, my partner had himself owned a charming house in the special place we shared, so that spending summers with me in the house *my* late husband had built did not seem a strange setting for him; the island was familiar, the house itself was familiar since he and his late wife had been social friends, and his adjustment, while having poignant moments for both of us, was relatively smooth.

The bond forged to a place called "home" or "special," can be a most enduring love — almost equal to the love of a person or a family, and often piercingly hard to leave behind to make a new life with a new partner.

In a charming memoir called *Dancing the Cows Home: A Wisconsin Girlhood*, author Sara De Luca tells of a first marriage in which her then-husband wished to emigrate to Australia. Believing it important to see the wider world beyond the farm country where she grew up, she eagerly went along.

But wisely understanding her modern situation, as opposed to her immigrant grandparents who came from Norway a century earlier, she wrote, "I was aware that I had choices. I could fly home in a single day if the reasons were compelling. Adapting was not critical to my survival. I could afford to mourn."

"And," she continues, "mourn I did. I longed to see snow-drifts, spring violets, white birches, and blazing sugar maples, red timber barns anchored by concrete silos, Holstein cattle dotting the Wisconsin countryside." (In her second marriage, her husband admired her home state and they returned to Wisconsin to make their new life — a happy ending that doesn't always happen.)

This mixture of longing for the physical beauty of a countryside one knows well and the symbolism of that place as "home" pulls powerfully on nearly everyone. It also explains the bitter tears of exiles, refugees, and other immigrants torn unwillingly from their home place.

Of course, there are many for whom the "home place" was never a happy and fulfilling part of their lives and to roam the outside world was imperative. That journey outward often made possible enriching love affairs, marriages, and careers.

All of these elements are part of the adjustment that newlyweds or long-married couples make in choosing to share their lives, but they also can add complications to late-life loves.

For example, seventy-six-year-old Kristi T., raised in Brooklyn, New York, always thought of herself as a "big city" girl and she loved Manhattan with its glitter and promise, but when she married a man who was determined to live in the suburbs, she went off to New Jersey and did, as she called it, "the suburban bit." She managed, however, to get back into the city as often as she could. After a long, close marriage of forty-two years, four children, and three grandchildren, Kristi lost her mate. After a lengthy period of numbed grieving, she decided to give up the struggle to maintain the big suburban house alone and to reclaim her first love: the excitement of Manhattan.

She found a pleasant apartment, smaller, of course, than her suburban house, but big enough for the grandchildren to visit. Soon she became an avid New Yorker, indulging long-submerged pleasures in the city's offerings of museums, theater, and concerts and taking her grandchildren for exciting adventures in Central Park and showing them the Christmas tree in Rockefeller Center.

The fly in this sweet ointment started buzzing when she met Paul S., who at seventy-two was an about-to-retire widower who had always owned a beautiful second home in Vermont. This home on a lake was, indeed, a gem surrounded by exquisite forests and mountains. Paul always intended to retire there after his teaching days were over, but it was hard for Kristi to think of leaving the city now that she had regained it so late in life.

When I met them, they settled on a commuting romance that found them spending part of each year in the other's home, but Kristi said that Paul was always edging her toward spending more and more time in his Vermont home, frequently grumbling that "most women would be thrilled with this place."

Kristi didn't especially appreciate that approach, and though they had much in common and Paul seemed to enjoy his time in the city with her to some degree, the last time I spoke with her, she was just not sure if this relationship was going to survive the "Your place or mine?" controversy.

All of these pushes and pulls —these tensions of love and opposition, all tied to specific places — are put under a very bright spotlight as one elderly couple, described below, finds each other, gives up and reacquires home places, and then designs solutions for the last lap of the journey.

"What Am I Doing Here?"

Emily T. and her husband, Henry, illustrate almost every facet of the "place" problem. Emily was sixty-six and Henry was seventy when they found each other at their high school all-classes reunion in a small town in Wyoming eight years ago. Emily had married, moved to Los Angeles to raise a family, and had been widowed the year before she re-met Henry, who had been one of her early high school "crushes." The feeling she had for him in those long-ago days she dismissed as puppy love, since he was a senior when she was a high school freshman and he graduated and disappeared from her orbit.

Henry was a widower for many years before he and Emily married, but he remained on his family's homestead ranch all the years that Emily was becoming a "big city" person, used to getting pizzas at midnight, her newspaper on her doorstep in the morning, and not driving more than fifteen minutes to go to a movie.

Their late-life romance, kindled in the very high school gym, now bedecked with crepe paper streamers welcoming back all the classes of the 1930s and 1940s, where Emily had once yearned after the popular senior class president, was a passionate and soul-filling revelation to both of them. They could not believe how much they had to say to each other, what a delight it was to reunite their lives, and marriage quickly followed.

Since Emily's two children and her grandchildren were scattered across the country — one in Denver and one in New Orleans — there was no real impediment to her moving into Henry's comfortable ranch home outside a small town in Wyoming. Henry's one son had been killed in the Vietnam War and this tragedy, plus a natural shyness Emily hadn't been aware of, kept him unmarried (though with one or two unsatisfying relationships) through the years since his wife died.

Emily left a wide circle of friends back in Los Angeles, but was determined to make the move to Wyoming and to bring some warmth and practical help into Henry's life, much to the delight of *his* friends and the few remaining relatives who still lived in the area.

After all, she reasoned to herself, she had been born and brought up in this very Wyoming area, her girlhood home having been only a town or two away from Henry's; they had gone to the same regional high school and knew some of the same people, or at least some of the few who were still living nearby.

She was sure her adjustment to this remote part of the country, which was, she pointed out on every occasion and to every visitor, very beautiful, would be just fine. The cottonwood trees near the river, the rolling sweep of hills, and the comfort and beauty of Henry's home would be the perfect setting for an unusually fulfilling and contented "third age."

And so it was, for three or four years, but after four snowed-in Christmases when no holiday merrymaking or exchange of gifts was possible in the way it is in a sparkling city, and after four years of driving three hours to hear some music or see a movie, the remote and austere beauty of the place began to pall.

"I didn't think it would be an especially hard move at all," says Emily, "because after all, I was a home town girl. I came from there and thought I could slip right back into the life there, but it didn't work out quite that way."

Henry admits, with the benefit of hindsight, that he, too, underestimated the changes the years had wrought in turning a country mouse into a city mouse and that the change of seasons at *his* home place might not hold the same charm for Emily it did for him.

To keep busy, Emily tried volunteering at the local hospital as an aide, but that, too, meant endless hours of driving in bad weather and was especially unworkable when Henry's longtime arthritis flared up badly and he needed her help at home.

When they both began to encounter fairly serious health problems, Emily began a real campaign aimed at moving them to Denver, where her younger daughter was a nurse and tied in to many health care resources in the community.

It was wrenching for Henry to sell the home he and his father had been born in (he had sold the cattle a good many years before) and to move to a city, but he recognized the wisdom of Emily's plans. Emily understood his sadness at leaving and tried her best to comfort him. Denver had no particular associations for her, either, but the presence of her daughter, her three grandchildren, and access to medical services was a comfort to both of them.

"I didn't like the idea that I had to be that close to doctors all the time, but Emily's daughter is just a crackerjack nurse and she got us set up with some medical people who are swell; I really like them, but I just keep hoping we won't need them all that much," says Henry, "but still it feels comfortable to know they are so handy."

Neither Henry nor Emily, now prepared to live out whatever time is left to them in Colorado, feel or think that they have settled the "place" problem particularly well, but their own relationship remains a vital, sweet prop in the instability and dislocation of leaving beloved places behind. In their case, the adult children are great resources. That is not always the case.

Little Kids, Little Problems; Big Kids, Big Problems

The two-edged sword of relationships with the adult children of both members of the couple — whether they are gay or straight — is one of the hardest to predict. Sometimes the adult children are genuinely thrilled that their solitary parent has a new relationship. Few would admit it, but not having to worry about widowed or divorced Mom or Dad is a pleasant reprieve, even if a very aged parent may eventually return to the family if they outlive their late-life partner. Some adult children even act as the matchmakers, as in the case of Mary Higgins Clark, the famed mystery writer. She was widowed for many years until her eldest daughter, a successful businesswoman, met a distinguished, retired corporate chief, a widower, and decided he was "just right for Mom." The match was happily made and when it was announced, Clark gave notice to other women that "the tuna casserole brigade can now retire."

But the two areas of trouble that seem the most insistent are: (1) the adult child's relationship to or memory of the absent (divorced or deceased) parent and his or her sometimes strong devotion to the remaining living parent and (2) the link between children and money, a potentially painful reality that older lovers must confront.

And the inheritance obstacle is not confined to very wealthy people whose children worry about stocks and bonds when Dad or Mom remarries or has a new relationship. It can also crystallize around the smallest object — a piece of jewelry, a pair of candlesticks — that symbolizes the absent parent and, from the children's viewpoint, the newcomer's usurpation of these symbols of the family's past.

"That woman using my mother's china, drinking from the beautiful wine glasses she brought back from Venice on her honeymoon? Over my dead body," is the way one recalcitrant daughter greeted the news that her father wanted to remarry.

There was no great wealth here to provoke intense greed in this daughter; but the artifacts that spelled "mother" to her were beyond price.

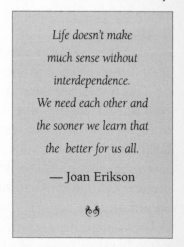

Life doesn't make much sense without interdependence. We need each other and the sooner we learn that the better for us all.

— Joan Erikson

These emotions can be so intense and so difficult to handle that many couples who would like to remarry don't do so because of resistance from their children, according to Eileen Simpson, author of *Late Love: A Celebration of Marriage after 50.* Christopher Lehmann-Haupt, reviewing Simpson's book in the *New York Times,* commented that "we are going to need a whole new set of fairy tales, ones that explore the behavior of the wicked stepchildren." The children's viewpoint, however, was poignantly expressed in a moving documentary created by filmmaker Terri Randall, called *Daughter of the Bride,* which was nominated for an Oscar in 1998. Randall made a film of her mother's remarriage some years after her father's death in 1989, stating that, while her mother likes the film as it finally emerged, she was doing it primarily for herself, to plumb the depths of her feeling about the new situation.

She tells, in a National Public Radio interview, how, after studying her mother's bedroom and seeing that the bedside photo of her Dad was moved to another place in the house, she realized that what she feared was that "my father's memory would just be pushed aside." As time progressed, that fear was conquered, but not until Randall, who is in her early forties, confessed that "no matter how old you are, you are always that lit-tle kid who wants to be with your Mom and Dad." Through mak-ing the film, she says, she understood that her mother was torn between the life she had and the life she would have and that an understanding slowly grew between mother and daughter.

Such understanding, says Dr. Robert N. Butler, chairman of the Geriatrics Department at Mount Sinai Medical Center (see Preface) and social worker Myrna Lewis, who have collabo-rated on several books encouraging public acceptance of elder sexuality, is often sabotaged by troubled histories.

"Problems can develop," says this team of experts, "if your children have grievances or hold grudges against you, which they demonstrate by refusing to condone your right to build a new life for yourself." The task of repairing such relationships often requires professional help, but direct, open attempts to understand and make things right again can be useful too.

Among the couples I interviewed, time was sometimes the change agent that made things work: by not pushing an immediate marriage plan, but having an ongoing romance that doesn't seem so threatening to the family's functioning, older couples sometimes can slowly alter such an unforgiving stance.

One canny divorced man in his late seventies, when faced with his seventy-four-year-old fiancée's children's correct, but very chilly, behavior, bided his time until the first grandchild was born. Then his role as surrogate grandpa, genuinely in love with the new baby, helped him slip into marriage with the new grandma in a comfortable way and made him more acceptable to the stepchildren.

Just the opposite reaction was registered by a seventy-six-year-old divorcée attending a senior center discussion group in Chicago on dating in late life. She confided to the group that she was thinking of breaking off a relationship with an other-wise appealing widower of seventy-three because she couldn't stand his *grandchildren!* She understood that he was very fond of these young adults and she assumed that if they married, she would see a good deal of them. "Once a year at Christmas, I could manage it," said Ruth W., "but not vacationing together or entertaining back and forth. To me they just seem like awful kids — demanding, undisciplined, and spoiled." "*He's* nice, though," she added wistfully.

How *do* the nearly quarter million people over fifty who remarry in this country each year make a go of it, despite the tensions of trying to mesh different family cultures? One way is to be certain within themselves of the validity of their new life and then communicate that to the children as Rachel and Dick did in the next story.

Tough Love: Not for Toddlers Any More

Rachel, seventy-three, and Dick T., seventy-nine, met at a cancer survivors' group where Rachel, an occupational therapist, was a member at the same time as Dick, who was attempting to deal with the death of his wife of fifty-one years. Rachel and Dick have now been married for three years and have some words of advice to help couples trying to assert their rights to a new life, no matter what their age, after loss and sorrow.

The answer, say Rachel and Dick, is "tough love." When they encountered bitter resistance from one of Dick's daughters ("I lost my Mom, I couldn't face losing my Dad, too," was her cry) and some initial foot-dragging from Rachel's son, they first tried patience and time, then coaxing and a few little bribes — like parent-paid vacations together and help with household projects.

When nothing seemed to work, they sat all the children down at a family conference, and announced, smiling gently, that they *were* going to be married, and that they hoped the children would share their happiness, but that the children must understand that this was, indeed, the plan.

"Sometimes this can be devastating and lead to an estrangement, at least temporarily," admits Dick, "but in this case, they just needed to understand that *this was going to happen,* that we were not asking their permission, but making plans about our own lives." He adds triumphantly, "They came around!"

Rachel reports that they continued grumbling for a while, but did attend the quiet, small wedding ceremony and the ice has been steadily melting. She and Dick advise tough love for almost all the problems older lovers face when elements of past lives overshadow the hoped-for new life.

Resistance from adult children, as family therapists, geriatric psychiatrists, and many of the couples we met in earlier chapters tell us, may have additional roots in unresolved subconscious sexual triangles involving the surviving parent and a new partner.

One young woman, the daughter of a friend, asked whether I planned to interview her Dad and his new wife for this book. Her mother had died suddenly of a heart attack while the twenty-eight-year-old daughter was on an overseas business trip, and her father had been a disconsolate widower for three years. In that time, he and his daughter, his only child, had become quite close. Later, he remarried, and chose a woman who was in every way an appropriate partner and a charmer to boot. My conversation with the daughter took place less than a year after the remarriage.

"Well, yes, I believe I will interview your Dad and Lillian," I answered. Virginia's response startled me with its vehemence: "I don't want to know about it," she said in an urgent tone, "don't tell me anything about it!"

"Oh, alright, I won't," I said calmly, thinking to myself, *If the young people can't stand the idea of their parents having sex, how are they going to handle their grandparents as sexual beings?* But life has taught older lovers lessons that might keep them from getting tangled in the Oedipus and Electra stories that Dr. Sigmund Freud has made part of our mental and emotional baggage.

The following practical steps are worlds away from myth-making, but are practical guides to reaching an understanding with adult children, distilled from much actual life experience.

Some Instructions for Winning Over Wary Children

The same parenting virtues that Moms and Dads have needed since the first newborn wail continue to be useful in this late-life stage, as well. Patience, sensitivity to the children's possible feelings of being an "outsider" in the new bond, and open communication have worked all along from the cradle to the children's own weddings, and most couples who have been through the wringer on this have a few suggestions. Here they are:

Tip 1: Recognize the children's tie to the missing partner and talk about it openly. Reassurance that the memory of a beloved parent or parent surrogate will not be moved aside in the new relationship can be made very convincingly, because in most cases, the surviving partner deeply feels the earlier experience as an immovable part of him- or herself. One divorcée, who had been her children's sole parent for many years before remarrying, explained it to the children this way:

"Look," she said, "you know that there is never a time your father is absent from my thoughts because of what a good Dad he is to you, even if he and I were not able to get along. I will always be grateful to him for that, and my new life is not going to go over those same tracks — it will run on a track *parallel* to the memories you have of how good your father is to you."

Even with clarity and straight talk, however, parents need to understand that acceptance may not come immediately.

Tip 2: Recognize time as an ally. Give the children time to adapt, to think it over, and talk it over — with you and among themselves. Don't spring a fait accompli on them; telling them you just got married when they didn't even know you were dating is a surefire way to make them feel left out and sullen, if not outright furious.

Tip 3: Siblings have a role to play here; try to estimate whether the resistance of the adult children is a unanimous reaction among all the children, assuming you have more than one. Sometimes one sibling is a ringleader in organizing opposition, but the other children may not feel so strongly as it appears. There may be chinks in the armor where some reason and affection can make some headway toward disarmament. In-law children often can be helpful here, as they have a less heated history with the parental generation involved.

Tip 4: After allowing time, sibling pressures, and candor to work on your behalf, if there is still resistance, then it is time for the tough love strategy referred to earlier. What is indicated then is a cheerful firmness about your own right to life and love, whatever your age and past history. The fact that one or both partners may have a troubled family history is no reason for older lovers to give up their chance for late-life happiness. If they need to do repair work on their relationship with their adult children, the new spouse or partner may be able to help — but whatever the situation may be, the rights and privileges of the elders also have to be respected.

> *There's no question that the outside of an individual does change…but very curiously, the inside does not change… Age is very mysterious because the essence of a human being, the soul, actually never ages.*
>
> — Beatrice Wood

Whether it's resistant children or money troubles or a variety of other problems, older lovers seem to have incredible reserves of resilience and strength to meet these challenges. How do they do it?

Prescription for Triumph: R$_x$ Courage, Love, and Humor

The stories of Emily and Henry, Betty and John, and the others have shown that a Pandora's box of troubles can erupt when older men and women — whether heterosexual or homosexual — try to carry the baggage of the past into the new country of late love.

Yet hundreds of thousands of straight, gay, and lesbian lovers contract late-life liaisons every single year and the majority live successfully together until death parts them, just as it does couples who only marry once and stay together until advanced old age.

What is the secret of triumphing over children's objections, money problems, culture clashes, and even health problems? The following stories of two couples who are dealing with fearsome physical health issues will help provide an answer.

Valor under Fire

Paul and Bea S., both eighty, were married onboard a cruise ship two years after their children introduced them to each other at a resort where both widowed parents were on a family vacation with their adult kids and grandchildren.

Both Paul and Bea are passionate travelers, always ready for a new trip and new adventures, so their compatibility on that score was quickly evident. And their wedding on a beautiful ship could not have been more romantic.

But they were candid about the fact that as they both entered their ninth decade, age had a deeply serious meaning: each was a survivor of bouts with serious heart disease and they had discussed this in honest detail with each other when it became clear they were falling in love and thinking seriously of marriage.

"Why marriage?" I asked, brave in the lessons I had learned from my New Age children and also from seniors who live together without marriage to avoid losing financial benefits or for other reasons.

Paul and Bea exchanged glances, and answered gently (as they would a not-quite-bright child), "Whatever happens, it's better to be together."

I found their courage breathtaking, but they were matter-of-fact about it, even kidding gently that "we did it for the grand-children — felt we should set an example for them," but the reality is that they weighed all their life experience with earlier marriages, family raising, and work lives; they knew something about their own needs and wishes and decided that, since each was apparently in good control of their heart problem, they would enjoy what time they could have together. When I interviewed them, they were about to set off on another trip, this time to scout Australia to see whether they wanted to aim for the 2000 Olympics. "Love," they told me, "is risky at any age."

Then there are Edith and Phil, whose story echoes a comment from Irish journalist Nuala O'Faolain, who wrote in her memoirs, *Are You Somebody? The Accidental Memoir of a Dublin Woman,* this analysis of older men and women: "How brave widows and widowers are! How resourceful people are, and how many secrets they carry around with them!"

Both the resourcefulness and the secrets are reflected in the story of Edith F., a seventy-seven-year-old widow who lives in a retirement community in North Carolina.

As she serves coffee and her special homemade cake in the tiny kitchen of her small apartment, Edith is a bright eyed, active partner in a romantic friendship with Phil T., eighty, a widower whose wife died many years ago, but who chooses to stay in a retirement community largely dominated by couples.

Although Edith is more than ready to tell about her romance with Phil and how she conducts it, she feels she should provide a little background. She confides that she has health problems that she has been successfully able to hide from Phil, even in their most intimate moments. (Sex plays an intermittent role in their lives, but is second to the pleasure of emotional intimacy and sharing they enjoy.)

Edith suffers from vision problems, chronic cystitis, Parkinson's disease, and borderline diabetes, and as a result, she carefully controls the amount of time and the settings in which she and Phil are together. But because she is not always as available to him as he might like, Edith makes sure their time together is very much "quality time," and she enjoys preparing special dishes he likes and accompanying him, when she comfortably can, to movies and concerts he enjoys.

Because she continues to invest a lot of psychic and a certain amount of physical energy in the relationship, she compensates for these outputs of energy by allowing her grown children — two of whom live within easy driving distance — to coddle her a little when she visits them or they visit her, and they are delighted to do a little pampering every six or eight weeks because they see the pleasures both Edith and Phil gain from the friendship, even though they do not live together and are not married.

In interviewing Phil separately, it is clear that he, too, is ready to claim space and time for himself, sadly based on a long unhappy marriage in which his wife was so demanding and difficult that her death could not help but bring him relief and liberation.

Even though he does not usually accompany Edith on visits to her nearby children, he is quite content that she makes these visits frequently and he enjoys visits from his only child, a daughter, but Edith and Phil make no attempt to mesh their children together; that would require much more stamina than either of them wishes to put forward at this time. They would, it seems, rather reserve that emotional energy for each other.

Although Edith is able to manage her illnesses — which she says can only be done because she has excellent doctors and pays close attention to their instructions about rest, medication, and exercise — her decision not to talk about them with Phil is, she says, prompted by a mix of motives. The first is that she doesn't want him to feel obligated to care for her should her health deteriorate; the second is the pride she feels in being able to take care of herself; and the third, she muses aloud, is that "I just don't want to admit that there is anything seriously wrong. I think a little denial is a good thing, don't you?"

Determining how *much* denial to indulge in is part of the skill of figuring out the best way to handle emotions and each couple meets this in their own way.

Not everyone has such a clear grip on what illness can mean to late-life love relationships.

Social worker Mary Cadden runs a class on dating after fifty at a senior center near Washington, D.C. One of her "students" a few years ago was a seventy-two-year-old twice-divorced retired government worker, whom we'll call Roscoe N., who told the group he had had a bout with cancer and had a heart problem.

He wondered aloud to his classmates: "In all fairness, do I want to bring someone into my life who is going to have to deal with this?" It apparently did not occur to him that he might "hide" his illnesses as Edith had done and perhaps his health problems were such they could not be hidden. However, he may also have been influenced by the fact that men of his generation continue to see themselves — albeit unconsciously — as the person to be *taken care of,* rather than the caregiver, and with some honor, he was wondering if he should involve someone else's life in that task.

In the end, Roscoe *did* remarry a year after he completed Cadden's session on dating; presumably both he and his new wife thoroughly understood the risks and rewards of what is called "proactive" aging in which very old people maintain the same number of *very close* relationships among age groups despite a reduction in the size of their overall social network.

Older couples who take the risk are often the winners in life's late-love lottery, as expressed by Katherine T., sixty-nine, who married Adam S., seventy-four, after each, in their late middle years, had lost cherished spouses, children, and siblings and had considerable baggage to carry into their new marriage. Still, Katherine was able to write to a friend who had been unable to attend the wedding, "the glow still remains,…leaving us to marvel at the wonder of how two people in later life could bond together so well."

The Anatomy of Bravery: Emotional Competency

From my own observations and from life span studies done by a large community of scholars and researchers, the mysteries of courage and risk taking seem to be explained by the fairly simple idea that older people *have learned how to live!*

According to Professor Laura L. Carstensen, Ph.D., of the Psychology Department at Stanford University, who is also director of Stanford's Institute for Research on Women and

Gender, and Robert W. Levenson, Ph.D., director of the Institute of Personality and Social Research at the University of California, Berkeley, older men and women have become "virtuosos" in regulating their emotions, in controlling extremes of behavior, and in avoiding negative situations and maximizing pleasurable interactions.

"Older people," reports Dr. Levenson, "are master emotional schedulers." He adds "that they become better at putting their emotions to work for themselves in effective ways."

Looking at the skills that Bea and Paul and Edith and Phil are going to need to handle problems, much encouragement comes from all quarters — from both individual couples and scholarly professionals in many fields.

One famous life span researcher is Paul Baltes, Ph.D., of the renowned Max Planck Institute for Human Development in Germany. Dr. Baltes has been willing to place himself on a direct collision course with geriatric researchers who claim that all is decline and loss in the older years.

Dr. Baltes's research shows just the opposite: while the mechanics of the aging brain may indeed indicate slower responses ("biology is no friend of old age," he says), the experience and cultural knowledge of the senior trumps the biological limits of memory and recognition. In other words, common sense smarts based on experience, knowledge, and cultural memory, compensate for physical losses. He points out that human knowledge and skill in using information helps us handle difficulties as they arise. "If people have hearing problems, society develops hearing aids," he says, pointing out that it is only in older years that we have enough sense to try to avoid emotional blind alleys and wasting our energies on unproductive emotions. Dr. Baltes further pinpoints the ways

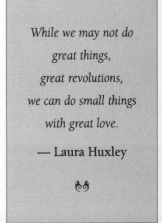

While we may not do great things, great revolutions, we can do small things with great love.

— Laura Huxley

in which older people balance using gains and losses. Using the late concert pianist Arthur Rubinstein as an example, he noted that the great musician admitted he could continue to perform well into old age because he (1) played fewer pieces, (2) practiced each piece more frequently, and (3) changed his technique so that by varying tempos in certain ways, he could maintain the sound of rapid notes.

Dr. Baltes cites this as an example of the three main ways in which culture and experience help older people to continue to function at high levels: selectivity (fewer pieces), optimization (more practice), and compensation (increased use of tempo changes).

Dr. Baltes comes to his conclusions from work with volunteer subjects in his laboratory, but in my talks across the country with older men and women aiming to include deep new love relationships in their long lives, I found just those processes going forward.

There are widows and divorcées living in small towns, big cities, and everything in between, including retirement communities, who are so surefooted among the shoals of aging, health, and emotional losses and gains, that it is not uncommon to meet women who have been married two, three, four, and more times, or who have had a similar number of monogamous-style but legally unmarried relationships. Since women still tend to outlive men by seven or eight years (though the gap is slowly closing, demographers say), it is not quite so common, but not completely unknown either, to meet older men who have been widowed several times.

These *emotional competencies* that living a long time seems to confer on both genders are so striking, says Dr. Robert Levenson, that early returns on some of his research projects suggest that even in long-enduring marriages that are not particularly happy, the partners manage a "better balance of positive to negative emotion" than in unhappy marriages of people a generation younger where negative emotions predominate.

Exit Laughing: A Coping Skill

One of the ways long-married couples *and* new late-life lovers demonstrate this greater equilibrium and regulation of their emotional lives is through humor. Teasing, laughing, and telling stories on themselves and each other, looking life right in the eye and figuring out what's funny and what shouldn't be taken too seriously — all these are coping methods that many older men and women delightfully demonstrate when talking about how they are facing togetherness in old age.

When older people laugh at themselves and couples fondly repeat ancient "inside" jokes that only they understand, these are ways of affirming bonds and revealing healthy perspectives on what's important and what isn't, a distinction young people — in the throes of ambition, acquisitiveness, and youthful love passions — often cannot make.

The laughter with which older lovers manage to greet the inevitable troubles, large and small, that life provides is clear in this story told by Gertrude Bernstein, eighty-three, of New York, who described a nervous moment when her fiancée, David Edelstein, eighty-five, was coming to dinner with his son. It would be Gertrude's first meeting with the man who would become her stepson.

"Now normally, I'm a good cook. But that night I burned the steak! If that had happened at thirty-five, I probably would have burst into tears, but at eighty-one, you see the humor in it," says Gertrude. She and David now say they wouldn't be back in their twenties or thirties for anything.

"It [love] is more pleasant now," says David. "When you're young, every imaginary slight can throw you into a funk. Now we look at each other, we smile. When one does something absentminded, the other one says 'it's okay — all of us do it.'"

"You laugh a lot more in your eighties," confided Gertrude to Lois Smith Brady, who covered their wedding for the *New York Times* in 1997.

Using humor to defuse tensions and conflicts and to ward off pain has been the principle technique of every clown from Pagliacci to funnyman Red Buttons and older people express a tremendous joy in life and love through this kidding and joking that seems to mark the good times they're having together.

> Ours is a long marriage,
> and we have found
> solitude together.
>
> — Carolyn G. Heilbrun
>
> ☙

One of the liveliest wits of all time was Mae West, the first Hollywood sex kitten. Born in 1893, she lived to flaunt her sexuality throughout most of the twentieth century and she did it with humor, jokes, and running gags that kept her out of trouble with the censors at least some of the time.

One of her most famous lines, delivered just a few months before her death in 1980, was given to the reporters who asked her to confirm a news story that she had had a stroke and fallen out of bed.

"Nonsense," she said, "I was dreaming of Burt Reynolds — and it [the fall] was worth it."

The humor expressed by older people when they talk about their love lives and aging in general has many emotional colorations — sometimes it is wryly cognizant of the troubles of old age ("a great catch in the retirement communities is not a man who is rich or handsome or young — it's one who can drive at night"); sometimes it is hilarious (although of questionable taste) jokes about Presidential scandals or the foolishness of people who want to be famous for fifteen minutes; and sometimes there's a kind of playfulness that reveals that older people have, as many of them described it, "time to kid around now — time we didn't have when we were working and raising kids."

Whether older people use teasing and jokes to ward off the mortality just around the corner, or whether they are more disposed to be reflective and introspective in older years, the possibility of using a long lifetime of experience, together with laughter, to enrich late relationships is firmly supported by virtually everything that is known now about the older mind and heart.

Even people who did not marry in the conventional family-forming years, sometimes find relationships of warmth and love, courage and humor, in late years that eluded them in the more turbulent decades.

Married and Unmarried: The Tale of Two Men

Two men who remained unmarried for many years during the time their peers were marrying and fathering children illustrate that hard-won emotional knowledge gained over a lifetime can eventually result in relationships of sweet contentment later on, a fact young people find difficult to believe.

Both in their forties at the time, Zack T., sixty-one, was a confirmed bachelor, living in Northern California when he spotted his now-wife, Mona, sixty-four, on the dance floor at a social gathering, and asked her to dance.

"As a bachelor for a long time, I was okay with rejection — it had happened plenty of times in my life and I was used to acceptance, too," he says. When Mona turned down his offer to dance, he waited a bit and then suggested that they "just talk a little." That's an offer that's hard to refuse, and dates followed. But each of them, as we know is likely, had heavy, heavy emotional baggage to unpack.

Mona was the single divorced mother of three children, who maintained close ties with her ex-husband, and Zack had never married or, as an adult, lived with children of any age on a regular basis. He is frank that Mona's child-rearing methods didn't match the structured and more disciplined family life he had been raised in, and although her children were soon to be out of the nest, they formed a formidable adjustment challenge, as did her relationship with her ex-husband.

For her part, Mona was devoted not only to her family and all the aspects of her earlier life before Zack, but she also wanted elbow room to pursue her interest in theater and dance.

Experts say that men who do not marry by age forty have only a one-in-six chance of ever marrying. (This was thought to be a generational issue and that the baby boom generation married so much later that the numbers did not apply to them. However, the latest statistics show it remains a reality: unmarried men in midlife seldom change their patterns.)

And Zack and Mona's two-year courtship during which they lived together sometimes, then separated, and then reunited, was indeed a stormy period of adjustment when they needed all the luck, flexibility, and perspective that their decades of living gave them.

Today, they have been married fifteen years and their union is as solid and rewarding as friends who are heading for their golden wedding anniversaries.

Zack and Mona chose to marry but another couple — Edward and Dorothy — utilizing some of those late-life smarts — chose *not* to formalize their close relationship.

Edward N., seventy-eight, who continues teaching English literature at a small college in Washington state, remains the same bachelor he has always been, but has now had for some twenty-five years, a wonderfully full and satisfying romantic friendship with Dorothy P., seventy-six, who is a retired teacher.

They maintain separate residences, but are definitely a couple who have linked their lives in every meaningful way, sharing each other's family and friends, traveling together, and being as supportive of each other's aging lives as any husband and wife.

This is how Edward described their baggage-laden past and their contented present. In a letter, he wrote: "My most meaningful relationship is one that came about for me well into my middle years. She, too, had been through, by then, the 'sturm and drang' of earlier relationships and love affairs. We came to each other as rather seasoned beings, not without needs and desires, but with having many of our youthful fantasies and expectations tamed by life experiences. By then, we both were ready to compromise some of our more unrealistic needs.

Though our needs for physical closeness and mutual attentiveness are important to our relationship, we nonetheless value almost equally our separateness and individuality. In other words, we know and respect each other's need for space, as well as intimacy."

Zack and Edward may be exceptional among older men in their ability to articulate that very "emotional control" that life span experts find over and over again in their research, but there are many men seeking — and some are finding — the contentment reflected in what the Zack-Mona and Edward-Dorothy pairs have shown us of their gallant ability to handle life's problems.

A Road Map for the Journey

If we look at the mastery of living that the couples in this chapter have exhibited, we can see in their experiences a sort of road map for late-life lovers. These are some of the roads they've taken, potholes, bumps, and all:

- Courage is a main highway. The risks, the pitfalls, and the triumphs stem from having learned and loved. It took bravery to confront physical and emotional health issues that all elders will meet at some point.

- Love and spirituality were found along the byway of learning to give and take, and to keep their eyes on what becomes truly important as time shortens.

- There's a bridge on the map that shows the way over troubled family relationships that may need renewal now; but, with increased "emotional competence," parents and children have a new chance to experience familial love.

- Take time out for laughter, older couples advise. Joy is contagious, humor a subtle way out of trouble, and private jokes a kind of good luck charm just for two.

Although this map was put together by couples who daily take their own prescription for courage, love, and humor, the spiritual and emotional realities they have dealt with apply to any older man and woman, whatever their love relationships may be as they age.

In the next chapter, we will see how this prescription can help older men, and the women and families who love them. There are special problems men face after the loss of a partner through death or divorce, and ways particular to men that they work out the coping skills and develop the valor they need as the years race past.

The triumphs we have detailed in this chapter were accomplished with two partners together. How men alone can either find new partners or win a good old age on their own will be described in their own voices in the pages ahead.

TRAILBLAZER

Carolyn G. Heilbrun

If courage, love, and humor are the answers, what is the question?

The question is: How do we go about living our lives as we age — both in our love relationships and in our relationship with ourselves?

One of the bravest, most loving (and occasionally the funniest) women to answer that question is Carolyn G. Heilbrun, Ph.D., seventy-three, distinguished author, retired Columbia University professor of literature, and, under the pseudonym Amanda Cross, creator of engaging mystery stories.

Dr. Heilbrun is the author of *The Last Gift of Time: Life beyond Sixty,* which was written after she passed her seventieth birthday. In terms of courage, it is one of the most candid observations on women, aging, and love that we could turn to for guidance and inspiration.

Dr. Heilbrun confesses, in essays, critical works, and biographies, that she had decided early in her life not to live past the biblical span of "three score and ten," that life after seventy would be too grim and depressing, and that she would take her own life because after sixty everything would be downhill.

Reaching the seventy milestone, she was astonished, she reports, to find that her sixties had been more rewarding than she ever imagined because she had achieved a delightful combination of serenity and activity. She now regards her seventies this way: "I find it powerfully reassuring now to think of life as borrowed time. Each day one can say to oneself: I can always die; do I choose death or life? I daily choose life the more earnestly because it is a choice."

Dr. Heilbrun, married to the same man for many

decades, mother and grandmother, a writer more than useful to the worlds of literature, feminism, and education, reports that her children are more rewarding than ever ("friends with an extra dimension of affection"), her circle of women friends one of the great joys of late life, and she seems to find no difficulty in acknowledging the love and support of her husband during a long-running marriage.

Her pithy humor is up-front, too. On marriage, she writes, "I have come to accept the fact that if one is married to a man, there are certain things to be expected on the debit side, just as if you have a cat for a pet, you expect the furniture to be clawed. I know you can declaw cats, and perhaps husbands, too, but I don't approve of it in either case."

Love, for Dr. Heilbrun, is capable of careful distinctions. She reports that, while she takes the great and conventional pleasures in her grandchildren that all grandparents know, she believes the pleasure she gets from her own adult children is even greater now that they are grown. To understand how charming small children are, she points out, you do not need to be old, but to savor the conversation of your grown children, one has to have a "special sense of present time" available only to those in their sixties and beyond.

Love, courage, and humor stand around this trailblazer like a stage spotlight as she unflinchingly discusses mortality: "The greatest oddity of one's sixties is that if one dances for joy, one always supposes it is for the last time. Yet, this supposition provides the rarest and most exquisite flavor to one's later years."

Chapter 3

Flowers in Winter
Men Speak of Elder Love

An old man in love is like a flower in winter.

— Portuguese proverb

I n the perfumed oasis of her [ship's] cabin, they made the tran-
quil, wholesome love of experienced grandparents...it was as if
they had leapt over the arduous calvary of conjugal life and gone
straight to the heart of love...they had lived...long enough to
know that love was always love, any time and any place."

This is the climactic scene in Gabriel Garcia Márquez's masterpiece, *Love in the Time of Cholera*, a novel that describes a
man who, despite many physical relationships, truly loved only

one woman all his long life. After, as he put it, "fifty-three years, seven months, and eleven days and nights," the couple consummated an incredible love affair. For today's older lovers, it is also a charming reality that Márquez has his seventyish lovers — who were married to or living with others throughout their long lives — hesitant and fumbling at first, until they reach that place where "love was always love."

The strength of the lover who sought the same beloved from youth into his old age amazed the captain of the ship on which they were pursuing a new life together. The captain, looking at Florentino Ariza, the aged hero, "his invincible power, his intrepid love," came to the conclusion that "it is life, more than death, that has no limits."

This gift to us from a famed Latin American writer whose stories are framed in magical realism is, under the surface of different cultures, different times, different histories, still recognizable in our own day. We can feel it in stories told and written by contemporary older men who, in their tenderness and their ability to renew life, suggest Márquez's hero.

In exploring the love landscapes of American elders, it became apparent that while older men struggle alone with loss, fear of aging, loneliness, and isolation, they often also find love, sex, romance, and companionship. In this chapter, we will consider their fears and worries and the hope that might be offered to those who have not found their way out of bereft aloneness to new relationships.

> *Eighty percent of life is showing up.*
>
> — Woody Allen

Michael M., a seventy-six-year-old retired film editor, headed an industrial film production company in Portland, Oregon, before his retirement. He was married twice before our meeting and was the father of three and the grandfather of four. Michael shared a journal he kept during the reappearance in his life of a new/old love. This is a woman with whom he had had a collegial work friendship, but not a romance, when they both were

English majors at the University of California at Los Angeles.

In his journal, Michael does not use her name, but refers to her only as "my love."

"In response to your request for an amplification of my personal friendships and love relationships, I must extend my statements to you in our interview about the woman who has become the center of my life in the last two years," he writes.

"My second wife's death at only fifty-seven [Michael was twelve years older] was absolutely shattering. I grieved in a zombielike state for a long time, going through my work days like a robot, though everyone assured me that work was the best antidote for grief. It didn't seem to be that way for me," he confided to his journal.

Anyone reading this passage will recognize the commonly-held belief that work is a helpful diversion through widowhood and grief. However, because Michael had had a completely different experience, I wanted to find out why and continued our interview through a long series of cross-country telephone conversations, since I was based in New York and Michael had moved from Portland to Northern California to be nearer two of his three children in the San Francisco area.

"I made a decision," Michael related, "to attend a college alumni reunion and while a number of old friends were there, the woman who is now my life's love was not. I asked about her — a premonition, maybe? — but all I could learn from other classmates was that she recently had been widowed and was still in mourning. The alumni people gave me her current address; happily for me, she lives in Southern California, but at least we are on the same coast!"

It turned out that the woman married one of Michael's college acquaintances and had four children of her own. Now bereaved, she was receiving many condolence letters and calls, Michael's among them.

"But she only sent a formal acknowledgement — one of those printed things — of my condolence letter and that wasn't a lot to go on," Michael said.

It was then that Michael made the courageous decision that changed him from a zombie into a man with a new life; he had her return address on the printed form and he called her.

It is exactly at this point in Michael's story that so many other men included in this book found themselves unable to move forward.

So many fears — of being old, of being too rusty at courting not to mention love or sex, of rejection, or of making poor choices — can paralyze older men who have led settled, conventional married lives and are now alone through death or divorce. These fears afflict both gay and straight partners who have lost longtime spouses or companions, and they seem to be universal in almost all cultures. African American, Hispanic, and Asian men all confide to ethnic gerontologists the reality that older love, while wonderful when found, may not be so easy to achieve as society and older widows believe. Men are so favored in numbers, as against the superabundance of elderly widows in all cultures, that it would appear that for men a new connection is easy to make, whether they live in Chinatown or in a beach resort frequented by gay men or in "Little Havana" in Miami, where elderly Latinos reside.

But many men must overcome paralyzing fears and if they have not been resilient, adventurous, and experimental in their previous life, it is difficult to begin in later life. And when they do try, they are often so inept, frightened, and desperate with loneliness that their choices are poor and create new struggles to be overcome, handicapping them further, just when energy and material resources must be managed carefully.

Sean T., who lost a beloved second wife at the age of seventy-eight, said, when we were discussing the difficult time an older man has in the first phase of widowhood, "I swear to you that if it had not been for our children, I would have married the cleaning lady six weeks after Mary's death; I was so horribly alone in the house we had shared for so many years. I just couldn't face that aloneness, but I was held back from doing anything crazy by some shreds of sanity that mostly had to do with not wanting to upset my grown kids any further; they were having a hard enough time with the loss of their mother and their own kids lost a perfect grandmother, too." At the time of our talk, Sean had been alone for nearly three years, though feeling that soon he might be ready to think of at least some modest forays into the new world of dating. "At past 80 — can you believe how badly prepared I am for this?" he asked.

George R., seventy-two, contracted an unhappy late marriage after his wife of nearly fifty years passed away, and in disentangling himself from a messy divorce, he explained the mistake by simply describing what he felt after his wife's funeral.

"The notion of going home to that empty apartment was absolutely unendurable," he said. He tried to manage that dreaded daily moment of putting the key in the lock at night by working very late and coming home so tired that he would sleep immediately; it didn't work. Then he embarked on a busy schedule of visiting all the friends and adult children he could cram into his vacation time. At that point, a divorcée in the office of the shipping company he worked for appeared on his doorstep with the proverbial tuna casserole (in this case, it was chicken soup) and he was married shortly thereafter, only to find that the quick effort to avoid the empty apartment had caused more problems than it had solved.

But even when men do not jump into a rapid remarriage, the dry throat and sweaty palms attendant on the first effort to call up a prospective date are as bad as ever they were in high school.

Michael, too, confessed to me that if he had not had the very thin thread of their earlier college days together (they were never in touch again after graduation), he isn't sure that he would have had the courage to call the woman he now says is "my life's love."

"That visit, a sunny weekend in early autumn, changed and joined our lives," he wrote in his journal. "I took a room at an inn near her home and we met for walks and quiet dinners."

As in so many similar stories, the critical reality here is not that she was a slim, dazzling beauty of thirty-five or even fifty, (according to her pictures, she is a matronly grandmother with pretty white hair who is exactly one year younger than Michael), but that they quickly reached a comfort zone of sharing confidences, pouring out their heart's grief and loss, showing each other pictures of their children and grandchildren, and remembering together the student days when they were going to each write the Great American Novel.

"We talked and talked...we opened up and confided, we caught up with all those lost years, we commiserated...like friends or siblings who had been parted for years," Michael wrote in his journal. "Her long, happy marriage was not like my more troubled marital history, but we each had nursed spouses through terrible, traumatic illnesses and it was amazing how similar was the crucible of emotion we passed through. She had never accepted her husband's heart condition and fought to get him a heart transplant down to the last moment of his life; I, for my part, had stood frozen when, in response to my begging my wife's doctor to tell me the real truth about her chances to survive a killer hepatitis infection, the doctor said, 'well, miracles *do* happen.'"

Many older men and women share the belief that young lovers cannot begin to imagine what it is like to share this experience with someone capable of compassion and empathy, someone who has, indeed, "been there." "At this stage of life," writes British novelist David Lodge, "common human kindness counts for so much."

What saves Michael's story from cloying sweetness or an unendurably happy ending is that they did not marry and they did not combine homes. They feel, warily, that with seven children between them, complex property and money assets, the best route is to keep their present domiciles, each near their own children, and go back and forth to each other as best they can.

This was Michael's last letter to me: "To the relief of our

kids, we are making no contractual plunges, and hope to live out our lives and stay as healthy as we can, as friends and lovers…my main goals are to reach authentic adulthood before it is too late, and to be grateful to the kindly fates for my great good luck. My love, who is perfect, doesn't really have to do anything but just be."

To some women readers, Michael may seem unlike any man they have ever known in terms of his resilience, kindness, and courage, but the tenderness and empathy of which he is capable is latent in many men if a bit of luck can be found that will reveal these traits, gleaming among the more typical masculine strengths of loyalty and hard work.

No one, for example, might think that a big gruff man who earned his living as a football coach would be likely to exhibit the tenderness and understanding that his daughter reported to best-selling author Robert Fulghum, when Fulghum was collecting stories of true love for a book with that title. His book *True Love* follows his now famous *All I Really Need to Know I Learned in Kindergarten*.

Most of Fulghum's interviewees and correspondents did not give their full names, as Myrna from Seattle did not, but she tells Fulghum that her mother, who is very pretty and had won beauty contests when younger, had given up the little vanity of putting nail polish on her toes when arthritis made it hard for her to twist herself into the bending necessary to apply this cosmetic touch.

To her mother's surprise, her husband of forty-five years volunteered and now paints her toes for her. "Why would you want to do that?" she asked her football coach husband.

"Because," he answered, "I love you and I want you to feel beautiful for as long as you live."

And not only are some older men capable of the full range of love and passion, but they often leaven it with that saving edge of humor that spices the warmth we feel coming from Michael and from Márquez's Florentino.

Invisible? The Diverse Lives of Older Men

Readers who are drawn to the images of the articulate and warmhearted men described above may be puzzled at why sociology professor Edward H. Thompson Jr., Ph.D., of Holy Cross College in Worcester, Massachusetts describes older men as "invisible." In his book, *Older Men's Lives,* Dr. Thompson points out that because the elderly population is predominantly female and because men appear to be — and in many areas of life, actually are — so much more advantaged than elderly women, both scholarly research and popular media have focused more attention on the needs and life challenges of older women.

But, says Dr. Thompson, "there are more than 13 million men over the age of sixty-five in America" and they are not a homogeneous group; they are as diverse now as they were when they were younger.

True, men are not obliged to bury their spouses and live alone as often as women, but, say gerontologists, we need to be sensitive to and anticipate the differences among elder men. For example, elderly black men are much less likely to live with a spouse than are white men or men of Hispanic origin. This diversity in elder men's marital situations, for whatever reasons, just points up that "old men" (which used to mean all males over sixty-five), live differing lives and cannot all be lumped into the same seldom-studied minority.

Another element of "invisibility" is that when older men retire from work they seem to disappear from the stage, even though they may continue very active family lives and are busy in their communities or with "worklike" activities, such as driving disabled neighbors to doctor appointments or tutoring children in underprivileged neighborhoods. But once the daily pattern of leaving home for work for a set number of hours is over (or society thinks it *should* be over), our culture views the retiree as either a constantly vacationing playmate or as uninterestingly inactive. But here, too, the view of older men as one homogeneous group is mistaken, says a research report on older men and work, done by Peggy A. Szwabo, Ph.D. and the late Kenneth Solomon, M.D., both of the Department of Psychiatry at the St. Louis University School of Medicine. The geriatric psychiatry researchers claim, first, that many men over sixty-five continue to work, either full- or part-time, and second, many embark on second careers often quite different from the first, a trend that is predicted to accelerate strongly when baby boomers reach sixty-five.

But in our popular culture now, men in late adulthood no longer occupy center stage, says Dr. Edward Thompson; their generation is no longer the dominant one. And with this comes the assault on older men of all the negative stereotypes that a youth-oriented society can develop, i.e., older men are asexual, passive, sedentary, and, in fact, not "men" at all. This stereotyping may help younger men retain their grip on power in the period of their own generation's dominance, but it bodes ill for developing healthier and more accurate "masculinities" for themselves when the young generation itself ages.

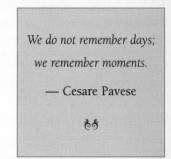

We do not remember days;

we remember moments.

— Cesare Pavese

The popular culture, which so worships youth, is even harder on those who have achieved some measure of success or fame. The Oscar-winning actor, Dustin Hoffman, who is now sixty-one, finds he must move behind the cameras as a producer since, he says, "by definition, leading roles are written mostly for people in their thirties and forties, not people like me. So you become a friend of who the movie is about, or you carry a gun in those action things, which I won't do."

Although Hollywood has long been famous for discarding actresses over forty until they are old enough to play grandmother roles, society seems not to have noticed that this ageism comes down hard on men as well.

"Our senior performers have all but disappeared from

television, and they're practically invisible in feature films" says Richard Masur, fifty, former president of the Screen Actors Guild.

Although the stereotypes would have it that older men suffer such significant losses — work, health, independence — that their lives would appear to be diminished beyond hope, the reality that men from sixty to ninety live with is infinitely more diverse, active, and engaged than stereotypes permit.

The "plus" time that ensues for older men when longtime work patterns end or change includes a very real sense of freedom, of doing things they've wanted to do for a long time, and of reinvigorating long-enduring marriages and reinventing relationships with children, grandchildren, and friends who may have suffered neglect during men's intense focus on work in their young and middle years.

Many mental health professionals have commented on how older men sometimes (not always) become more expressive, relate better to both men and women in friendship and love, and seem less hard-edged once the daily battle in the jungle of work relationships is behind them.

In addition, the great psychologist, Erik Erikson, said older men have a big task to do in their late years: they must pass on to younger people all they've learned and help the next generation to well-being and productivity. Erikson calls it "generativity" and many men — from carpenters to college professors — *do* find settings in which they can transmit their hard-won knowledge to others.

Both the increased sensitivity to others and the drive to pass on knowledge, skills, and understanding are also expressed actively by older men in a varied range of volunteer activities in big cities, small towns, and rural areas throughout the world and in many ethnic and culturally diverse communities. The ways older men find to accomplish these developmental growth possibilities are different in different ethnic communities and are not always easy.

The conventional notions, for example, that elders are

venerated in Chinese and other Asian cultures and their wisdom and experience is highly respected is not so true when these values bump up against the battering of popular American culture, which pulls American-born Asian children away from the old ways. Similarly, Hispanic men, often the patriarchs of closeknit families, can suffer role losses and disaffection on the part of their children because of differing American customs and pressures. How closely immigrants are tied to the old country and its values and customs, and how those ties are handled in collision with modern America, determines to some extent how well the older man can set about his later life tasks of warming and enriching his family relations and giving something to the next generation.

Caution: Men at Risk

It is true that for women, widowhood, diminished funds, and chronic illness often result in the so-called "feminization of old age." This iron rule of demographics causes most social policy and individual family concerns to be focused on the greater number of women who outlive their husbands and who can be alone at a vulnerable time.

It is true, in addition, that most older men are still living with caretaking spouses or other family members, they have more financial assets than women their age who frequently — in that generation — did not work outside the home, and that, in general, older married men score very high on life satisfaction.

It is appropriate, given these realities, that gerontologists and policy makers put older women at the top of the priority list.

But that focus of concern should not overshadow the fact that men who live alone suffer particular forms of isolation, emotional depression, and often, rapidly deteriorating health.

They are considered by social workers and community agencies to be at high risk, even when they have adequate income and adult children are not too far away.

Illustrating just how dramatically these factors can impact on the diverse lives of older men are these reports: "The highest suicide rates in the nation in 1996 were for white men over eighty-five, who had a rate of 65.3 suicides for every 100,000 people in the U.S. The national overall suicide rate was 10.8 per 100,000, and the elderly rate was five to six times more frequent even than the suicide-prone rage years. In spite of often living long lives of economic deprivation and cultural discrimination, the suicide rates for black men are much lower, stressing once more the diversity among life experiences of elders."

Of course, not all these suicides among elderly men are caused by loneliness or emotional deprivation; some were caused by severe physical illnesses, untreated depression, substance abuse, or specific mental illnesses.

Buried in these chilling statistics is another thought-provoking fact for the medical profession and family members of older folks: A large majority of older people, both men and women, who do complete suicide attempts, have visited some kind of health care provider within a month prior to their deaths.

This reality would seem to confirm a widely-held theory that many elder suicides are the result of untreated depression which, experts say, should *not* be considered a normal part of aging.

Barry D. Liebowitz, M.D., an expert on the emotional disorders of aging with the National Institute of Mental Health, emphasizes that "depression is not the outcome of natural processes and should not be considered normal."

Because older people often have other health problems, medical professionals tend to think that depression is the least of their difficulties, but even the most complex set of physical health problems can be helped by treating the companion depression.

George S. Alexopoulos, M.D., a psychiatrist at Cornell University Medical College, reports that treating a depressed patient with Alzheimer's disease, for example, improves both the depression *and* the dementia.

The National Institute of Mental Health, which keeps these statistics along with other government agencies such as the U.S. Bureau of Health and Human Services and the Center for Disease Control in Atlanta, points out, however, that suicide rates among the elderly — both men and women — continue to be *highest for those who are divorced or widowed*. Although women generally *attempt* suicide more often (in all age groups), men more often complete the act.

Behind the sunny untruths that postretirement years for men are all about dancing aboard cruise ships and improving golf handicaps lie some other difficult realities.

For more men than women, marriage is the sole deeply personal relationship in their life. By contrast, even happily married women who feel their husbands are best friends and important confidants, often have additional networks of close women friends and frequently have close ties to siblings, particularly sisters, as well.

Geriatric psychologists speak movingly of the need older men have to know, deep in their souls, that someone is "there" for them after they have lost a partner of many years.

This can seem on the surface to be simply looking for a housekeeper, since this need is often expressed by such laments as "who'll sew a button on my shirt?" and many men admit to being worried about what happens when the clean socks run out. Laundry, cooking, and shopping are not as comfortable for the generation of men who came of age in the 1920s and 1930s as for younger men of today, by and large, though of course there are exceptions.

A seventy-four-year-old retired businessman from Michigan, who had been widowed for two years, confided that going down to his usual wintering spot in Southern California was complicated for him now because a number of widows had indicated they would like to accompany him. He further reported that *none* of these women were ones he was interested in establishing a "couple" relationship with, but he admitted that the most persistent one probably would go to California with him for a couple of months, saying, "well, she could do the cooking and the laundry, anyway." This kind of pragmatism often hides an emotional neediness that men seldom will admit. Men often have to cast this need in mundane terms because this older generation was raised to believe that men should suppress feelings, not show weakness or vulnerability, and concentrate on monetary success.

"With age, the husband's close relationships with others outside his marriage practically disappear," particularly in blue-collar families, according to the late Mirra Komarovsky, a nationally known sociologist who did a groundbreaking study of working-class husbands and wives in the 1960s. There has been no data to refute these findings since, and we are left wondering, along with Komarovsky, why, as the years go on, husbands increasingly depend solely on their wives for emotional support. "Is it," she asks, "because the *need* for sharing diminishes with the decline of emotional vitality, or that the opportunities for contacts with male friends shrink [as work lives wax and then wane]?"

> The best thing about the future is that it only comes one day at a time.
>
> — Abraham Lincoln

Whatever the answers to those questions, we can say with reasonable certainty that some men have problems expressing feelings, that they have little emotional support outside the marriage, and that they are members of a generation in which the wife is the caretaker of the husband, the children, and the home, and are very often assistants in the husband's job or career as well. All these elements combine to put older men at high risk not only for suicide, but for poorly considered, rushed, postbereavement new marriages (divorce rates for older men are higher than the high national average), for alcoholism, and for depression as well. The effort to replace the lost partner, often arranged from the depths of panic and loneliness, doesn't always work out well, either for the isolated older man or his children. The adult children may see a poor choice of stepmother on the horizon, but most often they are so consumed by their own lives, they are unable to do much about it, since they certainly cannot drop their own responsibilities to step in where a perhaps ill-advised relationship is developing.

Children's roles also can be deeply compromised at this difficult juncture for the older man because of past history. Many men now in their late sixties, seventies, eighties, and beyond are often better grandfathers than they were fathers. Many men report they partially sacrificed their relationships with their children to the work and separation-of-genders atmosphere of their time. Dad was supposed to work and Mom was supposed to raise the kids; this doesn't leave Dad in a great spot when Mom is gone and the children are the only familial support he has, other than possibly his own siblings, who are roughly of his generational group and may be dealing with many of the same problems he is.

So, older men after they have lost partners fall into two categories — those who are living in intact, often long-running, marriages or successful late-life relationships, and those who are living alone — desperately lonely, frightened about who will care for them, and vulnerable and at risk in many ways.

Before we study the latter group and see how many of the men in that group go on to find solutions, we need pause for a moment to consider another group of men we have not discussed so far.

I call this group "swans," because they seem to mate for life, and when they lose a partner, adjust to a different life without seeking a replacement. Several of the men interviewed for this book described themselves as a "one woman" man. When the soul mate in a long marriage was gone, these men, often with considerable inner resources, made new lives with family, friends, and new activities and interests, and showed a peacefulness with their adaptations that was impressive. They did not seem unbearably lonely, partly because they enjoyed close relationships with children and grandchildren and had male friends, but also because they seem to have had life-long interests, hobbies, or activities that were valuable to them. During the course of writing this book, one of the six widower subjects who could be described in this way *did* remarry successfully, but the others seemed happily absorbed in the new lives they had made after very hard periods of grief and loss. These new lives occasionally included dating or romantic friendships, but these men apparently felt no need to rush into any longterm committed relationships. They appeared to be comfortable with themselves, their choices, and, most significantly, with a certain amount of solitude, something Americans of both genders seem to have a lot of trouble with. (See chapter 6, "Visions of the Future: A Newer World.")

Leaving aside this unusual group, admittedly a minority among single older men, what are the fears and worries that keep men solitary, or sunk in failed late-life relationships, even including long, but unhappy, marriages? And what are the characteristics of the men who successfully navigate these obstacle courses, and either find satisfying late-love partners, or, if they choose *not* to be in a committed or lengthy relationship, find life patterns that fit whatever social, psychological, and sexual needs they have?

Sex and the Single (Older) Man

Close your eyes and try to remember (or go find, if you're under sixty) the Glenn Miller record of "Deep Purple." (Never heard of that song? You probably haven't if you're young or middle-aged.)

Now open your eyes and try to guess what the terms *bobby-soxer* and *zoot suit* meant back in the 1940s and 1950s. Is the history of America before Pearl Harbor as far away to you as the Greek and Roman wars? Do you even know your grandparents' stories of the Great Depression or the 1929 stock market crash?

Just trying to wrestle with these artifacts of decades gone by gives the reader a tiny glimpse of the huge gulfs of memory, experience, social customs, and popular culture that separate people who came to maturity in these earlier periods and the young who seek love and intimacy in radically different times today.

For older single men who feel ready for new relationships, the first Mount Everest to be scaled is that *everything* in today's dating customs seems to require a revision of the earlier attitudes and conventions these men grew up with. After all, post-Victorian rules lasted well into this century, and many older men of today were raised with completely different "programming" about relations between the sexes in terms of both emotional intimacy and physical sex.

A glimpse into the different mind-set of lovers more than half a century ago is afforded by a collection of letters between a pair of sweethearts who met, courted, and married in Oklahoma in the 1920s. Their love story is chronicled in a moving account by their granddaughter, Keri Pickett, a professional photographer, who gathered pictures and letters together in a volume titled *Love in the Nineties*. She followed their love story into that final aged decade of their lives. The wife is named Josie Lou Lydia Walker and the husband is B. B. Blakey.

"Dearest JoJo," Blakey wrote in 1928, "The work and planning of a home entices me and I ache to try to make it nice and comfortable and enticing for you. Not a showplace, not an exclusive place but…an inviting place that says 'enter and rest and think.'"

Josie, who was a traveling religious educator for Protestant churches, wrote back, "I can truthfully say I should like to have a real home. You know how I like my work…but I think it is only natural that any woman should dream of a home…back in my subconscious mind, there has been that dream of a sweet Christian home."

Blakey writes in another letter: "JoJo, I want to help and encourage and protect you, to inspire and expand your ideals and services to the world."

Much of what we see in these letters could certainly be echoed among young lovers thinking of commitment today, but there is much that men of Blakey's generation and even the generation after him, will recognize as particular to their time and place and hard to reproduce today.

If an older man seeks a younger woman today, she very often is not dreaming of a home — sweet, Christian, or otherwise — she is dreaming of a way of life together that may or may not include founding a home in the manner understood by men now in their sixties, seventies, eighties, and beyond.

If a man seeks a woman somewhat in his own age range, presumably she was raised with some of the same attitudes and conventions that he was, but her life experiences have changed her goals and dreams in ways he is unsure of. What is a romantic friendship (which she may prefer to marriage)? He has no experience with that concept, since all friendships between men and women in his youth were seen as precursors to romance of some kind — whether a brief fling or a long-term "understanding."

The kind of true, nonsexual friendships between men and women that today's younger generation has had an opportunity to experience were largely unknown to the older man of today. Today's seventy-year-old has never lived in co-ed dorms at college, usually only encountered women in the workplace in the roles of secretary or clerk, and feels that Blakey's idea of "protecting" his love is the correct one, rather than the more *interdependent* notion of today's couples in which each partner looks out for the other equally.

In fact, psychologists say, many men and a few women use their close friendships with a spouse or lover as a substitute for all other cross-sex relationships in this age group.

So the first wrenching change for the seventy-five-year-old new widower is to realize that his ideas of the male social role may need considerable adjusting. In this new world of dating, women of all ages initiate phone calls and first dates, men need not feel they must pay for every movie and dinner (a change that might be quite welcome to some), and traveling together without marriage is now not only perfectly acceptable, but assumed without *necessarily* invoking intimacy and sex in the early stages of a new relationship.

The second mountain to climb is that the older man has to deal with himself as a sexual being in a whole new world and to struggle with societal stereotypes that affect the most intimate, personal part of his life.

Defining Sex: Then and Now

In this section we will look at some of the stereotypes and clichés that older men have come to believe as gospel and that they have internalized to the sad detriment of their sexuality. We will discuss the solutions that many men have pioneered in the new country of modern aging.

Cliché 1: Older men decline so much sexually with advancing years that it is normal to accept impotence and a decrease in desire and arousal. Of course, Viagra has helped with the mechanics of impotence, but no chemistry can help a man who believes it is *normal* to give up sexual interests, desires, and fantasies as he ages, or who is caught in an unsatisfying relationship, whether of short or long duration.

In China, which is just now discovering more liberal sexual attitudes, Viagra is called *Weige,* meaning "mighty brother," and for men with very real physical problems or who have been on libido-dampening medications, it is a vital brotherly assist indeed. However, the need to examine the entire relationship in which the newly-invigorated older man experiences sex remains as great as ever, according to James A. Pitisci, a Miami psychologist and family therapist. "If the relationship is in trouble already, Viagra is not going to change much and may become just another area of conflict," he points out.

Cliché 2: To the older generation, sex — with or without Viagra — is to be initiated and "managed" by the male, and his definition of sex is focused intensely on conventional intercourse, meaning penetration by an erect penis. Anything else, according to the norms of this older generation (which are often reinforced by cultural, religious, and historical beliefs), is not "the real thing" or is foreplay or is a tender and considerate "fooling around" because one's partner is ill or has suffered some sexual incapacity, but it is not sex as generally understood by men now in the "third age."

It won't be necessary to launch new investigations of Presidential sex scandals of 1999 to know that much of the socio-political traumas of that time turned on the issue of whether nonintercourse forms of sex truly constitute sex. The old-fashioned idea that only a bed — or at the very least the floor or a table — and penile penetration is sex brought the country to a constitutional crisis. Although older cultures in other nations were amazed at these goings-on, the notion that oral sex is not really sex is right up there with the flag and apple pie as American male preoccupations.

The sun continues to rise on the republic after this great debate, but these deeply ingrained ideas about how to make "real" love are serious hazards for older men and their partners and seem to rule out the thrillingly sexy, intimate touch and embrace that older lovers explore all the time.

Shere Hite, author of the much-discussed *Hite Report: A Nationwide Study of Female Sexuality,* said "I'm suggesting we call sex something else, and it should include everything from kissing to sitting close together."

Despite Hite's suggestion, "a hard man is good to find" was the beery anthem sung by young men at fraternity house and high school parties in the 1920s, 1930s, and through World War II and the suburban explosion of the 1950s, and it has not substantially changed as this older generation's definition of sex. This pervasive fear — recognizing on the one hand the very real declines in biological readiness and the increasing presence of health problems, but refusing on the other hand to experiment with any other sort of psychological or physically sensuous forms of sexual intimacy — leads to what psychiatrists and psychologists now call the "widower's syndrome."

According to Jack Parlow, Ph.D., a Canadian clinical

psychologist who has spent fourteen years treating impotence and other problems of sexual dysfunction, the "widower's syndrome" occurs when an older man is actually sexually viable but has disabling fears because he has been sexually inactive for a fairly long period during a spouse's illness and then death.

John H. Driggs, a clinical social worker with a private practice in the Midwest, has seen many patients who have such "performance" anxiety that they may withdraw from sex, rather than "fail" or they may be involved in an unsatisfying relationship and have suppressed their emotional needs for so long that the idea of failure is chronic in their sexual lives.

"Often," says Driggs, "the question older men struggle to answer is: What value am I as a person if I am not the stud I used to be?" Seeking younger partners as a youth elixir or passively shunning sex to avoid answering this question is often the fate of both straight and gay older men, reports Driggs.

Cliché 3: "It's not my medicine, it's not my disorienting retirement, it's just age — what should I expect?" is the mantra of men who left the gathering of health information to their wives over a long lifetime. When they lose that source of comfort and information, many men have no idea that drugs can have a negative effect on libido or that certain reversible illnesses can be erased or moderated through proper medical treatment, thereby improving sexual responses.

And anyway, say older men, passionate sex is for youthful bodies and good-looking people. When older bodies explore sex it is unattractive at best and disgusting and perverse at worst. Besides, older people have health problems and no one with health problems can be truly sexual.

All these clichés, and many more, once perhaps contained a tiny seed of truth; clichés are what they are because so many people have experienced something like what they reflect. But whatever tiny germs of truth these clichés may have once contained have now been obliterated by changing times, new knowledge, and advanced medical developments like Viagra.

Today's older men are overturning these clichés, and their partners and medical and mental health professionals are assisting them in fighting ageism in the sexual realm.

Deepening and Strengthening Love and Sex

The idea that is "normal" for sex to wane and then disappear as men age is a misreading of what actually happens when physical changes occur and a misunderstanding of how those changes can be modified and turned in new directions. In addition, the helpless "over the hill" feeling, all too readily embraced by men alone, ignores completely the resources of mind, spirit, and experience that can alter old patterns and lead to deeply satisfying new relationships.

There is no question that aging and sometimes oncoming but undiagnosed health problems, affect how a man functions sexually in purely physiological terms. In his later years, a man may indeed find that desire, arousal, and orgasm may not all occur together as they did when much younger; but he may also be surprised to find that women greet this change of pace with delight, finding a place for their own loving attentions to him to become more welcome. Women, too, in later years, freed from fears of pregnancy and the exhausting demands of childbearing and rearing, find it easier to explore their sexuality and accept pleasure in many different forms, as do gay and lesbian lovers.

In 1989, nearly two thousand men between the ages of forty and seventy, chosen to reflect race and ethnicity as represented in their communities, were involved in an extensive survey of their sexual lives as part of a long-term study on all aspects of the aging process conducted under the aegis of the National Institute of Aging. The study, known as the Massachusetts Male Aging Study, remains one of the most detailed and exhaustive analyses of male sexuality in mid- and later life since the Kinsey Report of many decades ago. The interviewers covered just about every manifestation of male sexuality encountered among normally healthy men who were living in their own communities, and were not institutionalized. The physicians and other health professionals who conducted the survey were affiliated with major Boston medical centers and they looked at everything that might affect sexual function — prescription drugs, work habits, availability of partners, attitudes toward a range of sexual activities other than intercourse, and half a dozen more.

What were the results of hundreds of interviews, months of work, and years of interpreting the data?

When men get older, the ability to have an erection, to maintain it, to control ejaculation, and to recover and be ready for further sexual activity all slow down when seen in purely biological terms and can be seen as a normal aspect of aging, although sometimes they are precursors of health problems.

However, the study also revealed a number of other not very surprising realities:

- Good health usually means more involvement and satisfaction with sex.
- Depression and repression of anger, taken together, were *"strongly associated with increased sexual difficulties."*

In other words, we are back, after getting validation from as precise an examination as we could hope for, to the basic facts that all the elements of a man's emotional setting — his fears and anxieties, his relationship with his partner or partners, his lack of knowledge about his own health status, and his frequent inability to understand his own emotions and express them — play a very big role in his perceived troubles and *these factors can be changed!*

The authors of one part of the Massachusetts study argued that while aging certainly influences some sexual slowdown, "a large

> *Here I am, fifty-eight, and I still don't know what I'm going to be when I grow up.*
>
> — Peter Drucker

number of social, psychological, and lifestyle phenomena taken together also contribute significantly to the variations across the age range."

It is in the area of social and psychological factors that the older men whose voices we hear in this book have tentatively begun to take new steps and to look at sex in new ways.

For example, the terrible "performance anxiety" that many health professionals have observed can be alleviated almost completely if older men are able to abandon the vision of themselves as eighteen-year-old hormone-driven conquerors and look closely for a moment at what it is their partners may really want in the way of sexual or any other kind of communion. This turnabout in lifelong attitudes and expectations is not easy or quick, but is warm and rewarding when accomplished (see chapter 1, "Banishing the Shadows: The Story of Sarah and Alex").

"I think men are often sex experts but intimacy apprentices," says John H. Driggs, the Minnesota social worker and human sexuality expert. "Men may have had lots of sex, know how special it can be, but are still learning the *ABCs* when it comes to connecting emotionally."

No less an authority than advice columnist Ann Landers has backed up, in easy-to-understand terms, Driggs's view that now, in older years, men may slow down enough to understand their partners' wishes for a closeness that does not depend on an erection or on conventional intercourse at all. In 1985, she asked her female readers "would you be content to be held close and treated tenderly and forget about the 'act'?" Some ninety thousand readers responded. Seventy-two percent said "Yes," and, interestingly enough, 40 percent of that group were under forty years of age.

This certainly suggests that for most of their lifetimes, men and women have often been "out of synch" in pursuing their sexual lives with each other and now, in their older years, perhaps at last perhaps their pace and wishes can be adjusted more lovingly.

The disjunction between what women have always wanted out of a sexual relationship — emotional closeness, as well as sexual pleasure — and what men have wanted — orgasmic release first, maybe romance later — was the subject of a witty observation by the late Dorothy Parker, the author-poet who often cast a wickedly amused eye on the eternal war between the sexes. "Love is woman's moon and sun, man has other forms of fun," she wrote in a brief poem, "with this the gist and sum of it, what earthly good can come of it?"

A similar bracingly astringent, if more scientifically-based, attack on conventional notions of what constitutes true sex, particularly as one ages, has been put forward for more than forty years by a pioneering authority on human sexuality, Dr. Richard J. Cross of the Robert Wood Johnson Medical School, New Jersey. A medical educator and administrator responsible for training generations of physicians and other health care workers, Dr. Cross, now at eighty-four an emeritus professor but still active in sex education, has strong and provocative ideas about the obsession with the male erection and about American attitudes about sex generally.

In introducing a study session for doctors in training on "overcoming erectile difficulties," Dr. Cross's approach was straightforward: "Why do older men need an erection? This is a holdover from the era when sex was seen as dirty unless used for making babies. Do older men and women really want pretend procreation? No, of course not. What they want is closeness, exciting touch, recognition that sexual interest, desire, and activity last throughout life and need to be adapted in new ways as biology slows them down in later years."

"Recent decades," says Dr. Cross, "have brought greater understanding of the many wonderful benefits of a good sexual relationship, but we still tend to regard penis-in-vagina sex as the best kind and *this needs to be reexamined*. It only happens because that is the way we were socialized."

"Can we change [this belief]? We can," he says, but warns that we can't make these changes easily or quickly. "The sex drive is powerful, primitive, and complex. It can't be turned on or off or diverted whenever it suits our convenience. For better or worse, we live in a society in which men are respected and honored for their competitive drive, their aggressiveness, their potency, their ability to 'get it up and keep it up.' We can't just decree that potency is no longer important and thereby eliminate men's concerns," says this wise and humane doctor.

Dr. Cross's writing, lectures, and views on sex education also reflect the secret (besides faking orgasms) that women have kept from their lovers forever. As this medical educator writes, "experienced women generally agree that skillful application of fingers, tongue, and/or vibrator causes far more enjoyable sensations and intense orgasms than does an erect penis. And men can learn to enjoy hugging, cuddling, kissing, sexy massage, and intimate talk, since many women say they'd like more of those things, too."

> *And now that I am 75, every fresh day finds me more filled with wonder and better qualified to draw the last drop of delight from it....*
>
> — Maurice Goudeket

Of course, Dr. Cross is not the only health professional who has been attempting to help men, and their partners, understand that the different nature of aging sexuality does not mean that older people are not sexual. Health professionals dealing with both physical and mental health problems in the U.S. and in many of the developed countries around the world are trying to prepare for the "age wave" that will soon inundate most services that deal with older people.

In Australia, for instance, researchers at two Australian universities have pooled their expertise in gerontology, health sciences, and epidemiology and have been undertaking large scale investigations of late-life sexuality among men and women in that country.

Their survey of one thousand men and women between sixty-five and ninety-three, the first ever in Australia, found that, while two-thirds of senior citizens polled believe that sexual relations are an important part of intimacy in later life, many lack knowledge in key areas of sexuality.

The researchers found that a large majority — 62 percent of older people — were unaware of the adverse effects that both prescription medications and depression can have on a person's sex drive. Only a little more than one-third of the respondents recognized that sexual activity in later life can have important physical and mental health benefits.

Two of the study authors, Professor Victor Minichiello, Ph.D., of the University of New England and David Plummer, Ph.D., of the Australian National University, strongly urged Australians to combat ageism by "treating older people as sexual beings and investing the same level of resources (as with younger groups) in sharing appropriate information about sexuality."

Back in the U.S., a poll of 118 people, taken at a senior center in Palo Alto, California, among men and women aged fifty-six to eighty-five, found that they are already learning and acting on many of the new findings that experts report.

One of the two directors of the survey, Walter Bortz, M.D., a Palo Alto internist and authority on geriatrics, reported that "intercourse is not highly ranked as a lovemaking technique" by the seniors he interviewed. He said, "other methods, such as oral sex, manual genital stimulation, and kissing were listed as alternatives."

Older people usually assume that those who are younger will always favor the conventional view of sex: only beautiful young people are good candidates for "real" love-making and old people are "out of it." But there are a few hopeful signs on the horizon that in all age groups, the single-minded emphasis on youth equals sex may be slowly changing.

In 1994, a small sample of fifty men between twenty-two and sixty-three revealed some startling developments toward a more mature view of things when *New Woman* magazine asked these men what they really found sexually exciting in women.

Most surprising to women readers was that physical perfection almost never came up, and that, in fact, some men said the gorgeous models in ads looked plastic in their perfection and were a turn-*off*.

Key for our interests was the finding that "as men age, their ideas about what makes women truly sexy apparently change. An older man may hardly notice wrinkles," the magazine's report said.

A fifty-three-year-old psychotherapist in Tampa, Florida, told journalist Sue Browder, who did the survey for the magazine, that: "I know I'm still supposed to find nubile twenty year olds in bikinis the sexiest women alive, but, to tell you the truth, I've begun to see all those girls as my *daughters*...and forget sex with a young twenty-something woman...I'd be thinking 'are you sure you should be doing this yet?'"

And a fifty-six-year-old Ohio novelist and screenwriter told Browder, "I used to want to touch all the parts of a woman's body, but now I want to touch her very soul. And of course that means that for a woman to be sexy to me now, she has to have far more depth."

During interviews conducted for this book with men from sixty to ninety-three, it became clear that, contrary to women's firm beliefs that men will always seek renewal in young flesh, older men who conquer their fears enough to undertake new relationships most often wind up with women somewhere close to their own generational group, and, according to a recent American Association of Retired Persons' survey, older lovers find their partners physically attractive way past middle age.

What happens is that women see only the first steps in a *process* that often begins with what I call the "candy store" phase of an older widower or divorced or never-married man finding himself alone and back in circulation.

During the first months and possibly years of being single, which he never anticipated or planned for, a man is astounded to discover, like a child in a candy store, that he has incredible choices for dating and romance among much younger women. On every side women in their twenties, thirties, and forties, seem eager to convince him that he is still attractive and virile, especially if he's endowed with money and power, those tried and true aphrodisiacs.

But even older men who lack those baits find that society smiles and approves when they take out much younger women, and for a while the older male is surfeited with sweets.

But then something else sets in, as wittily and touchingly portrayed in Olivia Goldsmith's clever novel-movie, *First Wives Club*. What begins to happen is that the experiential and cultural gap between the generations starts to shadow the "hot sex" era the older man thinks he is in. Since even the aerobics instructor who replaces the first wife in the movie has to get out of bed some time, the need for conversation develops. Then, both in the movie and in real life, the older man realizes she doesn't "get" his jokes (she never even heard of Milton Berle), and she thinks the Great Depression is back there with the Crusades in medieval history along with the great experience of his life, World War II. In my research, if she's as young as male fantasies often suggest, she can't even remember the Vietnam War, he discovers.

The candy store phase begins to wane (though older women have averted their eyes long since and aren't aware of it) when he realizes that his youngest daughter is not that much younger than the young partner he is with, and that *none* of his children are interested in this woman as a stepmother.

It is about at that point that the process of renewal changes. One such man I interviewed told this story: he is invited to the wedding of his closest male friend's granddaughter and there he meets a charming widow whose late husband turns out to have served in the same unit as he did in Europe during the D day invasion. They talk animatedly about those wartime years, they don't even notice the other guests, she looks into his eyes with warmth and sympathy when he talks of the loss of his wife of fifty years and *bingo*, the aerobics instructor or her facsimile is history. It turns out the widow has gray hair and is not a size four and has grandchildren of her own, but somehow they manage to slip off and drink champagne and decide that there is life after death and they best explore it.

This is actually a reflection of many older men's experiences, and while women find it hard to believe that men, given their greater choices, do not all automatically wind up with women half their age, the hard facts are that usually the age differences among stable older late-life lovers are not *all* that great. A minority of men do, of course, end their lives with much younger women and often it is an intense and very genuine love that binds two very substantial people, but that number is statistically much smaller than those who tend to choose companions of their own generation. Older women are so used to devaluing themselves as objects of love or sex that they sometimes seem to be willfully blind to this reality even though it is quite well known to social workers, senior center directors, and others who have insight into the dating and mating patterns of older men.

Older women also have little understanding of the other great fear of older men, which is often linked with the fear about sexual performance, and that is the fear of rejection.

A poem submitted by the New Yorker Irwin Hasen to the *New York Times* should elicit some awareness from their female age-mates that all is not "candy store" for older men, either.

"A Senior Citizen on an Uptown Bus"

He edged his way to where the
Lovely young woman was seated.
His eyes met hers, and in that
Moment, he designed a possibility.
Cocktails at the Carlyle,
Dinner at the Mark.
Suddenly, his sparse gray hair
Grew fuller and his liver spots
Graciously took refuge.
Then the lovely young woman
Rose to offer him her seat.

In a few short lines, the heart-tugging reality for older men is laid bare for older women to ponder; is there not some role there for the benefits the years have given older women? Is not the greater emotional depth life has created in them worth something on the scales of mutual attraction between both gay and straight lovers? The love stories we have tracked so far and those we will hear from long-married couples later on, suggest indeed that those roles do exist for older partners, and that the struggle to connect *can* be successfully waged at any age.

"Deep down," says writer David Foster Wallace, "we all know that the real allure of sexuality has about as much to do with copulation as the appeal of food does with metabolic combustion...[R]eal sexuality is about our...struggle to erect bridges across the chasms that separate selves."

"We're Still Here": Love Songs for Later

The older men we've tried to look at with a warm heart and a sharp eye, the older men who are numbers in a statistical study, the older men who are your parents and grandparents (and in some lucky cases, your great-grandparents) are, like all human beings, needful of connection and meaning as life moves them inexorably forward. "We are all members of a club we might have preferred not to join, but now that we have, we need to be as graceful as we can," said the late poet, Eve Merriam.

The resilience, power to love, and adventurous risk taking that are the hallmarks of older men who have successfully mastered some of the fears and anxieties mentioned above are demonstrated in the story of Peter N., who is now ninety-two, and his second wife, Sally, a vigorous, bike-riding eighty-year-old great-grandmother. They live in Tulsa, Oklahoma, where Peter once practiced veterinary medicine until he retired some years ago. Sally was a high school principal for many years, and although technically retired, remains active on the local school board and volunteers as a teacher's aide two days a week.

Peter and Sally seem on first acquaintance to be a serenely

perfect example of untroubled elder love. They are in unusually good health for their respective ages, and while not wealthy, are without serious money worries. They enjoy good relations with Sally's children, not so good with Peter's, but in any case, all five of their children are scattered around the globe and are not available for casual visiting.

The interview, which takes place on a pleasant sun porch that is part of a comfortable and tastefully furnished roomy house, is relaxed and pleasant. What is the subtext of this amiable conversation? How did Peter and Sally come to this seemingly calm, high plateau?

After much trouble and trauma, it turns out. Sally, particularly, believed she would never remarry, never find love again, and most definitely never enjoy much happiness in general when, after four children and twenty years of marriage, her then-husband announced he was in love with another woman and left her and the children. While he did not completely sever himself from their children, his contact was tenuous and not particularly loving or supportive. In the modern world, this is not such an unusual happening, but for Sally, as she describes it, it was the end of the world as she knew it. The devastation to her children, her self-image, and her ability to love and trust was "soul smashing" she says. Fortunately, she had a good job and much respect in the educational community, but she sees herself as a sleepwalking survivor in the immediate aftermath of an abandonment so complete she feared she might never regain her emotional equilibrium.

Peter's background was both happy and sad; his long first marriage was happy and fulfilling, but like many men of his generation, he had left care of the children to his late wife, had left their social contacts and friendships to be nurtured by her, and had left much of the practical business of their family life to her while he enjoyed and grew his veterinary practice.

When she died, he, too, felt abandoned as Sally did — but by death, not divorce. He and Sally met when she had resolutely determined to make herself strong and solitary and to look to no one — certainly not to another man — for help or healing or the care of her children.

Peter and Sally share many interests in outdoor life — camping, hiking, biking, tennis, and sailing — and they met when each signed up for a charity fund-raising bicycle ride across a portion of Oklahoma one autumn day when he was sixty-seven, newly widowed, and she was fifty-five, divorced for some time. Their meeting was about as far from love at first sight as they could get; Sally refused to accept Peter's help when her bike developed a problem at a rest stop on the prescribed route. She fixed it herself and caught up with the others by taking a shortcut she knew about and most of the riders did not. Something about her fierce determination to excel, to do it alone, and to finish the ride, in spite of an injured ankle, a balky bike, and rainstorms, caught Peter's attention.

The heart that loves is always young.

— Greek proverb

At that time, he says, he was experiencing every anxiety about a new relationship known to older men. "Being too old for sex was just the start," he says, "it was everything — I had been with one woman for nearly forty good years — was I capable of loving and relating to anyone else? I sure was shaky." But this is a man who has faced professional and personal crises, who is outgoing and adventurous, who has that necessary resilience not to be paralyzed nor to rush into anything ill-advised. He set about a cautious campaign to win Sally, but her distrust of even the possibility of love again was a serious obstacle. They look at one another fondly as they tell this story, but on her own Sally says very seriously that even though Peter talked to her calmly and reassuringly, it took her a long time to believe that he would not hurt her and that she could count on him.

As they now age together, they demonstrate how two very

rugged individual souls can maintain their own independence and emotional elbowroom while loving in a devoted oneness. Peter has been ordered to cut down on some of his more strenuous skiing by his doctor, and he grumbles because Sally is still active, but he has learned his limits and strengths and can go on well within them. None of this would have happened for either of them if Peter had not acted on that first impulse to find out who this gray-haired lady on a bike really was.

This determination not to give in, to announce to the world that "I'm still here," is movingly described by an old widower who has just buried his wife. His musings on what will become of him now after he has nursed her through a long illness and sat by her bed when she died are confided to a journalist who is collecting personal stories that will eventually be used in a course on aging to be taught at the Open University in England.

The author of the stories, *The Way We Are: Old People Talk about Themselves,* is Jeremy Seabrook, British writer, essayist, and social critic, and he speaks respectfully of the subject of his interview simply as "Mr. Cosgrove."

> *Love doesn't make*
> *the world go around;*
> *it makes the*
> *ride worthwhile.*
>
> — Franklin P. Adams
>
> ෨

This is what Mr. Cosgrove tells Seabrook: "I'm lonely, yes, but it's not that terrible loneliness that you see some old people suffering from when they've been bereaved. There's an old boy in this street, he neglected himself when his wife died, he wouldn't eat, he wouldn't bother. You could see him going downhill day by day, shuffling around with a vacant look on his face. *That isn't going to happen to me.* I go out now, I meet people up the Centre, there's a lunch club. I go shopping, I cook myself a bit of tea…*I'm not going to give in.*"

Mr. Cosgrove seems a living example of the old Irish

proverb: "Life may not be the party we hoped for, but while we're here we should dance." I salute his spirit and that of all older men who stay alive to the possibility of the dance.

The Music of Time: Learning the Steps Again

"After Mom died, my brother and I would drop by Dad's house after work and we would find him sitting in the living room without the lights on, in a sort of twilight. We knew this most likely reflected his sadness and loneliness. That was four years ago. A year ago, he met Rita and his life and ours have changed so much, it's hard to describe."

This tale is told by the forty-eight-year-old daughter of Larry S., a seventy-nine-year-old widower, whose story seems to feature every single aspect of the difficulties older men face.

Why was Larry successful in passing through all the stages of isolation, depression, ill health (he contracted pneumonia twice when alone), and fearful sexual paralysis (he wouldn't consider dating at all for the first two years after his wife's death) that are typical of widowers to reach a fine new relationship?

Part of the reason simply lies in his personality. He was usually an outgoing man, and had shown resiliency and stability in much of his earlier life and marriage.

But Larry's success, and that of many other solitary older men, is based on not "giving in," on channeling the life force in all of us into a constructive desire to learn new steps when one dances to the music of time.

This is what Larry and many of the older men we have met so far have learned and what they recommend:

For Men Only: Lessons in Late-Life Love

- If you feel overwhelmed with sadness and loneliness, *don't hesitate to ask for help!!* The importance
  of this tip cannot be overstated, especially since it

goes against the habits of a lifetime for most men,
who always saw themselves as the ones who
solved problems, not suffered from them.

• Whom do you ask for help? Many men would not
feel comfortable discussing sexual fears with their
adult children, even sons. The place to start on
that issue is with your primary care physician
who, after determining whether there is or is not
a physiological problem, can help you determine
the next step to take.

• You can also try talking with a psychologist, psychiatrist, social worker, or counselor, preferably
one who specializes in geriatrics. If there are family members you *can* talk to, seek them out.

• Read up on health information. If you left it to
your partner to remind you about vitamins or
when to get a flu shot or to research information
about how certain medications can depress the
sex drive, make it your responsibility now. Health
information floods into people's lives from every
quarter — newspapers, magazines, books, the
Internet, television — and it only needs your
attention and some separating of the wheat from
the chaff.

• Start slowly as you prepare to meet the world
again. A mad dating whirl is not necessarily indicated while you are still only painfully emerging
from grief and loss. But it would be wise to participate in at least a few family events and to see
some old friends occasionally for dinner or a
movie.

• Make an inventory of your lifelong interests,
both those you actively pursued and those you
meant to pursue when you had time. This is the
time! If you were once a joiner, you're lucky —
every political, social, artistic, and hobby group

needs participants and volunteers. If you're not a joiner, there are classes, sports, and community projects that can be done alone, but keep you in touch with others. Not only do these mean contact with the world but they often lead to making new friends and — who knows — new romances, as well. When people invite you, go! Even if just to get in the habit of not sitting alone and even if the inviters aren't your favorite hosts or companions.

• Believe that you still have love to give. It doesn't matter whether you are sixty or ninety or 100 — you once knew love and can know it again, but have to dredge that belief up from somewhere inside yourself, and that's hard work. It can, however, be the most rewarding work of your life. You can redefine love and sex to suit yourself and a new partner now!

These new steps, which older single men, can learn for their own enrichment, are not too different from the dance steps that both men *and* women learn together when they are doing the anniversary waltz in a long-lasting marriage.

Seeking help for problems, learning about each other's health in aging, reinvigorating sex and romance, staying in touch with the world — all the things that work for men trying to emerge from grief and loneliness also are helpful to long-married couples, too.

In the next chapter, the spotlight will be on men and women who have been together for decades and the special challenges they face as they age.

We will learn that the long-running marriage — now so common as longevity brings so many couples to the golden wedding mark of fifty years together — is far from a placid plateau. It is full of new ways to grow, to learn, and to deepen understanding of each other.

William Segal

By the time he was thirty, William Segal had founded two leading magazines of the 1940s and 1950s (*Gentry* and *American Fabrics*), made a million dollars as a publishing executive, and had a beautiful and accomplished wife, two loving daughters, and a fine home.

Now, at ninety-five, he is also a newly rediscovered painter, philosopher, writer, Zen Buddhist, and American wise man of a kind almost unique in our national culture. He lost his first wife after nearly forty years of marriage, and lives now with his second wife, French artist Marielle Bancou, in New York and Paris.

Most American men know only the path of everyday life in which they must earn a living, shelter their families, be responsible citizens, and say good-bye to too much introspection or expressiveness. There just isn't time, they think, for much flirtation with life's ultimate meanings.

The other path for some American men has been to enter one or another of the arts — music, painting, literature — and say good-bye to worldly success for the most part. (The number of fine poets who can support a family on the sale of their poetry alone is a fraction of those writing — a tiny fraction!)

William Segal, who has spent sixty years painting self-portraits in a search for the answers to "Who am I?" and "Why am I here?" believes there is a third way between these two poles of Wall Street or the monastery. (He has spent metaphorical time on Wall Street and literal time in Japanese monasteries.) He believes this middle path calls for all people to both look within and also to understand, appreciate, and "be present" in the world around them. He calls it "meditating in the marketplace" and the quest for the inner life has occupied his art and time for the better part of this century, while he continued as a business consultant until he was eighty.

Segal says that within many people are the "seeds" of spirituality and a wish to know themselves, but the demands of the clamorous world make it hard to embark on a journey of self-discovery, which is especially difficult for men against the background of the classic American myth of the strong silent male. John Wayne does not easily coexist in the psyche of American men with the Dalai Lama, but Segal now enjoys hard-won serenity from struggles to unite both paths in his life and work.

A 1999 exhibition of his self-portraits, which he began painting when he was a college athlete and includes recent paintings of startling power and courage, demonstrates in oils and drawings Segal's lifelong quest to understand himself and humanity.

Though he had some formal training at the Art Students League in New York and also studied with the renowned Mexican muralist, Jose Clemente Orozco, Segal's long arc of work, study and art, reflect, in a highly individual way, his own drive to "be awake and aware."

To a reporter who asked him whether the paintings had changed over time and why he had chosen self-portraits as the instrument of his search, he answered: "Well, the human countenance is very interesting. Every face provides a model of complexity...and these elements are fascinating because they can lead one to the recognition that there is something beyond the mere form — *it is the feeling of the greatness of each human being.*"

Ken Burns, the acclaimed documentary film maker (PBS' *Civil War*), has made three films with Segal as the subject, and comments "there is nothing as poetic as a man's genuine search for meaning in this world, and nothing as generous as the sharing of his findings."

Segal, whose philosophy encourages modesty and humility, says with a smile that while he tries to eliminate ego from his painting, he wouldn't mind if, after he is gone, his family might say "well, that old man was not too bad an artist."

And not too bad a seeker, either, in the eternal quest for the answer to "Who am I?"

Chapter 4

A Durable Fire
The Long-Lasting Marriage

But true love is a durable fire
In the mind ever burning;
Never sick, never old, never dead,
From itself never turning.

— Sir Walter Raleigh, "As You Came from the Holy Land"

Holding a long marriage up to the light like a prism, we can see reflected in a rainbow of colors — some somber, some softly shining, some brilliantly sparkling and gleaming — the incredibly varied experiences older men and women have as they reaffirm their unions after many years.

These experiences range from sweet longing that seems to be ever-present to stoic acceptance that "happily ever after" is, in fact, not a guaranteed outcome of that march down the aisle so long ago.

Former President Jimmy Carter writes in his memoir, *The Virtues of Aging,* that he and his wife of fifty-two years, Rosalyn, are "bound together with ever-increasing bonds as we've grown older and need each other more." President Carter writes touchingly that when he is apart from his wife for even a day or so, he feels "the same hollow feeling of loneliness and unassuaged desire as when I was away at sea for a week or more during the first years of our marriage." (Carter was a navy officer when a newlywed).

Not quite that candid and more stoic is Dwayne B., eighty-three, a retired salesman. Following the death of his wife after a long illness, Dwayne wrote a friend, "Well, it wasn't a forty-five-year joyride, but it was a forty-five-year marriage." This seems to suggest that whatever joys, sorrows, disappointments, and achievements were encompassed in their years together, the marriage remains an immovable rock in the center of Dwayne's emotional landscape.

The ready wit displayed so often by older people on this subject, as on so many others, is contributed by the late humorist Erma Bombeck, who said, "The secret of a happy marriage? It is forgiveness. For years now, I have forgiven my husband for not being Paul Newman."

A validation of sorts for longtime partners who are separated by death is given by Mr. Cosgrove, the British working man featured in Jeremy Seabrook's anthology of life histories titled *Aging and Later Life* (see chapter 3, "Defining Sex: Then and Now"). Mr. Cosgrove summed up his relationship with his late wife this way: "[B]ut she was my old girl and I was her chap, that's all there was to it, really."

But, as we will see in the personal stories to follow, the reality is so complex, so dense with layered meanings over time, that it would take Scheherazade more than a thousand nights to plumb all the depths of a relationship lasting many decades.

In earlier chapters, we focused on the challenges of new

late-life loves when men and women suffer the loss of partners after the age of sixty. But millions of women and men past that age are finding changing love relationships *within* the framework of unions that have lasted thirty, forty, fifty, and today, much more often than in the past, sixty years, and more.

It is true that half of women over sixty-five are widows, divorcées, or were never married, but that still leaves a large portion of the aging population in intact, long-lasting marriages that, in an amazing number of cases (given the national divorce rate of 50 percent), are the only marriages they ever had. Because of the increasing longevity of marital partners, it is even possible for *second* marriages to reach the golden anniversary mark.

Legend has it that when some friends who had been living together for a long time finally decided officially to marry, Dorothy Parker, the writer and fabled wit, sent them a telegram saying "What's new?"

On the surface, it might seem that finding late-life love for husbands and wives who have been together in a long marriage is a puzzle solved, a hunt consummated, a dream either dashed on the rocks of everyday life, or reasonably, sweetly alive and well.

> *Love costs. Love is not so easy…nor is the shimmering of star dust, nor the smooth flow of new blossoms…*
>
> — Carl Sandburg

But in fact, a long marriage is *mysterious* and ever-changing, requiring new adjustments, new lessons to be learned, and new growth every day as partners face the last years together.

Literary-film critic Stanley Cavell looks at the fictional marriages we see in movies — Katharine Hepburn and Spencer Tracy, Cary Grant and many beautiful actresses — and says that despite the dazzling attractiveness of these actors "sexuality is not the ultimate secret of these [film] marriages…it is that these relationships strike us having the quality of friendship."

For long-running marriages in real life, Cavell chooses the image of the marriage bed, not — as movies and TV would suggest — as the setting for sex, but rather to stand for "everything in marriage that is invisible to outsiders, which is essentially everything, or everything essential."

In *The Pursuits of Happiness: The Hollywood Comedy of Remarriage,* Cavell points out, as did many of the men and women who were interviewed, that it is "*re*-marriage" that makes unions last so long; the willingness to renegotiate the deal, to reaffirm the bond, even to see bickering as a form of caring. "The happiest marriages," he writes, "may not be the best behaved, and paying attention to each other in public at least indicates that a couple is involved in the relationship as opposed to ignoring it graciously or absolutely."

"You come to know you are married when you come to see that you cannot divorce, that is, when you find your lives simply will not disentangle," claims Cavell.

How do couples — both gay and straight — come to some stage where their lives cannot disentangle? What is their history, their pattern, and what do they need to do now, as shadows lengthen, to go the distance together?

Love Glue: The Elements That Make It Stick

For the aging parental generation that gave us the baby boom, there seem to be a number of elements that help revitalize long marriages. These grow out of all the major milestones couples have marked over many years. Forming a family, sharing work, homemaking and leisure, and sometimes reaching grandparenthood and even great-grandparenthood certainly fasten couples together with many links. This love glue is made up of three elements.

- *The first element is the weight of time itself.* That sound of the calendar pages turning reminds long-together couples of time past (more) and time future (less). When their children are not visibly present to remind them, many couples can hardly believe how many decades they have passed together and yet, in their very bones, they can feel the happiness, the joy, and the sorrow and trouble that those decades piled on them as the twosome they still are.

The golden fiftieth year used to be a remarkable achievement and was often covered by newspapers and radio stations, but today, hundreds of thousands of couples who married during and immediately after World War II are reaching their fiftieth anniversaries. These markers are still much celebrated in the couple's own circle of family and friends, but are no longer considered newsworthy enough for a front page feature story in the local paper. Poignant and touching observations of a half century together help soften the rough edges of mortality. Even where vitality has drained from the marriage — or the long monogamy of some gay men and lesbian couples — the sense of time at their backs often smoothes the bumpy road of various incompatibilities. One couple who consulted a marriage counselor over a period of time began to show encouraging signs of working out some persistent difficulties and when the therapist remarked on this progress, the wife said, "well, we're getting older, you know, and I don't know how much longer I will have him."

• *The second element that helps couples toward reaffirmation is a sense of comfort and familiarity.* They have adjusted to faults and foibles on both sides, often using that dependable ally, humor, and have reached a *modus vivendi* that permits an ease that young lovers and newlyweds will struggle to reach over many years. Mrs. Patrick Campbell, the famous British actress, described this as "the deep, deep peace of the double bed, after the hurly-burly on the chaise longue."

- *The third part of the emotional glue that holds long relationships together is the gratitude and appreciation each partner feels for the other* when they look back over everything that life has thrown at them and each realizes that the other was steadfast through the bad parts, as well as sharing in the good ones.

This mind-set was described by Rich T., who, when he turned eighty-three, suffered a series of major health problems. He recovered after many months and wrote to friends and far-away relatives about how marvelously well his wife of fifty-six years had borne the troubles and how she helped him regain his health. Now that he was better, he was hoping, he wrote, to reward her with a respite, perhaps some travel, since, "Susan's good health and happiness are, as always, the principal objectives of my life."

Perfect love sometimes does not come until the first grandchild.

— Welsh proverb

In another family, an adult daughter, an attorney, watched her parents dancing cheek-to-cheek at their golden anniversary party and observed that "Mom and Dad are renegotiating the deal — it'll be better than ever!"

These familiar comforts and shared journeys are reflected in the moving title poet Mark Strand gave to an account of the days and nights he spent by the sea with his love in a poem he called "Our Masterpiece Is the Private Life."

If we think of such lives as music, these masterpieces are often audible in the voices that speak in this chapter. But for each song that describes a couple using time to enrich their bond or expresses the comfort and gratitude they feel, there are, sadly, many others who deny both time's tolls and its gifts.

Many remain unable to express appreciation of their partners or take comfort in the familiarity of domestic patterns.

Some longtime marriages are shells of former relationships, held together only by convention, habit, and perceived lack of alternative lives. How do the words of the wedding vow that say "for better or for worse" sound when the "worse" part almost outweighs the "better" part?

Going the Distance without a Fairy Tale Ending

In talks with long-married couples, I found that even when the marriage is a shadow of its former self, there is often a force that keeps many couples together in some semblance of home and family, whatever the emotional tone and texture. That force could be described as a love/hate symbiosis; the couple aged in place within a sometimes torturous set of complex dependencies. This may be truer for the World War II generation than for contemporary couples, who seem to spend less time in marriages they perceive as unsatisfactory.

While the children or friends of troubled couples now in their seventies and eighties may wonder and speculate endlessly about how they stay together, the husband and wife deal with a third party: the marriage itself, which takes on strength as an almost separate entity, exacting its price in misery and sorrow.

For every private life that is a masterpiece, as Mark Strand suggested, there is another marital pattern illustrated by another poet, Robert Lowell, who wrote a poem titled "To Speak of the Woe that Is in Marriage." (Lowell here was quoting an old sadness that goes way back to Geoffrey Chaucer's famous "Wife of Bath" poem.)

What are these woes that have accumulated over the years and that bring to late-life love within long-lasting marriages difficult new problems to face and resolve as older couples decide how the final lap of the race is to be run? Unresolved problems that make the late-life search for love within marriage more complex include:

- The pressure of everyday concerns — money, work, or retirement; worries over adult children; fear of aging. All these concerns appear differently through the circumstances of later years than they did when the couple was young. The earlier methods of coping may not be useful now. Couples might have been able to skate over money worries that didn't appear formidable when there were a lot of working years ahead — but now they can be frightening. Retirement, too, opens new chapters in terms of changed income levels and so, perhaps, changed life styles.

- Difficulty resolving the ever-present conflict between the wish to be together and the need for some solitary time alone. This problem is present from the very beginning of the marriage but becomes intensified by late-life changes, such as retirement and possible health problems. These changes require an even more careful balance between togetherness and aloneness and often mean changing long-held habits.

- A history of infidelity that caused wounds that never quite healed and that now must be dealt with in definitive ways that can enable trust to be reestablished.

- A lack of support from society and from conventional habits and customs as older people try to understand their aging sexuality, and to reach new depths of both physical and emotional intimacy. For heterosexual older women, the lack of age-mates as they reach their seventies and eighties means shifting attention to new kinds of sexual expressiveness and a devotion to other forms of sensuality — music, art, food, wine, nature, animals, children — that have traditionally been available to women as well as to men. Lesbian couples usually are closer in age, but, of course, also must face widowhood and loss of a sexual partner at some point in a long relationship.

• The natural fears about aging, ill health, caretaking, and being left alone that, again, each couple must solve in their own way. Many I talked with firmly refuse to pay any attention to the problems, beyond occasionally making sure their financial affairs are in order, but many other long-married couples *have* talked frankly about their feelings — each one often saying they want to go first and not live without the other. A warmhearted approach I encountered frequently is that many women want to continue, in a sense, the caretaker role for their husbands even after they are gone, giving him permission to remarry in the event of her death. Twice I talked with couples where the second wife had been handpicked by the first wife when she was terminally ill, and in one case I heard about, the wife, knowing she did not have much time left, stocked the freezer with prepared meals and left notes in her husband's closet about which ties went with which shirts and suits! (Unusual, but not completely unknown in retirement communities and senior centers.)

Older women and their partners deal with the search for late-life love within the marital marathon in varied and often imaginative ways.

Money Troubles Come in the Door; Love Flies out the Window

The world-famous acting couple, Ossie Davis and Ruby Dee, recently wrote a candid memoir of their fifty-year marriage titled *With Ossie and Ruby,* each taking turns with memories and advice. They shed some light on some of the stresses young couples must face that are not unknown to older partners, either: "As everyone knows," writes Davis, "sex, even at full blast, is not enough to sustain two blazing, blinding appetites, no matter how marvelous and ethereal it appears at the very beginning. It is no substitute for food and rent and work and a weekly paycheck which define the world in which two lovers must live...all honeymoons must finally be abandoned, as other things come knocking at the bedroom door."

Older couples nod sagely at this, and then Dee chimes in with "the idea that a good marriage is made in heaven and swung down on a golden cord like a gift from God did not coincide with my observations...the wedding is just an event that precedes the marriage...we have to *learn* how to live together. To arrive at love is like working on a double doctorate in the subject of LIFE." Davis credits their marital longevity partly to luck, to love, and also, as he describes it, "a talent for knowing, when we stumble, where to fall and how to get up again."

The issue of stumbling, falling, and getting up again was echoed by Tom B., seventy-nine, who said, when his wife was not present, that the first postwar years were rough, after he got out of the army and was trying to make a life with his wartime sweetheart whom he married before going overseas. They both were natives of small towns in Arkansas, but thought job opportunities might be greater elsewhere, so they moved to a larger southern city after his army days.

"The problem was," Tom says over a drink at his neighborhood bar, "that I was completely adrift about making a living. I didn't finish college because of the war, and was too dumb and worried to take advantage of the G.I. Bill and finish my education." He studies his drink thoughtfully for a few minutes.

"I sort of drifted into sales because in those days you didn't need a college degree as much as you do now," he continues. "Well, Mary and I had some hard years and even now, we aren't what you would call worry free. I never did get a pension, really, so Social Security is really important to us, and Mary worked some, off and on when the kids were bigger, so she has a little

Social Security too, and she's a great manager, so we have some savings."

But seventy-two-year-old Mary's view of their lifelong financial worries echoes the process described by Ossie Davis of loving, being lucky, and stumbling, falling, and getting up again

"I was raised with a little more money in the home than Tom was," she begins, "so I really felt bad when we couldn't get nice things for the little house we got under the G.I. Bill mortgage." She pauses. "When I hear young people today talking about how they have to have their silver and their matched china before they get married, I just don't know what to make of it," she laughs.

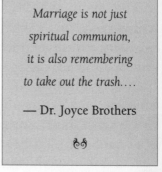

Marriage is not just spiritual communion, it is also remembering to take out the trash....

— Dr. Joyce Brothers

"But we have three healthy kids and we got them fed and raised and they now have good families of their own, so there's no way I could really say that my Tom was not a good husband and father — he was and is — he was always great with the children, and now his grandchildren just love and adore him."

"And does being the matriarch of a loving family make up for the lack of some of the material things that one might expect to have in late life?" I ask.

Mary is silent for several minutes, trying to decide how far to trust the promise of anonymity and identity disguises. Her bright blue eyes, ringed by the dark lashes that the Irish say are eyes "put in when God had a sooty finger," look directly at me. She takes a deep breath and says slowly, "I thought of leaving Tom two or three times over the hard years. I really did, even after I had three children. I just was so tired of the constant struggle and I felt part of the time that he wasn't trying hard enough; part of the time that I ought to figure out a way to bring in some money, even though we didn't have, like some of our friends, any family nearby to help out with the kids; and

part of the time, I let that big world out there push me around
— you know, neighbors with new cars, people on vacations we
couldn't afford, and lots of things I wanted for the kids that
they couldn't have."

She stopped and remembered: "But he's such a *good* man —
he worked hard, he really did, and he was always so kind and
loving to me and the kids. When I saw physical abuse of other
wives in our neighborhood, and when he always was there at
parents' night at school, I picked myself up and said we just
had to make this work."

Mary flashed a look of triumph and added, "All three of our
children finished college and they're doing fine. They worked
their way through with loans and jobs — we couldn't help
much — and I know they'd be there for us if we ever got into
real trouble. But I don't think we will if we have a little luck
with our health." She shrugged with a what-can-you-do expression and then confided shyly, "we had a lovely fiftieth anniversary party the kids made and Tom gave me a new gold wedding
band — see?" She held her hand out proudly with the shiny
new ring, like a young girl with her engagement diamond.

Stumbling, loving, falling, and getting up again? That happens with another part of older couples' late-life quest, too —
the part that has to do with how much solitude and how much
togetherness to have after the work-
ing years are over. It's a brand-new
problem women feel especially
acutely, whether they worked or
stayed home or some combination
of the two, they were used to having
many hours when their husbands
were at work and their time at home
was their own. This change in roles

> *People change and*
> *forget to tell each other.*
> — Lillian Hellman

and activities becomes even more difficult to sort out when the
husband and wife both work and the husband retires while she
may be just approaching the peak of her earning power.
Women frequently started to work later than men in this older

generation, often waiting until the children were nearly grown to earn a steady paycheck and perhaps have some benefits.

Actually, the question of how much space and how much togetherness a couple needs — which is a paraphrase for how to balance mature individual growth with the need for intimacy in long-married couples — has wide individual variations with some couples wanting from the beginning of their marriages to do everything together, and others needing much more "apart" time.

Whether they are ancient sages like Kahlil Gibran or modern psychologists like Erik Erikson, many observers of marriage recommend a balance of time alone and time together. Gibran instructs poetically, "Let there be spaces in your togetherness," while Erikson points out the need to balance isolation with intimacy as couples age and as material and health circumstances change.

The hope couples have that their marital intimacy will deepen as they age — both erotically and in everyday matters of companionship — is part of the lifelong quest for love and closeness that goes on to the very end of the journey.

Alone Together: Apartness As Love

Although many long-married couples spend most of their waking hours together participating in household chores, sharing outside activities, and relating to family and friends, many also express the need to have some hours apart — either for activities their mate does not enjoy, or simply for "breathing space," as one wife put it.

One of the most inspiring models for the balance of isolation and intimacy in contemporary life is the unusual marriage fashioned by the late novelist Iris Murdoch and her husband, the author and critic, John Bayley.

Between the onset of her struggle with Alzheimer's disease and her death in 1999, Murdoch's husband wrote a loving memoir about their life together, which he titled *Elegy for Iris*. In it he described how these two busy people — she a world-famous philosopher, teacher, and novelist, he a distinguished British man of letters — pursued their interests while remaining as emotionally close and physically intimate as a couple could wish.

Thinking back to their honeymoon and their early newly-wed days, he wrote, "So married life began. And the joys of solitude. No contradiction was involved. The one went perfectly with the other. To feel oneself held and cherished and accompanied, and yet to be alone. To be closely and physically entwined, and yet feel solitude's friendly presence."

Many older women, particularly, feel that the constant need to tend to their husbands or companions rules out much needed solitude and that if they verbalize this need out loud, it is a form of betrayal or abandonment of their partner, even when there are no health issues present to induce guilt about proper caretaking.

Bayley's vision of the solitude that is possible *within* marriage is quite different. "Apartness in marriage," he writes, "is a state of *love,* and not a function of distance or preference or practicality."

Older people seeking to hold fast to mutually satisfying patterns of *inter*dependence they forged in their earlier years of marriage must deal with the changes that retirement, relocation, and possibly health problems, whether major or minor, bring to their long-established equilibrium.

"The importance of intimacy and mutuality cannot be overestimated...a capacity for intimacy is the real goal of most people. Without it, lives which are otherwise successful will seem wanting. With intimacy, even the most difficult lives can be judged worthwhile and satisfying," according to pioneering gerontologist Dr. Robert N. Butler.

Psychologist Erik Erikson points out the difficulties in re-integrating the capacity to love and yet to bear isolation when spouses and close friends die. "It is a challenge to the individual to develop and maintain relationships of mutuality with people in *all* generations," he says.

Helen N., eighty-two, is a veteran of a fifty-six-year marriage with Herbert, eighty-one, and both are in reasonably good health and enjoying life in an assisted living community near their children on the West Coast. But clever Helen, knowing that the long, sweet idyll of a marriage in which each partner is completely comfortable with his or her separate role, could be threatened by change — in health, in living arrangements, in money problems — has begun (in secret, she says) a little campaign to teach Herbert some household and social skills in case anything should happen to her. She, like many women of her generation, has been the homemaker par excellence, kept the lists of the children's new telephone numbers as they moved through school, work, marriage, and parenthood, and maintains most of the couple's social contacts. She understands that Herbert would have to reconcile a sense of closeness to someone — children, friends, a new partner — with the experience of being alone, should she not be on the scene.

Their marriage has been strong from the beginning, and seems to have been little threatened by the "twenty-year dip" — a phenomenon reported in a 1997 study in the *Social Psychology Quarterly*, which interviewed 3,600 spouses. Researchers found that after the first fine rapture of the newlywed stage wears off, marital satisfaction takes a downward, if not a belly flopping, turn, reaching the lowest point at about twenty years. At that point, says a commentary in the University of California health newsletter, couples start thinking of divorce though even, in most cases, they don't actually get a divorce. Then the curve turns sharply upward, according to the study. No one is quite sure why the bumpy road to love gets much smoother as the silver anniversary looms, but speculation is that as parental responsibilities lessen, money issues are stabilized and the couple has more time for each other. And then there's the ability to "maximize outcomes" that develops with age (see chapter 3, "The Anatomy of Bravery") and realizing that maybe the marriage has some strengths after all.

But what about the marriage that finds an extra pothole in

that road? The marriage that is surviving infidelity on the part of one or both partners is also struggling with issues of interdependence, commitment, and individual freedom and "apartness." These are issues that become urgent to resolve if couples are to enjoy some measure of trust and stability as time hurries them forward to old age.

An Affair: Escape from Intimacy?

There isn't a great deal of dependable information on adultery in the 1990s in the U.S., even after the 1999 Presidential sex scandal. ("Marriages are hard. They are hard work. I'd be the first to tell you," said First Lady Hillary Rodham Clinton at a women's meeting in Buffalo, New York, in May 1999).

But what meager information exists mostly comes from a well-respected study done in 1994 at the University of Chicago, which suggested that 25 percent of men and 12 percent of women were unfaithful at some point in the marriage. (Recent research, according to Joseph Hooper of the *New York Times,* suggests this gap is narrowing, but men are still much in the majority of adulterers.) There's no evidence that these kinds of threats to marriage are any worse as the millennium turns than they were in the "let it all hang out" era of the 1960s or during the vogue for "open marriages" in the 1970s, reports Hooper.

Women have greeted their husbands' straying with every possible psychological reaction: cynicism ("What do you expect — he's a man"); gallows humor ("If my husband is late and I think he's either lying dead in the road or having an affair, I hope he's lying dead in the road"); or posttraumatic stress syndrome, which can lead to depression in varying degrees that, in turn, can lead to a range of destructive behaviors including suicide and, rarely, murder — but often leads to stumbling forward to some kind of rebuilding of trust.

Why does it happen, even in a marriage lasting twenty-five years or more? Attitudes of therapists, psychologists, and marriage counselors have changed somewhat over the past generation. It used to be thought that an affair was a sign of a troubled marriage and that the unfaithfulness itself should be ignored and the underlying difficulties of the marriage be addressed.

Now, among some therapists, it is thought that the infidelity itself matters, and that it causes troubled marriages, rather than being the result of them.

In the 1980s, Frank Pittman, M.D., an Atlanta psychiatrist, wrote a book titled *Private Lies: Infidelity and the Betrayal of Intimacy.* He argues that many men are not good at intimacy (see chapter 3, "Defining Sex: Then and Now") and that they flee it. Some female psychiatrists say that the strongest indications a man will have an affair is how he views monogamy and male rights and privileges, and for women, a fairly accurate predictor is marital unhappiness.

This image of "male rights" is especially strong in some older cultures, including the well-known conventions in Italy and France, where men keep mistresses with the full knowledge of their wives. When the late French President Francois Mitterand died after a long illness, photos of his funeral shown around the world featured his longtime mistress, illegitimate daughter, and his legal wife standing together at the casket. Americans haven't quite accepted the idea on such a large scale yet, and when these older, more "macho" cultures are transplanted here, wives face difficult decisions.

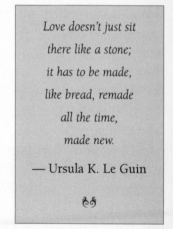

> Love doesn't just sit
> there like a stone;
> it has to be made,
> like bread, remade
> all the time,
> made new.
>
> — Ursula K. Le Guin

In filmmaker David Collier's 1993 Academy Award–nominated documentary film, *For Better or for Worse,* and in the book that was inspired by the movie, Collier and his crew focus on thirty American couples — both gay and straight — who have been together more than thirty years, some more than sixty years.

A Mexican-born couple named Tomas and Elme Bermejo, who are in their early sixties and have five children, were among the couples Collier photographed and interviewed for his book *Living Happily Ever After.*

"Monogamy?" says Tomas to Collier, "What is that? One woman all your life? I don't believe in it. It's not natural." His wife, Elme, knows about his "flings," but says that he has settled down now, a little bit at least, and she stays with him partly because, as a Catholic, she believes marriage is forever and partly because "he has a good heart."

The "cool" that Elme is able to summon in the face of her husband's quite notorious (in his younger years) infidelity is also partly due to their having grown older and built a LIFE, in capital letters, together. The cumulative weight of children they raised, of a business they run, and of having "made it" in this country together, and possibly most of all, Elme's intuitive understanding of the culture into which they both were born — all add up to a decision to do the last lap together. Elme is not a doormat, by any means. She is a spirited, energetic woman who has drawn very definite lines in the sand and there are a number of things she would not countenance, including any kind of physical abuse, which has never been present in her marriage. She is content with what she calls a "traditional Hispanic marriage," which, she says, is a bit more egalitarian in the U.S. than some of her female relatives find back home. This, combined with Tomas's kindness to her and his hard work, would seem to make her old age unthreatening and would account for a marriage that may be better now than it was at the midpoint in their forty-five-year span together.

While being interviewed for this book at a senior center in the Midwest, Jeff S., eighty-two, and his wife, Millie, seventy-six, both American-born of pioneer stock, were horrified at the idea of the casual infidelity that Elme and Tomas seem able to keep from shadowing their later years. Though both described themselves as without any strong religious affiliations ("Church was social, when I was a girl," says Millie), they strongly felt some kind of binding code that would not allow them to be unfaithful during the more than half century they have been together. "Oh, I was tempted here and there," says Jeff and then, in a charming effort to be politically correct, he hastens to add "and I'm sure Millie was, too." She nods vigorously, a little to his surprise. "But now there's a nice, well,..." he struggles for words, "sweetness?" Millie supplies. "Yes, we have something special now — an understanding, I guess you'd say," adds Jeff.

Although Jeff and Millie can only generally describe the sense of loyalty and knowing "the difference between right and wrong" that accounts for their marital fidelity, other observers have described more precisely the ideas that they believe contribute to faithfulness in marriage.

California psychologists, Kenneth Robert Lakritz, Ph.D. and Thomas Morrison Knoblauch, Ph.D., in an effort to explore all aspects of love and loving as elements in a better community life, gathered a circle of elders to hold discussion seminars about different kinds of love and spirituality.

Among their participants was a couple who married each other after unhappy first marriages, and who, at the time they participated in the discussion group, had been married nearly twenty years. The wife, Elizabeth Leonie Simpson, seventy-one, is a retired psychologist with a background in linguistics and literature, and the husband, John Wurr, seventy-five, is a retired engineer.

In the book, *Elders on Love,* which features transcripts of the seminar discussions, the first task accomplished by Wurr was a definition of love: "Romantic love," he said, "is a fantasy that most young men and women have and it's very exciting. But that intensity isn't going to last. I remember how much I enjoyed the giddy fantasies of infatuation when I was young, but I think I always knew that these were not real love...I thought: when all this great excitement is over — and it's absolutely marvelous while it lasts — I want it to mature into this thing which I consider real love...I always felt that the real thing, real love, the permanent thing, has to grow slowly and is based on helping, struggling, and succeeding together...this is what I think love is."

Dealing with preserving that love within the tricky challenges of how to combine personal, individual freedom with commitment to another person, Simpson said: "What's good is *controlled freedom*…you are constrained by the need not to hurt the other person…the freedom has to include an awareness of the needs of the other partner." Wurr pointed out that "total freedom is as incompatible with marriage as it is with a civilized society…you don't do things that would hurt the person you love…and it is very important that this discipline comes from within, that you know you are controlling your own freedom." This seemed to reflect the "you just don't do things like that" feeling that Jeff and Millie had tried to describe when we talked about fidelity in marriage. Faithfulness is especially important to Jeff and his wife as a core value of their shared sexual life; the notion of betraying that with another person seemed to be outside anything they could envision.

Does late-life love include another language of love, of sex? While Jeff is absent from the interview, Millie explains in a circuitous fashion (clearly sex is not a subject that can be discussed easily with outsiders for this couple) that this question happens to come at a delicate point in their reaffirmation of their sexual bond. It seems that her husband had been on medication that was known to dampen the sex drive and since he had to take it for a good many months, they had adjusted to that situation with some lovemaking she described as "ingenious." Then, out of the blue, his condition improved to the point where he could go off the medication and, after a period of readjustment, they could once more consider the more vigorous love life they had always enjoyed. With a laugh, a blush, and a twinkle, she added "and all that was without Viagra, and at our age, too!"

Jeff and Millie illustrate one of the key elements that arise in the life of long-marrieds: the exploration of the new country of aging sexuality. Here, as we have seen in earlier chapters, the older couple battle conventional attitudes and stereotypes that decree that they either have no sexual desires, fantasies, or interests, or if they do, they should be faintly ashamed and embarrassed about them and do all they can to douse those fires of autumn.

Because members of this generation, like Jeff and Millie, were largely socially programmed never to discuss sex outside the intimate world they create for each other, it has been difficult to track the exploration of older couples' sexuality as they age together after long marital histories.

Sex, Affection, Love, and Caring: The Kautz Study

What role do health problems play in changing patterns of lovemaking? Do old emotional problems — such as the infidelity discussed above or festering feelings about the partner that are never really aired and resolved — shut down physical expressiveness as people age? What about those partners whose sex lives were always somewhat muted, neither partner feeling the need for much more than quiet physicality?

Many of the people who were interviewed for this book, both couples and men and women who were single due to divorce, death, or were never married, hinted at "adapting" and "getting around the problems," and men who used Viagra were not shy about whether it helped or had no effect on relationships, but in-depth probes of the strategies older couples use to face the effects of age and health on their sexual lives have been scarce.

However, while a graduate student of health services at the University of Kentucky in 1995, Donald D. Kautz completed a hitherto unpublished study of seventeen older men and women — eight couples and one husband whose wife refused to participate in the survey — aimed at looking at the maturing of sexual intimacy in older adult couples. The men and women he surveyed for his doctoral thesis were between sixty-five and eighty-five, and the strategies Dr. Kautz examined were those that the couples adopted to deal with physical problems only; psychiatric difficulties, other than depression, were not included

> *And when will there be*
> *an end of marrying?*
> *I suppose, when there is*
> *an end of living.*
>
> — Quintus Tertullian
>
> ୫ଡ଼

in the study. Seven of the couples were white, one couple was African American. The latter couple had each been married before; the white couples were in their first marriages. Most of the men in the survey had served in the armed forces in World War II.

The findings of this study reveal an overwhelming sense of love, caring, mutual understanding, and helpfulness, each partner to the other.

Where ill health such as acute arthritis for the wife or impotence for the husband force a new set of sexual plans, couples showed these emotional responses:

1. *Emotional commitment:* "We are married for keeps" seems to be their theme. Since most of the couples had been together for half a century, their summary of how deeply entwined they feel is articulate and moving. Says one husband (Tim): "I'm sure I come first in her life and I'm sure that she's first in my life...it's always been that way. She was the girl I wanted. I got her and I still want her...we try to please each other." His wife (Teresa) says: "I couldn't live without him...I like to touch him, I like him by me in bed, I like him...I just like him...Tim married for keeps and so did I...there's not just one, it's not just Teresa, and it's not just Tim, it's Teresa and Tim."

2. *Acceptance of aging:* Most of the couples indicated that while they slowed down sexually, they remained active, and that conventional intercourse was less important than a variety of other sexual expressions, especially touching, kissing, and embracing as a sign of closeness. The couples Dr. Kautz and his assistants spoke with described a

range of physical activities — walking, swimming, biking — that they tried their best to continue despite knee, back, and hip joint problems. Accepting the slowing down of aging, but working hard to keep active and keep going was a major strategy that fed into improved sex, they felt.

3. *Adaptability:* The role of the men in initiating sex was a clear reflection of the social norms these men and women were raised with. Several clear patterns were found in this realm, as well. While the husbands initiated sex, they did not force it at all if their partner was not well or not encouraging at the moment. The wives were grateful. "He's a very sensitive and sweet person" said one wife. Half of the men in the survey did everything they could to fight the effects of aging — primarily intermittent bouts of impotence — by consulting physicians and trying various pre-Viagra treatments for erectile dysfunction. The other half of the men in the group simply accepted health problems and substituted other forms of sexual contact if conventional ones were not possible.

4. *Protectiveness:* "We care for each other." This mutual sense of caring and protectiveness was carried out in many ways. Couples were greatly sensitive to each other's needs and seemed to intuit when sex shouldn't even be discussed, but rather transformed and transcended if health problems were too severe. For one couple, this was brought about because severe arthritis made the wife use walkers and wheelchairs, but did not daunt either her own or her husband's positive attitudes. They carry over warm memories from the past, and he reads books and magazines to her and then they discuss them. They play cards, do crosswords, watch TV, share good jokes — in

every way, they protect each other from the worst impacts of a chronic illness. This couple believe they have become more as a couple than they were when they were younger because of their experiences. (Couples interviewed for this book said such experiences either bring husbands and wives closer together or, in some especially difficult life experiences such as the loss of a child, they destroy the marriage).

Older couples use the following strategies to help themselves mature sexually in their advancing years:

- Older couples draw strength from their commitment and being "married for keeps."
- Couples learn to accept what they can't change and to feel the sense of shared normalcy that makes "things okay."
- When men continue to initiate sex, they often take additional steps toward keeping themselves and their wives healthy and active.
- Long-married couples protect each other; they don't attack vulnerabilities (as they might have when young) and they often can transcend their physical problems with sex. Tim expresses it this way: "What I can't understand about it, usually love and sex go hand in hand...well, I love her better and more since we stopped our sex life. I think more of her now than I did then...I appreciate her more."

It seems clear from this groundbreaking study that elder love and sex are intense realities and that when there is a long history couples can overcome a great many of the difficulties that life throws in their path.

Ron B., seventy-two, and his wife, Miriam, also seventy-two illustrate exactly how many crises long-marrieds survive and what the costs are to remain together and look toward a fiftieth anniversary.

Ron and Miriam have lived through the death of a child, marital infidelity, another child's drug use, and the illnesses of their own parents, which strained budgets and emotional stamina.

Yet today, they are in a special place of peacefulness together. This is their story.

Marriage As the Keeper of Souls

Ron and Miriam have been married for forty-eight years and are renewing their marriage today in ways neither could possibly have imagined when they, like millions of other returning World War II veterans and their brides, crowded into marriage license bureaus in the years immediately following the war.

They are such a textbook example from the America of Eisenhower and Truman that they could serve as an illustration for the cover of one of the many books on the 1940s, 1950s and 1960s now flooding coffee tables. They are both retired now, but have chosen to remain in the Pennsylvania suburb where they raised their family.

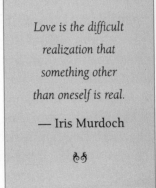

Love is the difficult realization that something other than oneself is real.

— Iris Murdoch

The trek to the suburbs when jobs were plentiful for Ron, who used the G.I. Bill benefits to become an accountant (the first of his family to go beyond high school), the little tract house where two sons and a daughter came along; then the better job and bigger house — all were familiar patterns for many American middle-class couples who now are looking toward their golden wedding anniversaries. In those years, working-class couples were able to make some gains, as well, before manufacturing and heavy industry gave way to technology and the information age, requiring much more training and education beyond high school.

Miriam went back to work as a secretary when her children left home, joining the burgeoning wave of women returning to work. Miriam did not read *The Feminine Mystique,* the book by Betty Friedan that was largely credited with launching the contemporary women's movement, until a decade after its publication in 1963, nor was she forced by necessity, like many middle-class women of the 1990s, to take a job to maintain a house–two cars–college for the kids standard of living. Ron was supporting the family, even with two of the three children in college; it could be done on his rising salary in the 1950s and 1960s.

"I didn't need a book or a friend to tell me that I had to get out of the house," Miriam reports now with a disarming grin. "So for a lot of years I juggled the job, house, family — it was tiring and I'm not sorry that's over," she says about her retirement from her well-paid administrative assistant job.

But, of course, Miriam and Ron are not "typical" — no one is. Every couple experiences life, love, and aging in a long marriage in a singular way — as unique as their fingerprints.

Though superficially, the backyard barbecues and the Little League games where they yelled encouragement to their boys — girls didn't play Little League in those days, so their daughter sat with them in the stands — were life events exactly like those of their neighbors, but Ron and Miriam had their own darkness and sunlight.

A mid-life crisis that brought a tumultuous affair into Ron's otherwise steady life, then the death of a son killed by a drunk driver in a car crash, and later, fears (since conquered) that their daughter was drug addicted — all these experiences make it clear that no one's life is "typical."

Today, in their mid-seventies, they are quite recognizable from their wedding pictures, in spite of the obvious changes. Miriam is not quite the tiny doll she was back then, but is still trim, perky, and optimistic. Ron has all his hair, now quite white, but bad bouts of pneumonia two winters in a row have left him thinner than usual for a big man. On the whole, they are able to continue the golf they enjoy and long walks and occasional bike rides.

But what is special about this couple is the warmth and tenderness underneath the dry jokes and the teasing, a rock-bottom kindness not always visible in long-together pairs whose comfort zone sometimes includes a wariness born of what they know of each other's vulnerabilities.

Both born and raised in Maine, Ron and Miriam are deeply conventional people and they share that notable style of reserve and understatement. It became clear that the deeper intimacies of love as one ages were not going to be discussed in the context of a simultaneous interview as they were strongly invested in presenting a united facade of a long, stable marriage with no cracks in the sculptured figures — at least to a virtual stranger.

Things went better in a series of separate interviews, though Miriam made clear certain trouble areas that Ron would not discuss and that would cause him distress if he knew Miriam had talked about them to anyone. The main circumstance he did not want known was about a serious infidelity with a woman who came quite close to destroying their marriage. She was the wife of an office colleague of Ron's and their affair nearly resulted in two divorces before it ended with both marriages still in place, if somewhat battered.

> *Love is what I'd call metaphysical gravity. It really holds everything together.*
>
> — Buckminster Fuller
>
> ☙

Commenting that women seem able to progress to self-revelation in conversation more quickly than men, Miriam says, "it's only in the last few years I've understood *myself* well enough to even try to guess about the subjects you are asking about — love as we get older. I really didn't feel free enough until I was in my late fifties and early sixties to ask myself if my life was what I wanted it to be — or what was reasonable to hope — especially about marriage and our family."

"What are love, sex, and romance like for us, after nearly fifty years together?" she muses in response to questions.

"Well," she laughs, "I'm from Maine, so I'll say it in very straightforward words: the sex is quieter but sweeter, the romance is more playful and the love," she stops, pauses, and her eyes fill with tears.

She goes on, "I realize now that I have always loved him, and love him now more than ever. It's deeper and better because now I know for sure how short a time is left for us to be together. When he nearly died of pneumonia last winter, I had one of those bargaining talks with God that people have when they're in bad trouble. I promised that if he lived, I'd never take happiness and love for granted again...that I would never take him for granted again. He is the same hero to me that he was when he came home from the war with a medal for bravery, not just the Purple Heart, everybody who was wounded got that, but a real medal. But he's been brave in so many other quieter ways, not in public, that nobody but me knows about. When Ron Junior was killed by a drunk driver, he kept me from going over the edge while nearly crazy himself; when we had drug problems with Annette, he was calm and got help for her...those things made him a hero to me. I admire and respect him more every day."

Why didn't she walk out on him during that rocky time in the marriage when he confessed to being with another woman?

"Oh, a lot of reasons," she answers. "Maybe I was too scared; I had three little ones then. I had never lived alone for a day. Like they say in the books, I went from my father's house to my husband's house. Maybe I just couldn't accept that he might love someone else the way I thought — the way I know now — he does really love me. Or, maybe," she flashes a blinding smile, "or maybe I just love the big, dumb jerk so much that I wanted to go on and try to make our lives together, after he swore that he did not want to leave me or the kids and that it would never happen again."

She pauses for long minutes of silence, hearing in the

stillness, the echoes of what she just said. "So I said I'd take him back — without recriminations, without bitterness, which was the hardest part. But you know," she pauses again, "something like that either blows your marriage right up in your face, or, in some funny way, it can bring you back closer than you ever were. We both tried to understand what had happened, what had gone wrong at home: Too much of small kids never giving us any privacy or time? Too much work pressure? Too much sameness in the suburban routine? — which, by the way, I always hated, but we convinced ourselves the kids needed it."

Problems at work, maybe?

"Yeah," Miriam answers. "There were some work problems. But that's too simple and easy an explanation," Miriam says, the Maine twang getting stronger as she gets more emotional, "it was probably just… " she searches for the word, "just…life. It happens."

She quickly recovers her poise and humor. "But the important thing is *now.*" Then her voice softens again, "Ron Junior has been gone for a long while now, but you never get over it; you never really heal from losing a child, but at least we have each other. Annette, thank God, is happily married and has two beautiful babies of her own. It's time for *us,* for Ron and me."

She leans forward over the kitchen table: "I can't tell you how deep is the contentment we have now. It's something kids will never know about until they're together for a long, long time. We have a *knowledge* and a sharing of each other that — " she looks away embarrassed, "that is well, sort of soulful…or …spiritual, you might say."

"I don't know," she continues, "it's like remarrying. All I know is that we've renewed our marriage for the rest of the way we have to go together, and I do *not* regret for a second that I took him back."

Did it ever happen again?

With a keen eye and the smallest smile, she says, "I don't think so, but do I really know? If he wants to deceive me, he will. I think I would know though, and I feel very easy, so easy, in what we have now that, quite honestly, I don't worry about it — it seems unlikely at this point and I don't find any false notes in the way we get on together day-to-day. I've been tempted, too, from time to time, over nearly fifty years, but I never met anybody who seemed worth hurting Ron for."

The only part of their rocky road that Ron was willing to discuss stretched from before his son's death, through that tragedy, and a short time afterward (before the extramarital affair).

In the cozy room that once held guitars, sneakers, soccer balls, dolls, and tricycles, but was now his den, Ron begins by saying, "I don't know what Miriam told you," and laughs knowingly, adding, "Of course, you're not going to tell me and that's okay."

"I really don't know how you or Miriam — or any woman, for that matter — explain love or try to tell what it's about," Ron says earnestly, trying hard to overcome the awkwardness of discussing love with a stranger. "But, I see one big thing now that I didn't know when I was younger, and I think it's a combination of aging *and* the special affection my wife and I have."

Marriage is not a matter of creating a quick community of spirit by tearing down and destroying all boundaries, but rather a good marriage is that in which each appoints the other guardian of his solitude…

— Rainer Maria Rilke

"And that is, that I'm just more ready to talk about things that hurt than ever I used to be. Maybe it's Miriam's loyalty, maybe it's my son's death, maybe it's finally being out of the rat race at work — whatever it is, I don't feel so bad talking about mistakes — or about the anguish when we lost our son. I guess I'll always feel that to some extent."

"Miriam and I both grew up believing that you should always keep your troubles and worries to yourself and never,

never do anything except keep a stiff upper lip and stay away from any subject of conversation that wasn't pleasant and easy," Ron continues.

"But the rocky parts of our marriage, then losing one child and worrying about another — only our eldest has been the responsible, easy one to raise — have made us so *close,* so *fused* that it's sort of a wonder," he shakes his head almost in disbelief.

He asks, "Do you think young or even middle-aged people would understand what I'm talking about?"

"Nope," he answers his own question, "I think what we understand about each other now, the kids can't know until life kicks them around a little, right? Or until they finally understand that this is not a rehearsal and they're not going to be here forever. It's beyond anything they can know when they're young and think they're immortal, or even middle aged and they're so caught up in work and college tuition bills and worrying about money and fixing the roof — if you ever get beyond that, as Miriam and I have been lucky enough to do, you see there are different kinds of ways of caring about each other."

Maybe Sophocles Was Right: Different Strokes

It is clear that the sexual component of Miriam and Ron's marriage was ever-present, despite the changes their emotional roller-coaster may have wrought over the years.

But the Greek philosopher, Sophocles, is often quoted about his release, in old age, from "the tyranny of sex," and there are many long-married couples who share this view, who are glad to have the turbulence of that driving force fade from their lives.

We know that sex, love, and romance have always been more complicated constructions than we may admit; they are influenced by race, class, gender, family attitudes, religious doctrine, popular culture, and many other factors.

Whether for these cultural and social reasons, or for other psychological or physiological reasons, men and women who have been quite content with a subdued love life, or who have rejected sex altogether, presumably do not change dramatically in later years, although there are women who say they did not fully enjoy sex until well after menopause.

Sex — not love — has been oversold as a therapeutic activity, like vitamins or a good brisk walk ("I think I thought sex was like aerobics when I was young," said sixty-five-year-old feminist leader Gloria Steinem); it's been seen in some quarters as a guarantor of physical health, even if it is viewed as unrelated to emotional needs.

But scientists have shown repeatedly that many people past sixty have allowed this part of their lives — if it was ever active — to be put aside, and they are perfectly healthy and happy, satisfying whatever sensuous or sexual needs they may have in other ways.

Physicians and psychologists say that no one, at any age, should be pressured into thinking that if they are less interested in sex than popular culture suggests they should be, there is something dreadfully wrong with them that needs drastic correction.

Modern professionals, who are perhaps more humane than those of a generation ago, are well represented by English geriatric therapist-researcher J. M. Kellett, M.B., who, while on the staff of a London hospital, did a survey of sexuality among the elderly in 1991. Kellett wrote that the elderly must feel free to alter their sexual practice to *"suit themselves."*

"Our role as therapists," wrote Kellett, "must be to avoid putting pressure on patients to conform to our ideals. Equally we should prevent others from destroying intimacy by interventions which ignore the sexuality of the patient. *The elderly have earned the right to decide for themselves."*

The Magical Mystery Tour: Friendship and Memories

Whether it's a sexual passion continuing into advanced old age or simply each partner loving the sight of the other, we know from the couples we've met in this chapter that older people seeking love in later life within the framework of a long-lasting marriage have mastered certain "facts of life."

These are the guidelines they can give to all older lovers, whether they are newlyweds at eighty or celebrating many decades of marriage:

- "Happiness is being married to your best friend" is a well-worn motto that doesn't begin to touch on the profundities of married friendship. Transmute that first fine madness of betrothal and love into a steady, unblinking friendship, along with the sex, along with the passion, along with the longing. That is probably the single most important piece of advice that long-marrieds give.

  The elements that make married friendship so potent include the fact that each partner can be the most dependable champion, advocate, and all around cheerleader for the other because if he or she wishes, the partner's very best qualities can be the ones emphasized in the marriage and to the world. After all, friendship is almost always a benefit, while love can sometimes hurt, as all long-marrieds know.

- Celebrate your marital self-esteem. Look back on your memories of tough times surmounted, crises survived, and achievements recorded; it strengthens the fabric of late-life love to glory in what you've accomplished together. Even when the road was rough, you made a home, often raised kids, and together helped the grandparent generation where you could, and each helped the other to whatever worldly successes were possible.

  Led in some cases by church and other religious bodies, there is now a formal "renew your marriage" movement in the United States, which is somewhat based on the Catholic Church's Cana projects (named after the Biblical story of Christ's participation in a wedding feast in the city of Cana), that now has moved beyond religious affiliations. Couples involved in more New Age ceremonies are also setting up renewal rites during which newlyweds or long-marrieds repeat their marriage vows, share their stories, and renew their erotic attachments through whatever private rituals are significant to them.

- Acceptance grows more secure as time rushes ever faster; the reaffirmation of "just the way you are" love is an important ingredient of late-life marriage. In first young love, each partner may think they will change the other in the few "little" ways they need changing. By the golden anniversary, they are laughing over the idea that they ever could change the other spouse, and have long since ceased to try, while perhaps retaining teasing rights about who leaves the cap off the toothpaste.
- With patience and new knowledge about health, fitness, and medications, there can be a "second language of love" in late-life sexuality; older couples must be pioneers in overturning the stereotypes about older people as sexless and lost to physical pleasure, when actually, their need for touch is greater than ever and continues to the end of life.

With these helpful guides in hand, older lovers in whatever setting — long marriages, new relationships late in life, third and fourth new marriages — can often look forward to constant growth and development.

The challenges they will meet — ill health, loss, and dependency — are helped by the approaches listed above, but ordinary Americans can also learn something from a community to whom they do not often turn for models of growth and learning: the homosexual communities of gay men and lesbians.

Because of the AIDS epidemic, these communities have much to teach about loss and also about caretaking, one of the major challenges of older years.

Because gays and lesbians have been often stigmatized by society, they can help elders learn some ways to cope with ageism, with being ignored, left out, stereotyped; and with the struggle for human rights.

These are lessons that can be taught by members of many minority communities who are stigmatized and excluded, but the homosexual community has been especially successful at building friendships and networks of support and help outside the standard ones that, in some cases, are denied to them; the support of families is not always forthcoming, nor of employers or colleagues.

Some of these strengths will be helpful to gay men and lesbians as *they* age and seek love in their later years, but they must also face discrimination as they age — prejudice both within and without their own communities.

In the next chapter, we will look at how ageism is an equal opportunity discriminator — coming down hard on straight and gay elders and everybody in between — and how homosexuals are dealing with aging and love in ways both the same and different from the larger society.

TRAILBLAZERS
Ossie Davis and Ruby Dee

Do you want to share with the world the secrets of your fifty-one years of marriage? You know, the quarrels, the misunderstandings, even, yes, the infidelities? Maybe you want to share the love and the children and the grandchildren, but not the bad stuff that stamps reality on your marriage — right?

Wrong — that's not the way to do it, say Ossie Davis, eighty-two, and Ruby Dee, seventy-five, the world-famous acting couple who marked their golden anniversary in 1998 by publishing a book of memoirs that was unusually candid about their lives as theatrical icons, civil rights and social activists, and parents who sometimes made mistakes with their three children. They have seven grandchildren, too.

In many publicized interviews and in the book, *With Ossie and Ruby: In This Life Together,* they told that they had "scavenged among the changes thrown up by the sexual revolution that swept across the country to find what suited us and what could be left alone." In the 1960s, they each strayed briefly, with each other's permission, finding their way home again, and they feel strongly it is important to serve future generations by helping them understand the problems of real life.

"If we leave children to explore their own sexuality unguided, we end up with…[those] who haven't the slightest idea what they're doing or the consequences of their sexual actions," Davis told a reporter, "so now we cannot do without absolute sexual frankness, whatever our previous reservations might have been." His wife strongly concurs, saying "it's a strange new time coming and we need somehow to get out there and test the waters for the people coming after...to make it easier for our children and grand-children."

Davis and Dee take turns telling the struggles of marriage, family raising, and two careers, and Dee is frank about how hard it was to adapt her career and her burgeoning self to the demands of wifehood and motherhood. The picture she paints of child care, work opportunities passed by, and the domestic grind while her husband seemed not to "catch on" to all she was doing is familiar to many wives and is the reality of the early years of marriage for many couples of their generation. In a touching description of what he has learned in a half century of marriage, Davis writes: "Sex is an errant stroke of God's most choice lightening...love on the other hand, is the maker — and keeper of our humanity...Marriage is the place which love calls home." Dee, with the wisdom of an earth mother, says "just staying together is not a real virtue if you're not happy ...then you're just there out of habit and that doesn't work, no matter how many years you stay together." They no longer give each other elaborate anniversary gifts, although they have one traditional present, a handsome poinsettia plant, because their wedding anniversary on December 9 comes in the Christmas season. They need nothing more, they say, because they have what they most want now: each other.

Chapter 5

Love and Mortality
Gay Men and Lesbians
As They Age

If anything happens to Clarissa, she, Sally, will go on living but she will not, exactly, survive...what she wants to say has to do not only with joy, but with the penetrating, constant fear that is joy's other half. She can bear the thought of her own death, but cannot bear the thought of Clarissa's. This love of theirs, with its reassuring domesticity and its easy silences, its permanence, has yoked Sally directly to the machinery of mortality itself.

— Michael Cunningham, *The Hours*

Perhaps all aging lovers — whether together for half a century or newly discovering late passions — are "yoked to the machinery of mortality," as Cunningham puts it so eloquently in his moving novel of gay and lesbian life. Is this struggle to wring joy from the lengthening shadows any different for homosexual couples than it is for the graying heterosexuals who make up the mainstream majority? Aren't the punishments of an ageist society — the discrimination, the stereotyping, the impatience — the same for every man and woman who has the temerity to live beyond sixty-five or even into their nineties, regardless of their sexual orientation?

Getting old in America is tough on everyone — a sort of equal opportunity oppression that many older people have come to rationalize and accept in a sort of "what can I expect, I'm old" fatalism. But that very social and economic age discrimination so familiar to older workers dismissed summarily and to elderly widows no longer invited by old friends — is it similar or different for men and women of the homosexual community? The answer is: both. There are many similarities in the way aging gay and lesbian couples are treated by society, and also, sharp differences. There are many similarities in the emotional texture of long-lasting love relationships and many differences. In order to examine those similarities and differences with intelligence and compassion and really determine whether there are lessons to be learned between the gay and straight worlds in these matters of love, aging, and mortality, an historical perspective is vital.

History As Illumination

Homosexuality is as old as heterosexuality, and so has been equally exposed, everywhere and at all times, to states that have an interest in regulating their citizens' sexuality. At different times in our historical past, different demands have been placed on homosexuals by the state. Laws and popular custom have imposed taboos on heterosexuals, too. In earlier periods of U.S. history, there were both religious and legal injunctions against masturbation, which was particularly condemned by religious groups as going against biblical injunctions. The persistence of these taboos was dramatically demonstrated as recently as 1994 when the Surgeon General of the U.S., Jocelyn Elders, was dismissed for publicly raising the question of whether masturbation should be discussed as part of sex education programs for adolescents.

In fact, sexual variance is whatever society says it is. In the nineteenth century, "abnormality" was applied equally to gay, lesbian, and straight people who had sexual contact for any purpose other than procreation. Professor Charles O. Jackson, associate dean and professor of history at the University of Tennessee in Knoxville, is the editor of a comprehensive historical review of sexual variance, published in 1996. Dr. Jackson's study, *The Other Americans: Sexual Variance in the National Past,* points out that today's repressive attitude toward homosexuals, while somewhat lightened in the past thirty years, is not a new development. The period of intense antigay attitudes and activities that was begun in the Reagan era, supported by New Right groups of both political and religious background, was, in fact, the third wave of such repression in the twentieth century.

According to Dr. Jackson, the first was in the 1920s when an early feminist movement, which resulted in women winning the vote in 1920, was perceived as a threat to the traditional family. This alleged threat prompted a mass campaign against lesbians but also included homosexuality in general. The second was in the 1950s when gay bashing was part of the McCarthy era of cold war hysteria about all nonconforming ideas. Many scholars agree with those historians represented in Dr. Jackson's study that the "threat to [the] American Way" — nonheterosexual behavior — remained a "stock theme in the nation's political culture and partisan rhetoric" through most of that decade. The 1950s also saw extreme discrimination against homosexuals in the military and in government jobs, which was institutionalized by President Dwight D. Eisenhower's executive order of 1953 barring homosexuals from *all* federal jobs. (This ban was not lifted until 1975.)

And, according to political scientist and author Andrew Sullivan, in his book *Virtually Normal: An Argument about Homosexuality,* Western society is still "in the midst of a tense and often fevered attempt to find its own way in the matter."

Describing precisely where society is today, Sullivan goes on to say, "Amid a cacophony of passion and reason, propaganda and statistics, self-disclosure and bouts of hysteria, the subject is being ineluctably discussed," and for the sake of all elders seeking to find love and to battle ageism, we will discuss it, too.

Social Earthquakes and the Homosexual Generational Divide

There is little doubt that the positive changes in today's cultural scene are extensive. Michael Cunningham's gay novel, *The Hours,* won the 1999 Pulitzer Prize and the TV sitcom *Ellen* in which comedienne Ellen DeGeneres, an open lesbian, came out on her show and later publicly announced her partnership with actress Anne Heche, ran for four seasons. In politics, gay leaders are detecting a subtle, but more tolerant, acceptance of their political contributions from the Republican party, which used to return their checks. In 1998, the first open lesbian ever to be elected to Congress as a nonincumbent — Rep. Tammy Baldwin (D-Wis.) — took her seat in the House of Representatives and will run for reelection in 2000. Meanwhile, two openly gay legislators — Rep. Barney Frank (D-Mass.) and Rep. Jim Kolbe (R-Ariz.) — are currently serving in the House. Two other openly gay Congressmen who formerly served — Rep. Gerry Studds (D-Mass.) and Rep. Steve Gunderson (R-Wis.) — have retired from Congress.

All these developments are hopeful, indeed, but they do not erase the past, nor make the future assured for gay men and lesbians, much less the bisexual and transgendered people whose lives are outside the scope of this book. The social earthquakes that have shaken American society in the past fifty years and have forced disorienting changes in sexual mores have a direct bearing on how older gay men and lesbians confront aging and the possibility of new love at the start of the new century.

War As a Catalyst for Change

The history of discrimination in the recent past notes World War II as the turning point in modern gay history. Up to that time, there was a flourishing subculture of gay life in some urban centers, well-hidden from general view. But during the war, millions of young people left homes, families, small towns, and tightly-knit ethnic communities to serve all over the world, and others went to strange cities to work in wartime factories.

This tearing away from roots was accompanied by new freedoms in the heterosexual community as well; contraception had now completely severed sex from procreation and the Jazz Age had begun a sexual revolution that would come to fruition everywhere in the developed world in the 1960s. All these forces shape the lives and loves of homosexual people now in their sixties, seventies, eighties, and beyond — as well as the AIDS tragedy of the past decades — and their inevitable sweep toward freedom for the gay rights movement was fought at many points along the way by increased repression and discrimination.

When, more than forty years ago, President Eisenhower banned gays and lesbians from federal employment, many state and local governments followed suit and so did private corporations. This meant there was a witch hunt in the homosexual community somewhat analogous to the political blacklist in the McCarthy era that destroyed the lives and careers of those thought to be Communists or Communist sympathizers. In this period of antigay frenzy, the FBI began a surveillance program against homosexuals.

Progression and Regression

That was the backdrop against which the second watershed in modern gay history occurred — the Stonewall Riots of 1969. In June of that year, New York City police raided a gay bar called the Stonewall Inn in Greenwich Village. To the astonishment of police, the patrons fought back and three nights of riots ensued. Fueled by the successes of the civil rights movements that radicalized blacks, women, and students, slogans of "Gay Power" appeared on buildings and the modern gay liberation movement was born almost overnight.

Since then, there has been a strong forward movement toward civil rights for members of the homosexual community. This momentum has seen gay and lesbian publishing houses established and flourishing, gay theater become mainstream, increasing gay and lesbian influence in the arts and politics, and gay rights organizations becoming more visible and useful than ever, both for their members and the general public.

President Bill Clinton, over Congressional objections, appointed the first openly gay diplomat, James Hormel, former dean of the University of Chicago Law School, to a post as Ambassador to Luxembourg. A number of large churches of various religious denominations accept and support gay and lesbian members. There are even a few that are primarily for lesbians and gays (while welcoming everyone), such as Congregation Beth Simchat Torah, a Reform synagogue in New York.

But for every religious institution like Temple Beth Israel in West Hartford, Connecticut, New England's largest mainstream synagogue, which, in 1999, hired an associate rabbi who is a lesbian, there are many more churches who refuse to have clergy or members who are homosexual.

Even clergy who are themselves heterosexual heads of conventional families have been ousted or suspended by their congregations when they took steps to support gay or lesbian couples by officiating at ceremonies of commitment by the two homosexual partners.

The United Methodist Church of the United States has a rule against same-sex unions and suspended the popular minister of a Chicago United Methodist Church in early 1999 when he officiated at the union of two gay men. The Reverend Greg Dell, with the support of his wife and son, refused to take a pledge that he would not conduct such ceremonies again because, he said, it would "contradict my understanding of my responsibilities as a pastor." The church's antigay rules will be up for discussion and possible revision at the central governing board's next meeting in 2000. The possibility that gay men and lesbians could live untroubled by prejudice and discrimination, even in the twenty- first century, seems to be strengthened or weakened in a "two steps forward, one step backward" pattern of historical development.

On the one hand, the very spot where the modern gay liberation movement was born, the Stonewall Inn in New York, has been placed on the National Register of Historic Places. Stonewall joins seventy thousand other landmark listings around the country. It is marked by the U.S. Department of the Interior, which supervises the National Registry, as a site crucial to the task of "recognizing the national significance and contributions of lesbians and gay men."

On the other hand, at the very time that Interior Department officials were saying that they hoped the listing would spur "additional advances in tolerance," researchers at Children's Hospital at Harvard Medical School were releasing a research report showing that teenagers who are gay or bisexual are more than three times as likely to attempt suicide as other youth.

Writing in the *Archives of Pediatric and Adolescent Medicine,* Robert Garofalo, M.D., a pediatrician at the hospital and the lead researcher for the report, said he saw the results of the study as a "cry for help." A second pediatrician, David H. Kaplan, M.D., at the University of Colorado School of Medicine, discussing the findings, said "it's about engaging the kids and making them feel that they really matter... there is lots of homophobia these days."

This alternating picture of dark and light for members of the homosexual community is only one of the many dichotomies facing all gay men and lesbians, but older homosexuals have special problems — particularly in their choices of lifestyle and life companions — that stem from their becoming citizens of the world of the aging.

While gays and lesbians now in their twenties and thirties have proudly "come out of the closet" (acknowledged their homosexuality to the world) and marched in Gay Pride parades, the sharp differences between their experiences and those of older gays become more marked with each year that passes.

The Generation Gap

Despite the link of their sexual orientation, old and young gays and lesbians' connections are fractured along generational lines. This has the sad effect of disrupting their shared historical continuity and generational *inter*dependence, which is a vital prop in the lives of many heterosexual elders.

Many older homosexuals never "came out" to family, friends, or coworkers; pressed by family and church, they often had conventional marriages and parented children, and they often have only "come out" to themselves and a few friends late in their lives. Many of these elders, who most frequently lived their sexual lives in secrecy and who even today seek anonymity and refuge in gay-only organizations, look upon the more openly gay lives of today's younger generation as largely irrelevant to their own experiences.

"When these seniors were young, they were labeled sick by doctors, immoral by the clergy, unfit by the military, and a menace by the police. [If they were openly gay] they risked loss of jobs, homes, friends, and family. If they were parents, their children could be taken away," explains Arlene Kochman, of New York, a social work gerontologist and leader in organizing social services for the elderly.

"The history of social harassment was such that many [gay and lesbian elders] could not bring themselves to trust fully even the increasingly numerous broad-minded members of the heterosexual world," adds Kochman, explaining why so many older homosexual men and women do not seek out general community services as they age and confront ill health, loss of lovers and companions, and financial worries.

Phyllis Lyon and Del Martin, who have lived together for more than forty years in San Francisco, are among the pioneers of the gay liberation movement. Together they founded one of the earliest lesbian social activist organizations, Daughters of Bilitis. They met in the 1950s and illustrate the "closet" into which lesbians were firmly closed at that time.

"Back in the fifties, we didn't have any place to build self-esteem. We were considered illegal, immoral, and sick. That's a lot to deal with. So we had to build acceptance. We were okay, no matter what other people thought," says Del. In a biographical sketch of the couple that appears in *Women Together: Portraits of Love, Commitment and Life,* published in 1999, Del explains that "back in those days nobody talked about sexuality, let along homosexuality. We didn't have the vocabulary to even look it up — what we were feeling — in a dictionary or the library."

When Del and Phyllis' own book, *Lesbian Women,* was published in 1972, libraries couldn't keep it on the shelf because people were too embarrassed to sign it out and simply stole it.

The Country and the City: Different Worlds

In addition to the generational divide, there is another divide, and that is geography. The large urban centers have always been places where gay life and culture could exist strongly, if secretly. But small towns, the south, and many other regions of the U.S. have long histories of intense homophobia and only those men and women (among the older generation) who were strong enough to leave had a shot at a slightly more open lifestyle in the big cities.

As Andrew Sullivan, author of *Virtually Normal: An Argument about Homosexuality,* explains: "the experience of a gay fourteen-year-old in a white, rural family is light years away from that of the HIV-positive activist in his thirties in a major urban center."

And the aging lesbian or gay man who has selectively "come out" late in life, finds at least the *possibility* of a different life in a city with gay social service agencies, gay social and professional organizations, and gay health centers than he or she has known as a still-closeted older homosexual in a smaller town in the Midwest where few health care providers, for example, are comfortable dealing with homosexuals at all.

Norm B., sixty-five, is a gay attorney in a large Illinois city who is a partner in a mainstream law firm where his closest associates know that he is gay, but it is not openly discussed and he has not come out to staff or clients. Nevertheless, his private life with a longtime companion is discreetly comfortable because of the large number of other professional men in this urban area who provide a supportive network of friends and surrogate family. The large gay community in this urban setting enjoys its own versions of popular culture, with gay newspapers and magazines, gay film festivals, and popular gay comedy clubs and theaters. Norm's gay community is multicultural; Hispanics and African Americans have their own gay groups and institutions as well.

By contrast, Ken S., seventy-two, is a retired pharmacist in a small town in Louisiana where no openly gay groups exist. He

> *It's better to be black than gay, because when you're black, you don't have to tell your mother.*
>
> — Anonymous
>
> ૯ઙ

has never acknowledged his homosexuality to anyone in his family or to his friends, and has lived a closeted gay life only made bearable by occasional vacations and visits to larger cities where casual encounters are possible. Unlike many gay men of his generation, Ken did not marry and so has no conventional family structure either to constrain him or to support him. But he has made his peace with his limited affectional life and enjoys the esteem in which his town holds him; he has retired now from what was one of the last small independent drug stores in his area, and can take more frequent trips away. That, with the love and support of his siblings (who may suspect, but never discuss his homosexuality) and a large group of nieces and nephews, seems to be the pattern he will continue. In conversation, he is quite serene, but wistful about a different life that might have been possible in a big city.

To Tell or Not to Tell

Divulging one's homosexuality is an issue that gay and lesbian people meet every day, almost regardless of their age. As *Virtually Normal* author Andrew Sullivan puts it, "most homosexuals are not in or out of the closet, they hover tentatively somewhere in between."

Others — gerontologists, psychotherapists, and social workers — observe that this problem is handled in three major ways. The first way, followed by many older homosexuals, is to remain firmly closeted, except within the "safe" confines of special organizations that have grown up in the past decade or two to meet the health and social needs of this aging population or in exclusively gay social clubs or professional, leisure, or sports groups.

The second way is to selectively acknowledge one's sexual orientation to family, friends, and work colleagues where this can be done with some, but perhaps not overwhelming, risk.

The third way, favored by the youngest generation, is to be "gay and proud" and live as openly as possible. This latter course has now become almost a matter of political correctness, with those who choose to remain somewhat concealed, encountering considerable pressure to come out, no matter how difficult this might be and despite the repressive environments in which some gay men and lesbians earn their livings.

This issue of "coming out" or not has been sharpened for gays and lesbians not only by ambivalent policies in the military, but also by the AIDS plague, which has made life, again, especially difficult for older homosexuals, who frequently have lost family ties, are no longer in the workforce, may have lost companions of many years, and are even afraid of coming out to health care providers.

While sexual identity revelations are problematical within the homosexual community itself, ageism in the straight world also causes men and women to lie and conceal — not their sexual orientation — but the other terrible secret: their ages. Lying about being past sixty-five to keep a job or spending money on face-lifts and hair dyes to keep the world from knowing what seventy looks like are straight versions of *passing,* a term gays and lesbians use to describe one's sexual identity. Gays and lesbians often "pass" for straight to keep their jobs; straights often "pass" as younger to keep theirs; but both want to avoid inclusion in that stigmatized group — the old.

Like their heterosexual agemates whom we met in earlier pages, however, the record of aging gay men and lesbians in meeting these challenges to life and love is an amazing one of immense creativity, crisis competency, and a growth in self-affirmation and self-sufficiency that is inspiring.

These qualities of creativity and self-affirmation are found within virtually all human communities, of whatever sexual orientation, but there are both striking similarities and striking differences in the way gay people and mainstream people engage in the search for late-life love. (These differences and likenesses may help us understand better what each group can learn from the other.)

Love Is Love, Aging Is Aging: What We All Know

Here is a little quiz. Read this passage carefully, then answer the question at the end:

"Beginning an intense relationship at this [older] time of life is good in many ways. Neither of us needed to idealize the other. How wonderful to know at all times that the loved one is a whole person, with a few bad habits, an imperfect disposition, some hang-ups, and with well-developed likes and dislikes — a whole person and not a fantasy image, and not a reflection in a mirror. Coming together at this time, all the successes, distresses, all of it — we know how to value not only each other, but also the relationship itself."

Was this account of a newfound late love written by:

1. One of the older straight men you met in an earlier chapter?

2. A lesbian?
3. An older heterosexual woman?
4. A gay man, in his seventies?

Kind of hard to guess, isn't it? It could have been written by any of the four, but was actually written by an older lesbian woman who told her story in therapist Marcy Adelman's book, *Lesbian Passages*. The writer had given up hope of another deep and lasting love relationship in her older years, but she did find such a love, and wrote about it in this fashion.

Reading over this journal entry a second time, we can see that it is a demonstration of *exactly* what we learned earlier — both from experts and from interview subjects — that older people of all backgrounds learn how to accept things as they are, how to change things if they can, what to leave alone if they can't, and some wisdom to know the difference.

This wisdom is only one of many similarities between the straight and homosexual worlds, and there are others that should disabuse both groups of the notion that they are somehow living on different planets. If they are getting older but still hoping for love, romance, sex, or intense friendships, they are *not* living on different planets, no matter how they may express their sexuality. Other similarities like gender influence, family history, and emotional and sexual intimacy patterns grow out of the commonality of aging and meshing spirits with another human being.

Gender Influence

The concept of gender — whether one is born male or female — regardless of eventual sexual identity seems to be just as strong a factor in the lives of gays and lesbians as it is in the lives of heterosexuals. Heterosexual women of virtually all ages, complain that their boyfriends, lovers, and husbands are often less willing to discuss the state of the marriage or the relationship than they would like. Men tend to shy away from big soul-searching conversations on the state of their hearts. Since lesbian families consist of two women, what seems to be a strong *female* wish to work on relationships can show up in both partners. Women's traditional role of being the caretaker of relationships is a commonality in both worlds.

In discussing therapeutic issues specific to lesbian couples, Barbara M. McCandlish, Ph.D., a Harvard-trained clinical psychologist who has specialized in psychotherapy with gays, writes that "women who have previously related to men often report a sense of relief that the burden of keeping the relationship vital no longer rests on their shoulders alone." Heterosexual women who have done much of the emotional work with husbands, children, and other family members — often through many years — will understand that relief very well. Men, on the other hand, whether gay or straight, do not seem to spend a great deal of time "processing" their feelings about their relationships.

In addition, males, whether gay or straight, see themselves as more sexually aggressive than women. Raymond W. Berger, Ph.D., a social work gerontologist, university teacher, and sexuality researcher, authored a pioneering work, first issued in 1982 and updated frequently since then, titled *Gay and Gray: The Older Homosexual Man,* in which he comments on this reality.

Dr. Berger reports that "men often feel that...sustained sexual activity is a test of masculinity and self-concept." While this "conquest" mentality is common among men of all sexual orientations, it is rarer among women, testifying once more to the powerful influence gender has on relationships.

Dr. Berger, who is also the author of a popular social work research textbook, points out how potentially traumatic the issue of aging is for both gay and straight men, with its implied threat to the virile self-image many men cherish, whatever their sexual identity.

Another measure of the possibility that gender is a strong determinant of how men and women differ in their approach to loving and making families is the different rates at which each seek help if the relationship is in trouble.

Gay men, possibly at least in part because traditional therapists presented their homosexuality to them as something to be "cured," do not consult mental health professionals as often as lesbians do, according to a recent study of long-lasting couplehood among gays and lesbians.

Gay and Lesbian Couples: Voices from Lasting Relationships is a study of seventy-two individual partners in thirty-six committed, same-sex relationships that have lasted for more than fifteen years. The authors, Professor Richard A. Mackey, of the Graduate School of Social Work, Boston College, and Professor Bernard A. O'Brien, associate professor of developmental psychology in the School of Education, Boston College, earlier studied long-term heterosexual relationships and are now attempting to find similarities and differences between those and homosexual unions.

They confirmed the persistence of gender differences in the way men and women approach their love lives, whatever form of sexuality they may express. In other words, women are women and men are men, and whether gay or straight, they have their own gender-based approaches to intimacy.

Dr. Mackey, Dr. O'Brien, and their assistant, Eileen Mackey, found that lesbians wanted to talk about their relationship in detail; they wanted to discuss its values, its meaning, and its problems.

But according to the Boston researchers, "gay partners *did not talk in the same way* about the value and importance of mutually reflecting on what had occurred in their relationship."

Some jokes that circulate in gay-lesbian groups reflect the attitude that "women will always be women, regardless," and ditto for the men. Gay males joke that after the second date, lesbians call in the U-Haul trucks and move in together.

For their part, lesbians joke about "What second date?" referring to how casual men can be about even their long-term relationships relative to the intensity women invest in theirs. Lesbians' similarity to overcommitted straight women, who still spend enormous psychic energy covering all the emotional bases in their family-friends circle is striking.

And in straight circles, another joke circulates that high-lights the same gender influences. This one asks, "Does your husband/lover/boyfriend have a sleeping problem? Does he have insomnia? If he does, try this: sit straight up in bed when he's having trouble falling asleep and tell him, very seriously, that you think the two of you should work on your relation-ship. He'll be asleep in no time."

Family History Counts

A second area where life experience persists in putting its imprint on both gays and straights is family history. Parents are as influential in providing models to gay companions as they are to straight — not so much in terms of sexual behavior (a majority of homosexuals have straight parents) — but in terms of emotional patterns.

Just as straight people may say "I looked at my parents' marriage and made up my mind that mine would be very dif-ferent," so do gay people look at their parents' marriage and say they want their love relationships to be different.

Brian and Barry, a gay couple in the Boston study, felt they wanted to improve on the models presented by their parents, which they felt were the old-fashioned heterosexual pattern of a dominant husband and a submissive wife. They have strug-gled, instead, for real equality and mutuality in their relation-ship. They have been together more than twenty years.

Similarly, where straight people have had *good* parental models — ones they felt were loving and responsible — they try to incorporate those good values into their own enduring partnerships and so do gays and lesbians.

In the Mackey-O'Brien survey, one of their interviewees, Beverly, had been with her partner, Betsy, for twenty-eight years. She believes that her parents had a good marriage and she wants a similar relationship for herself, say the researchers. Here is what Beverly told them: "My parents have a very similar relationship to ours. My mother and father have been married for fifty-five years and they're each other's best friend." It would be impossible for anyone to come upon this quotation by itself, with no cues from a context, and know whether the speaker was gay or straight.

Emotional and Sexual Intimacy Patterns

A third similarity in the lives of gay and straight people is establishment of emotional and sexual patterns within the relationship. These patterns include those derived from earlier unhappy marriages, divorces, and breakups. Heterosexual and homosexual groups are the same in wanting, working, and hoping for better experiences the next time around. Hope springs eternal, regardless of sexual preference. Additionally, sexual patterns that evolve over long periods of time also express a similarity between these two communities.

The Boston researchers found that lesbian and gay couples experience almost exactly the same "dip" in their sexual activity that heterosexual long-marrieds do in the middle part of the relationship. The pressures of work, family, and outside demands make homosexual couples slow down just as they do heterosexuals. Alice, one of Mackey's interview subjects, who has been with her lesbian partner for twenty years, said, "Sex is important…it's really connecting, but sometimes…we're just too tired!" And like heterosexual couples, homosexual couples often find their sex lives reviving when health, work, and other problems are ameliorated a bit as the union progresses in time.

In addition to these similarities and others, both groups are alike in facing isolation, loss, health and financial worries, and community neglect when they reach old age, as well as facing the stereotyping of elders of all backgrounds. So we can see that gender, parental role models, life experiences, and sexual patterns in long-enduring relationships have the same impact on gay people as on straight — but what of the sharp differences between the two cultures? In earlier chapters, we have seen how ageism and sexism, along with racism, have affected aging straight people as they seek to find and cherish love late in their lives.

But there are differences between aging gays and straights that add additional layers of difficulty onto the lives of homosexual men and women. Discrimination, prejudice, sometimes even a frighteningly deep, visceral hostility — all can be the daily lot of homosexuals. (When straight people try to understand these burdens, we can only "see through a glass darkly" under the most empathetic circumstances.)

Uniquely Burdened, Uniquely Prepared: Gay People Meet the Many Faces of Discrimination

Older men and women — of whatever race, ethnicity, or sexual preference — share worries about aging. They worry about having enough money to live comfortably and care for themselves through illness and disability; they worry about losing friends and family, living in a safe environment, and remaining independent for as long as possible.

But for aging gays and lesbians, these worries are compounded in particularly cruel ways that highlight the differences between the ways that straight men and women can meet issues of love and aging and the ways homosexuals must meet those same questions.

For example, most older people have health concerns, but how will health care providers treat their patients when they find out they're gay?

Jean K. Quam, Ph.D., director of the University of Minnesota School of Social Work, wrote in a 1993 report done for the Sex Information and Education Council of the United States that as older members of the homosexual community need to seek more and more health care in their later years, their earlier orientation toward secrecy and concealment makes it especially hard for them to reach out for the services they need.

She cites the poignant case of a frail eighty-seven-year-old woman, whom she called Ellen, who had lived with a companion who was also her caretaker for many years. When the other woman died, Ellen entered a long-term care facility and, while there, overheard two young aides discussing lesbianism.

After several months, Ellen got up her courage and asked the aide about the meaning of the word "lesbian." After more time had passed, she told the aide that her partnership with her deceased roommate "may" have been a lesbian relationship. The aide was not judgmental and Ellen seemed to gain some relief from the discussion and from exploring her grief over the death of her companion. Nevertheless, her attempts at discussion soon gave way to panic and extreme anxiety that her story would be told to other residents in the facility without her consent. She died a month later, Dr. Quam reported.

Another aspect of aging and living in love relationships that is so different for older gays than for straight elderly couples is that many old gay people never defined themselves as homosexuals — certainly not to the world and often not to themselves. Women now in their eighties may have lived safely in coupledom with other women, but society accepted the arrangement, with benign approval, as one of sharing costs and insuring safety in the presence of a "roommate," while many families extended love and care to eccentric old, unmarried Uncle Fred who was just a "confirmed bachelor."

The pressure of aging on lives so concealed creates very different problems with family members, too.

Dr. Quam reports on a sixty-three-year-old lesbian who confided her real sexual identity to her daughter some years ago without rupturing the relationship — except that the daughter asked that the grandchildren not be told. How much support will this lesbian grandmother

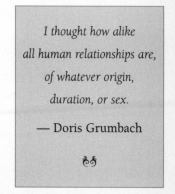

*I thought how alike
all human relationships are,
of whatever origin,
duration, or sex.*

— Doris Grumbach

get from her family should she reach a very advanced or needy old age? While it's true that bad family relations can separate older straight people from their children in later years too, it is not usually around issues that arouse the high level of inner shame and guilt about love and sex that older homosexuals experience as a result of interiorizing society's disapproval.

A seventy-two-year-old lesbian physician, who was marking her fortieth year with her partner, said her family's reaction would not be disastrously rejecting, but more a simple drifting apart, *if* she, the homosexual daughter and sibling, made her different lifestyle known to the "folks back home." In many cases, the gay man or lesbian has left the confines of a small town, a rigid family upbringing where emotions were strictly repressed, or some other setting where homophobia was simply a given fact of life without much discussion, along with racism, sexism, anti-Semitism, and anti-Catholicism.

Selma T. is one of three siblings, all of whom are tenuously in touch but, separated by much geographical distance, seldom see one another. Selma and her partner, Susan, came to Los Angeles in the 1950s and shared the same sense of uprootedness and loneliness when they first met, both having grown up in small towns in the Midwest and South. While their relationship shares many similarities with straight couples, they are now, as they age, looking hard at such issues as ensuring their financial well-being in retirement. Since they will not be able to claim the Social Security survivor benefits or any other spousal benefits granted to heterosexual widows and widowers by professional groups, academic institutions, or businesses, they must cooperatively determine how the survivor of their long, monogamous relationship — a marriage in every sense except the legal — will manage when one of them dies. This set of worries is especially hard on working-class women whose wages and salaries, even together with a lesbian partner, do not reach those of straight couples. Since women in all fields earn less than men, two working lesbian companions often do not make as much money as one man and one woman in straight pairs.

The problem of not being able to claim these kinds of benefits is equally difficult for gays when the issue is owning a home or property together. Many times gay men have not looked after the legal requirements of naming each other as co-owners of an apartment or home on the deed, but even when they have, or when they have made specific arrangements in their wills that the home is to go to the surviving partner, many long lost siblings, parents, or friends appear to contest the partner's right to the home, on the theory that the survivor was only a "roommate."

A straight widow, by contrast, seldom has such difficulty in inheriting a home that may never even have been in her name, but which is left to her in her husband's will.

Different also, unless very clearly outlined in a break-proof legal document, is the gay man or lesbian woman's right to make decisions for an ailing partner or even just visit a critically ill companion in a hospital where "family only" is the visiting rule, and the partner in a thirty-five-year-relationship is seen as merely a "friend."

It is true that many more companies and government employers are providing "domestic partnership" benefits today than was ever dreamed of half a century ago, but it has come too late for many senior members of the homosexual community, now retired, widowed, and minus spousal benefits. The continuing controversy over gay and lesbian marriage shadows the future for committed couples, and remains another hurdle same-sex couples have to overcome.

Committed couples face ageism in another area of discrimination: the AIDS catastrophe. Since many senior gays would rather risk isolation and illness than come out and risk rejection by care providers from social service agencies and health centers, the era of the AIDS plague has made life even more difficult for older gays than for aging straights who face life-threatening illnesses.

The initial problem for senior homosexuals relative to the AIDS crisis is that many doctors and other health workers simply assume that *all* older people are not sexually active. Therefore, even if they suspect a patient is gay, they sometimes do not pursue an investigation of AIDS very thoroughly, thinking the patient is not at risk for HIV infection due to age. One social worker at a health facility in New Jersey, who *does* deal with older, infected gay men, grumbled "doctors just don't believe older gays have sex or do drugs."

But in fact, according to the University of California medical center health newsletter, 10 percent of all new cases of AIDS each year are in the over-fifty population. The potent dual oppression of ageism ("old people aren't sexual") and fear of antigay rejection ("will my nurse treat me differently if she/he knows that I'm gay?") combine to make coping with AIDS and other serious illnesses very different for senior homosexuals than for straight seniors, or even for young gay people.

In addition to issues of health, there are several other differences between aging as a gay man or lesbian and aging in the mainstream community. These touch many matters of everyday life that straight people are never forced to think about.

- Housing is more difficult for same-sex couples since landlords often equate same-sex relationships with unacceptable lifestyles, no matter how responsible, financially able, or courteous (in other words, "straight") the gay couple's demeanor may be. New trends, not yet nationwide, suggest that in a few very large cities gay retirement housing may be on the horizon, but it is not widely available yet for the estimated 10 percent of the U.S. senior population that is gay and lesbian.

- Gay people who are partnered with foreigners and have been separated by visa or passport problems cannot solve these problems through marriage as heterosexual partners can, even if the gay relationship has been ongoing for years. Immigration rules, by contrast, allow straight couples to gain residency rights for foreigners when they marry, even if the spouse entered the country illegally.

- For all human beings, rituals that address the key moments of life — births, weddings, funerals — are important links to past generations and to the future. Because homosexuals are so often stigmatized and made outcasts, the larger society often attempts to deny them the solace that heterosexuals find in mourning rituals. (Gay men and women have made their own rituals in creative defiance of this stigma, of which the famous AIDS Memorial Quilt project is an example.) Bereaved straight people are supported through their losses by society's sanction and understanding of their status as widows, widowers, or bereaved parents and siblings.

But for gay men and lesbians, society attempts to make their loss and grief invisible. In many cemeteries, gay and lesbian couples who have been together for decades cannot be buried together in "family only" plots. It is only fairly recently in the largest cities that obituary notices refer to a "long-time companion" or "close friend" among the survivors; most obituary notices still do not mention the person who may have cared for the deceased through terrible illnesses, when families abandoned them.

The families of older homosexuals — both their families of origin and families they have created themselves — present to the mainstream community some of the most startling rebukes to conventional wisdom about gay men and lesbians.

Stepping back and thinking about the emotional reality and complexity of straight families helps us sympathize with older homosexuals who bravely create very real families for themselves, as well as the way they interact with their original families and earlier ones they may have founded before acknowledging their sexual orientation.

Enlarging the Family Photo Album with Gays and Lesbians

The notion of family life stands at the center of America's self-image; repeatedly, polls show that Americans place family at the very top of their list of most vital concerns.

Yet this idea of family — often wistfully mythical and set in time among good old days that never quite existed in reality — is one of the most difficult of images for straight people to apply to gay men and lesbians.

The conventional notion of what constitutes a family is so rigidly set in most mainstream cultural artifacts (family pictures, films, television) that it is often almost impossible for them to understand what family — past, present, and future — means to the homosexual world.

The majority community is often surprised to find that homosexuals, most often gay men but very frequently lesbians as well, have, at some time in their lives, been husbands, wives, and parents in conventional-appearing marriages and now, in their older years, are grandparents as well.

This surprise stems from two sources:

The first is that both gay and straight people often have inflexible definitions of sexuality and divide people into either "homo" or "hetero" groups and that's that! But as anyone who has taken Biology 101 or done the slightest work in anthropology, human sexuality studies, gerontology, or any other of the natural or social sciences knows, sexuality is a fluid concept, moving easily across time, human development, and biological phases. The professor emeritus of human sexuality at the Robert Wood Johnson Medical School, Dr. Richard J. Cross points out that young infants enjoy genital stimulation and are uncaring as to who provides it; but many adults have been programmed to believe there is only one right way that yields pleasure. Both gay and straight people share in the belief that their way is the most pleasurable way or even, they may occasionally claim, that their own mode of expression leads to greater emotional communion with a partner, when in fact what's needed is some recognition of how tremendously varied sexual behavior can be at different times, different places, and different cultural moments. Feminism, for example, intersected with the modern gay rights movement making it possible for lesbians not only to understand themselves better as women, but to also fashion life companionships that were freer than during periods of lesbian persecution.

A majority of heterosexuals have had one or more homosexual experiences in their lives; a great number of homosexuals have had experiences with the opposite sex as well as their own. This fluidity of sexual behavior was documented in Alfred C. Kinsey's groundbreaking studies a generation ago, and reaffirmed many times since then.

The second element is that, without any knowledge of gay history, many heterosexuals do not understand how important it was for gay men, particularly, to "pass" as straight when the current group of seniors came to maturity before and between the two world wars. By denying their homosexuality, men in those eras founded families as insurance against social discrimination of the most intense sort — in jobs, in the military, in the clergy, in society at large, as well as in their families of origin who pressured them to give up what was seen as selfish bachelorhood and "settle down." This was facilitated by the way in which gay men now in their seventies and eighties accepted society's dicta that they were immoral or sick, and hoped that by marrying and living "normal" lives, they could continue to deny their true sexual orientation. Many of them now know that orientation is not a matter of conscious choice, but an intrinsic part of their very being. The larger society may try to figure out causes: genetics? family influences? early formative experiences? Possibly all or none of the above apply, but what we know for sure is that sexual variance has existed since earliest times in the march of *Homo sapiens* out of the cave, and today we know that homosexuality and heterosexuality are not even the entire story since men and women can also be bisexual or have some other variant of sexual identity.

Lesbians in the early and middle years of the twentieth century had it a little easier, because two women living together were often interpreted as being vulnerable, unmarried women who formed a household as a safety measure or as a barrier to loneliness until they would marry, though long-lasting liaisons were gossiped and whispered about as were those of unmarried men who, however, were less often able to set up housekeeping together and not fear for their jobs.

These stories of past times are extremely important because they explain, in large part, why aging gays and lesbians, now in their "third age," are finding it so difficult to change the patterns of concealment that determined most of their lives. Those who find the courage, late in their sixties, seventies, and beyond, to tell their spouses or ex-spouses and their children and grandchildren that they are gay are still rare souls, though they are increasing in number and, in many cases, are surprised at the acceptance they are finding, especially among younger members of the family.

Even public figures — artists, political leaders — whom we could assume enjoyed some acceptance for their contributions to society were in the closet and did not come out until very late years. The poet May Sarton and First Lady Eleanor Roosevelt are two examples of public figures who in mid-life or later, either explicitly stated their homosexuality or allowed themselves attachments and relationships that were deeply emotional and possibly sexual with other women. For older women today, there exist a growing number of social supports that are on hand to help aging homosexuals with these difficult decisions.

A social service agency named SAGE (Seniors Aging in a Gay Environment) is headquartered in Manhattan, with branches in other New York boroughs and in Florida and other states. One of their social workers recounts how a lesbian in her seventies finally told her daughter of her secret life and was pleased to find that her daughter, in turn, was willing to share this information with her own children. "Grandma is gay," the daughter told the postteenage children. "So what's new?" they answered.

This was not a dialogue that could have been imagined by seniors who kept their sexual and their family lives separate for fifty years in some cases.

Because of this secrecy, it is difficult to know exactly, for instance, how many lesbian women in their sixties, seventies, eighties, and beyond are mothers and grandmothers or how many older gay men are fathers and grandfathers. However, we can try to imagine the pain involved if gay people have to choose between acknowledging their homosexuality and risking rejection (or revulsion and scorn) by spouses and children in whom they have invested many years of love and devotion and whom they do not want to hurt. It is not infrequent to learn that many of these men kept their double life secret, having homosexual encounters when away from home, remaining devoted to their families when with them. Frequently these men do not identify themselves as gay until separated from lifelong spouses by death or divorce or until their parents die.

Bernadette: A Study in Conflicting Loyalties

Bernadette, a sixty-nine-year-old lesbian grandmother, is the mother of six children. She decided in her sixties to acknowledge her true sexual identity in a selective way — coming out to her husband and children, but to few outside the family. Since she lives in a small southwestern town, the information did seem to percolate — in the time-honored manner of small communities — to the townspeople. However, she has been given a certain limited acceptance since, even though they live separately, she and her husband are not divorced and she cares for him during his frequent bouts of alcoholism and drink-related illnesses.

Discussing her complex system of loyalties over lunch at a coffee shop near her workplace, she explained why she had stayed so long in a marriage that — even aside from her sexual preferences — was incompatible from early on: "In my day, that's just what you did. You got married and you had kids and you *stayed* married, no matter what. Religion played a role in it, I guess [she is no longer an observant Catholic but admits the pull of the church is psychologically 'still there'] and then pressure from my parents and the town — girls got married, period, with a big emphasis on not becoming pregnant before you landed that wedding ring. My family was no different from any other in our church and I was a pretty youngster — it wasn't even pressure, it was just so completely *assumed* that I never questioned it in a million years."

When did she know she was attracted to her own sex? "I denied it to myself for years and years — a long, long time," she answers truthfully. She doesn't wish to discuss her private sexual experiences with other women once she came out to herself, but is currently living alone and feeling unhappy that her small town affords little socializing with other lesbians, much less finding a companion-lover for this last part of her life. The nearest medium-sized city is more than two hundred miles away and though she has reason to believe there is some kind of gay life there, her loyalties to her husband, children, and community (where she is an activist volunteer in many town projects) make moving there an unlikely option.

And what of her relationships with her children and grandchildren? The grandchildren, she says, are not a problem — most of them are quite young yet and her adult life is not part of their understanding of having fun visiting Grandma and going on trips with her. Two of her own adult children maintain a grudging neutrality about her lesbianism, neither accepting nor rejecting, but keeping a wary emotional distance. The other four seem quite accepting, with one daughter being especially supportive and helpful.

There is much stereotyping of gay men and women that says they *have no* family life, that they live lonely isolated lives when they are older, and that fate "punishes" them for their sexual role by denying them the solace of children. (Children are not always a big solace to heterosexuals, either!) In addition, stereotypes picture gay men as friendless and never able to maintain long relationships.

It's unusual for straight people to understand how *family* is affirmatively defined in the homosexual world. By listening to gays and lesbians who are living in deeply family-oriented settings, we can appreciate that *family* may have a much broader meaning than is commonly understood.

What Is a Family? Lesbian and Gays Answer

One of several definitions of *family* to be found in standard dictionaries is: "fam-i-ly, n. the basic unit in society having as its nucleus two or more adults living together and cooperating in the care and rearing of their own or adopted children." (No sexual identity mentioned here; just "two or more adults.")

This dictionary definition applies to many contemporary homosexual couples. Gay men today can legally adopt children in many states; they can ask a female friend to bear a child for them with their own sperm, either naturally or with modern artificial insemination techniques; and they occasionally win custody battles with ex-wives to have their own children live with them and a male partner. All this is new in American society, and it applies equally to lesbians, too. In the 1999 Gay Pride parade in New York, two female police officers, a couple for many years, who had each borne a child by artificial insemination from the same anonymous donor, marched with their children in double strollers.

The scenarios made possible by some degree of increased social tolerance and by modern reproductive technology are light years away from the experiences of today's aging homosexuals. The older men who did not take some period of refuge from society's harshness by starting conventional families and the aging lesbians who never married are now forced by passing time to consider the issue of family life in their late years and many of them are doing so in courageous and creative ways that force mainstream men and women to rethink the concept of family.

There are many ways in which homosexual men and women create a supportive framework for living that strongly resembles conventional family life.

They live together as couples in long-enduring relationships that straight society says simply can't happen, but they do and on a very large scale. In *Gay and Gray: The Older Homosexual Man,* author and sex researcher Dr. Raymond Berger, surveyed 112 men from widely varied backgrounds and found that none of them fit the stereotype of the depressed, lonely, and isolated older gay man. Nearly a third of his sample had been married and had family or community ties from that period even if they were now living alone. Another third, at some point in their lives, had been in monogamous relationships and some were in such relationships at the time of the survey.

Even those men who were not currently in a committed relationship were living with others and had steady sources of companionship and support. Whomever they lived with shared the functions of a family — nurturance, help, economic assistance where possible, companionship in leisure, and shared interests and values. Making a home and sharing domestic activities are the same projects in gay as in straight households, with the same need to work out equality in who does what in the way of cooking, laundry, and other household chores. On these issues, older heterosexuals might take a cue from homosexual couples who are freed from the traditional gender roles that decree that women cook, men do carpentry. In gay households, couples apportion housekeeping duties based more on each person's interests and competencies and help expand for everyone the ideas about what jobs are appropriate for each gender.

For lesbian couples, the two women together define themselves strongly as a family, whether there are children present or not, thus defying the dictionary definition that stipulates the presence of children.

After all, says Andrew Sullivan, author of *Virtually Normal: An Argument about Homosexuality,* when heterosexual couples are issued a marriage license, it is not made conditional upon a pledge to have children. Some couples do and many today do not, and lesbians believe that in all respects — bonding, care, financial support, emotional interdependence — their lives together demonstrate the main elements of family life.

Suzanne Slater, M.S.W., a lesbian psychotherapist and author of *The Lesbian Family Life Cycle,* stresses the strength with which lesbians create and sustain this family life pattern in the face of unrelenting pressures from the larger society to become invisible. If they do have children, they are denied family member-ships in clubs and recreational facilities; if they do not have chil-dren and focus much of their ener-gy on their relationship, their work, and their friendships, they are denied family benefits there as well.

The heart has its reasons that reason knows nothing of.

— Blaise Pascal

Slater points out that the prevailing assumption that the heterosexual family model is the only one or the only normal one is difficult for both younger and older lesbians.

The lesbian and gay couples who constitute families — whether with children or not — live in their main outlines exactly like all other families — making and maintaining a home, looking after each other, participating in a network of friends, and sharing in community activities.

There are two problems for homosexually-based families that have called forth great creativity and that have required considerable emotional equilibrium from gays and lesbians.

The first is that, while heterosexual families enjoy a well mapped-out pathway for their life together with reinforcements and approval in moments of accomplishment and support in predictable times of stress, societal assistance is denied to homosexual families and they therefore seek and obtain these reinforcements within themselves and their network of friends and supporters.

The second problem is that younger gay couples are cut off from the intergenerational support that grandparents often give their heterosexual children and grandchildren during life's storms. That gay grandparent generation either remains firmly closeted, or, even if out to some extent, may belong to the group that never had children.

So, there are fewer mentors available among gays and lesbians in their seventies and eighties to help strengthen young couples facing society's disapproval.

The parenting issue divides the generations in other ways, too. Older lesbians who never had children see the contemporary trend toward technologically-driven lesbian pregnancies or adoptions as unrelated either to their earlier lives or to the problems they face now as they age.

If we add to this discontinuity between the generations the fact that the new youngish middle-aged generation — men and women now between thirty and fifty-five — has been sorely ravaged by AIDS and become a real "lost" generation — we can begin to see some of the enormous courage and strength required from gay and lesbian families to maintain their structures in the absence of so much of the mentoring help that is available to mainstream families.

One possible source of support, over time, may become available to younger gays and lesbians from their own families of origin. Although many, many families still reject their gay children, there seems to be a growing understanding and acceptance of their kin by younger, more modern parents and siblings. Many parents march in gay pride parades throughout the country, join parent organizations that lobby for AIDS research and education, and join support groups for parents who may be having difficulty accepting their children's homosexuality.

Given their unique burdens, what is the outlook for older gay men and lesbians as they attempt to age with a modicum of health and joy and dignity and to — quite possibly — find late-life love?

The Times They Are A-Changin': Hope for the Future

Finding new love and romance is an ideal that can come from traditional and nontraditional networks of people and groups, in just the same ways that straight lovers find each other. The society that once so thoroughly oppressed older homosexuals that they either attempted to "pass" as straight men and women or sought life and happiness only in the most restricted gay-only environments — that society is changing in small and large ways. In spite of antigay attitudes so extreme they can lead to violence, in spite of an unfriendly military and a religious bloc that threatens to visit hellfire and brimstone on gay people, there are hopeful signs for older gay people in three main areas: health care (including help with problems of self-affirmation and "coming out"), social services, and new attitudes toward family and love relationships in later years. These important achievements also apply to straight people who must triumph over issues of ageism, sexism, and isolation as well.

Health Care: A New Look

Until 1973, the American Psychiatric Association carried homosexuality on its list of mental illnesses; it removed it from the list that year.

Until 1991, the American Psychoanalytic Association did not accept students for training as psychoanalysts if they were gay men or lesbians. That has changed so completely that at its 1998 annual meeting, the association held an open forum to analyze homophobia and see how society could rid itself of this prejudice.

Since self-affirmation — accepting oneself as a homosexual and moving on to enjoy love and the fullness of later years — is one of the most difficult tasks aging gay and lesbian people have to face, this change in the mind-set of leading mental health professionals means that psychological help is available from sources it never was before. It also means that questions of intimacy among same-sex partners can be broached and discussed, perhaps as never before. In addition, many large cities now have a cadre of well-trained therapists with backgrounds in psychology and psychiatry who specialize in providing gay and lesbian patients with help on many life management issues.

Then there is the problem that other life-threatening illnesses besides AIDS need to be treated with sensitivity and insight for gay people. Lesbians, for example, see breast cancer as big a threat in their community as men see AIDS in theirs, and in the past five years, special clinics have come into being to deal with their health concerns. More research is needed to determine whether the incidence of breast cancer is higher in lesbian patients or not, and also to determine what other health issues may be more paramount in the lesbian community than in society at large.

Traditionally, homosexuals of both genders have shunned mainstream doctors and other health care providers, not wishing to discuss their sexual lives and activities with medical people who, they felt, would not understand or be interested in their problems. Underground lists of gay-friendly physicians circulated or lesbian/gay patients sought out alternative treatments with nonmedical specialists.

Now, mainstream hospitals and medical centers in New York, Boston, San Francisco, and Los Angeles have sponsored special clinics, staffed with trained health professionals, to help lesbians handle health problems. Early in 1999, the Institute of Medicine, a division of the National Academy of Science, issued a report on lesbian health that urged the federal government to sponsor studies that would definitely establish the validity of various theories about which illnesses pose the greatest risk to gay women.

At one East Coast lesbian clinic, a sixty-one-year-old patient, Lillian S., who had contracted hepatitis, was comforted and relieved to be able to talk openly with her doctor there about what dangers her illness posed for her partner. "I wanted to know whether we could kiss or drink out of the same glass, not to mention sex. There was no way I would have asked a straight doctor those things," she told a reporter.

Since shunning mainstream institutions of all kinds has been a heavy burden on older homosexuals and since health concerns often accelerate as the years pile up, these new developments seem to indicate a positive trend toward improved health care.

Social and Service Resources: New Agencies Flourish

One of the most promising developments in the past two decades has been the growth of community and social service agencies designed specifically to deliver services to the often very aged gay and lesbian population, who may have lost partners of many years, be fearful of seeking help from public agencies, and be encountering housing problems as neighborhoods change and become less friendly to old people.

Outstanding in this field is SAGE, which has pioneered such services, first in New York and now in Florida and other elder population centers. It is the oldest and largest of such agencies and in its mission statement SAGE says it is dedicated to "honoring, caring for, and celebrating senior lesbians and gay men." The social work staff arranges a huge range of medical, social, and community services, not the least important of which — to older gay people — is providing a setting for socializing and meeting others of their generation. The acceptance that SAGE enjoys among seniors is so great that it is able to bring out into the open — at conferences as well as at informal get-togethers — such sensitive issues as the ageism that exists within the gay world itself and antiblack and other antiminority prejudices, as well.

SAGE cooperates with government agencies at all levels that seek to aid the elderly, co-sponsors many activities with other national gay groups, and offers "drop-in" centers where oldsters can begin a search for romantic involvement — or just fun-filled friendships. Many couples begin their new late-life love affairs at the SAGE centers, primarily because the setting relieves the social isolation that older gays, in sharp contrast to today's young homosexuals, often encounter in late life.

One of its most important activities, carried on by qualified social workers, is running training programs for mainstream agencies to sensitize them to the special needs of the gay population.

At birthday parties, holiday gatherings, and special anniversaries, gay lovers are celebrated in SAGE's meeting rooms, and new romances flourish. Although SAGE does not exist everywhere in the nation, it is serving as a model throughout the U.S., and it is expected that perhaps smaller programs, designed for their own specific problems and opportunities, will be appearing soon in small- and medium-sized towns and rural areas. The hope is that these types of social situations will provide an avenue — much like the Internet or classifieds — for men and women to meet in a safe setting.

Older Gay Activists: The New Breed

Some years ago, a then seventy-four-year-old lesbian named Christine Bolton, inserted a personals ad in a gay publication, seeking a partner-lover-companion. She received this reply from the newspaper: "Unless you made a mistake in your birth year, you are over fifty. Women are not looking for someone as old as you."

This staggering bit of ageism drove Bolton — who had already had five successful careers as a farmer, a businesswoman, a teacher, a writer, and a public speaker, and who didn't retire until slowed down by a stroke at age ninety — to start a group, now international in scope, that would serve as a worldwide social network for older lesbians.

Golden Threads is the group Bolton founded when she was eighty years old, and which has brought a new world of friendship, romance, and exciting adventure and travel to aging homosexual women. It has been the subject of TV documentaries and endless articles and interviews, and won Bolton SAGE's Lifetime Achievement Award. From her office in Burlington, Vermont, she issued this statement: "I believe we're all in this life together, although in amazing diversity…all ages, sizes, colors, shapes, ethnicity, talents…like threads in a fabric, we are woven inextricably into the human condition."

Bolton is a leader and a role model for a new group of gay activists among the senior population who are embarking — in their eighties and nineties — on new projects unheard of half a century ago. They are collecting records of gay history including drawings, photos, and paintings of the gay life that flourished underground; they are establishing "friendly visitor" volunteer services for housebound older gay and lesbian people; and they are joining with other human rights organizations in political battles on various gay rights issues including legalizing gay marriage.

Surely with the vision of a newly empowered senior gay community in front of us, mainstream men and women can learn something from the history and experiences — full of both joy and sorrow — that we explore here. What can straight America learn from these "wildflowers that grow randomly among our wheat," as Andrew Sullivan calls homosexual men and women?

Gays Sharing the Rocky Road to Wisdom

Aging people, of whatever sexual orientation, spontaneously and somewhat unself-consciously review their lives and seek to find meaning in the patterns of their days and years. If they have big unresolved questions about family relations, work goals, or internal conflicts, they often work on them, with or without professional help, with a renewed interest as time shortens. Taking a leaf from the book of gays, straights might glean these lessons:

- Society seeks to push older people aside, just as it seeks to make gays invisible. "Gay people build their own internal structures of meaning and value because they exist outside of a lot of the ordinary roles and structures," says Mildred Byrum, Ph.D., a New York–based therapist who deals with both gay and straight men and women. Perhaps in accomplishing this task — of building our own values and roles, of insisting on our worthiness as we age — we can borrow from the creative ways in which the lesbian and gay community supports gay families, pushes for antidiscrimination laws, and fights for a human rights agenda that we could also use to combat ageism.

- "Coming out" is the central dilemma for gay people; they struggle to acknowledge themselves, who they really are, in a hostile world. Is it not the same for older people? Can we "come out" to ourselves and to the world, perhaps not as homosexuals, but as the aging people we actually are? And also, doesn't "coming out" to ourselves mean thinking through things about ourselves that we have not wanted to face? The bravery of older gays in facing themselves is a lesson to all of us who hate and fear our aging bodies and our slowing pace in love and work, and who don't want to "come out" to ourselves that we are getting older.

- When gay people do affirm their sexual reality, they give us a photograph of what self-affirmation and self-esteem can mean for successful aging for everyone. The flexibility of gender roles, their competence in managing crises over many years in which they were always outsiders — all are useful to adapt for anyone's older years when we, too, are outsiders.

- The gay community's response to the horrifying number of deaths that the AIDS epidemic has caused among its members of all ages offers a picture of mutual support and caring that anyone can emulate. Since friendship networks many times stand in for family in fatal illnesses, the many friends and lovers of gay people who have stood by them to the end differ from straight caretakers only in terms of the number of deaths they have had to endure. Many straight partners show the same devotion to ill spouses and companions, of course, but seldom have had to suffer the high *number* of losses in a given year that gay men and women have encountered since the AIDS plague was identified in 1981. Naturally, both gay and straight partners do not have a perfect record of saintly behavior — many in both groups have left the sides of ill partners. But gay people have had to face intense emotional trials over and over, with hardly time in between for healing. This has led to a close examination of the human ability to deal with death and dying and with grief and mourning, and a keen sense of life's importance in the time that is left that is especially relevant to older people.

The historian, Martin Duberman, was asked why he — a gay white male — was considered the correct person to write a biography of the late Paul Robeson, a black artist in a different field from his own, who was indisputably heterosexual.

Robeson, the great Black star of the 1930s, 1940s, and 1950s, who conquered the concert hall with a magnificent baritone, the theater as a riveting Othello, and even the football field as a star for Rutgers University, nevertheless, in middle life, saw his career in shreds because of his political beliefs. He had a romance with Russian Communism after he encountered brutal racism in this country, and was never able again to regain the leading role in American cultural life that he once briefly enjoyed. Looking at this rise and fall, Duberman said: "Like

Robeson, I know about the double bind of being accepted and not accepted...and I know about concealment...and about buried anger. I know about loneliness."

As elders seek to transcend loneliness, loss, ageism, and the role of outsider, we must reach out to everyone in the human family who will help us come inside to stay. We do not want to be "spies in the culture" as Duberman called himself and Robeson, and as all outsiders are, but to belong in our final years to the mainstream of our world.

Ned Rorem

The composer Ned Rorem, at seventy-six, one of the "elder statesmen" of American music, has lived a life many gay men would envy as they learn of his association with world-famous musicians, writers, and artists in Paris, New York, and other capitals of glittering gay life.

But though renowned for his choral works and chamber music, for his brilliant and sometimes scandalous writings of memoirs and confessions, Rorem's music now echoes the poignant bittersweet late years of life, deep love, and loss that strikes chords in the hearts of many older gay people, and of all people who hear his music.

Rorem lost his companion of thirty-two years, James R. Holmes, an organist and choir director, to cancer early in 1999, and one of his first concerts after Holmes's death featured music dedicated to his partner that garnered praise from music critics and audiences alike.

The Rorem-Holmes relationship, like so many long-enduring love affairs, meant stability and enriched creativity in both their lives after a wildly philandering youth that Rorem spent in international art, music, and literary circles, and about which he wrote in honest and brilliantly entertaining fashion (while spilling the beans on many youthful affairs) in books and essays.

Holmes, the anchor in Rorem's life after their meeting in 1967, was himself a composer of considerable skill and was long associated as organist and choir director with an important Episcopal church on Manhattan's Upper West Side, the Church of St. Matthew and St. Timothy.

Interviewed by Melanie Rehak, a reporter for the *New York Times*, during the period immediately following Holmes's death, it became clear that his relationship with his lover had changed Rorem's life from one of youthful excess to one of mature achievement in a calmer, sweeter life that presents a model for all older lovers, regardless of their sexual orientation.

Now, with his companion of three decades gone, Rorem continues to think creatively of new projects, while admitting to deep mourning. He told Rehak that "I want to write a song cycle for Jim's memory. I'm looking around for texts that will be half in anger and half in resignation." While saying that he probably would never really stop mourning, Rorem said, "I could welcome another love affair, and I don't see why not, but that doesn't grow on trees for anybody at any age... [but] I don't want to stop living."

His personal and musical life force are reflected in a statement he made to another interviewer, James E. Oestreich, some years before Holmes's death.

Rorem said: "I do think about death...I'm not afraid of it...and I don't want to kill myself because when you're dead, you're dead. Out of millions of galaxies and trillions of light years, our little romance on earth is all we've got."

That "little romance" infuses his music with light and illuminates the path for all aging lovers.

Virginia Apuzzo

Virginia Apuzzo, of Kingston, New York, a former nun, a nationally famous gay rights activist, and once the highest ranking avowed lesbian in the Clinton Administration, is still not exactly a household name across America.

But perhaps one day she will be, for her record as a highly professional management whiz, who formerly had an office next door to the White House and the title of Assistant to the President for Management and Administration, is combined with one of the most unusual résumés in all of politics and public service.

In her White House job, Apuzzo ran the three-building, eighteen-acre campus that contains not only the quarters of the President and his family, but also offices for some two-thousand staff members. She was responsible for payroll, for security, and for the ultimate Washington perk: parking spaces at the White House. She also coordinated communications between the White House and the other federal agencies it needs to work with, such as the National Park Service, the Secret Service, and many others.

She stepped down from that unique vantage point in June 1999 after two years service to take an endowed chair in New York at the Policy Institute for the National Gay and Lesbian Task Force, a think tank focusing on gay rights issues. In her new job, the fifty-nine-year-old Apuzzo combines two driving forces in her life: her struggle for human rights and her ability to "make the trains run on time," as she described her administrative work in Washington. She left after two exciting years, she says, in order to be closer to her family, her partner, and her home in Kingston, and to step up her work on behalf of the homosexual community as well as human rights in general.

One of the most significant aspects of her long career in government and politics — she was formerly president of the New York State Civil Service Commission and an associate deputy secretary at the U.S. Department of Labor — is that her appointment to the White House job had no relationship to her work as a gay rights activist. She was hired, according to Lou Fabrizio, publisher of *OUT Magazine* and a longtime friend, for her management skills and her professional ability. (Another gay rights activist, Richard Socarides, was the official White House liaison to the lesbian and gay community while Apuzzo was serving as "mayor" of the White House complex.)

Many gay/lesbian leaders point out that Apuzzo's administrative job next to the most powerful office in the world was a real example of the good things that can happen when people are judged strictly on merit, and that it constituted a big step forward for all gays and lesbians hoping to be judged in the workplace for their professional skills and competencies.

Apuzzo's eye-popping background also included, when she was twenty-six, a stint with the Sisters of Charity, an order of nuns noted for their commitment to social justice, but she left the convent to devote herself to the gay rights movement, then just in its formative stages.

Apuzzo has been quoted as saying that she acknowledged her homosexuality to herself when in her late teens, but did not come out publicly until after the Stonewall Riots in 1969. Since then, what friends call her blend of "compassion and commitment" has made her a role model for Everyman (or woman).

Chapter 6

Visions of the Future
A Newer World

'Tis not too late to seek a newer world...
Though much is taken, much abides, and though
We are not now that strength which in old days,
Moved earth and heaven, that which we are, we are.
One equal temper of heroic hearts,
Made weak by time and fate, but strong in will
To strive, to seek, to find and not to yield.
— Alfred, Lord Tennyson, *Ulysses*

Love and aging are the twin peaks of our lives now, whether we are newfound lovers, long-married, or alone with loves of other kinds — family, work, ourselves, our friends, our communities. Still before us are possibilities for striving, seeking, and finding, to paraphrase Tennyson. If, as older adults, we are fortunate enough to know love, either with a specific partner or, in a larger sense, with the world, then cherishing that love, nourishing it through sunlight and shadow, is certainly a feature of the hills and plains spread out in front of us from the height of our years.

Also in view is the possibility of aging in a way that preserves our most important values, which, of course, are different and unique for each person. Some older people value independence above all; others are comfortable with a measure of dependence, if they can keep their spirits sweet and benign. Some value closeness with family or special friends; others have traveled far away from that goal, and are reaching for final summits of achievement and performance, no matter the years they number.

However aging lovers approach the last part of the journey, life does not let us put away — as long as a modicum of health and strength continues — our list of chores, of things we must try to accomplish while it is still possible. What is our vision as we seek and treasure love in all its forms, from whatever source it flows to and from us, and as we strive for a good old age? We have to consider these questions seriously because, as one vigorous ninety-year-old black woman announced at her senior center, "If you live, you're going to get old!"

The most important task before us, arching over questions of love, sexuality, health, work, and family, is *actively* to *choose our old age.* Scientists estimate that our genetic inheritance alone is only about 30 percent of how we age; lifestyle, personality, environment, and a host of determinants that *we can influence* will shape more of what our old age is like. Do we intend for it to be all terror and blackness, fear of decline, anxiety about becoming a burden, and worry over pain and suffering?

If we are women, are we doomed to live out our lives loathing our aging bodies, apologetic because we are no longer youthfully beautiful (but perhaps beautifully older), and almost eager to withdraw from the erotic fray on the theory that it is undignified and pathetic for older women to be interested in sex and romance? If we are men, are we doomed to live out our lives wondering what became of the focus that work provided before retirement or feeling abashed in the bedroom because sex is now different from the patterns of our thirties?

Is an alternative approach to tune in to nurturing what remains to us of life, of physical pleasure, of joy in touch and song, where we can find them?

How can we push our aging in the direction we want to go, how we can reinvent ourselves as the old people we want to be — with our lovers, our families, our friends?

There are as many formulas for successful aging (defined as good physical and emotional health and active engagement with the world) as there are scientific disciplines attacking the problems of aging. Most older adults, if they wish to be, can be inundated with health and fitness information. This, of course, is a key concern and one that can be pursued in a thousand venues as health information — some good, some bad, and some really ugly and exploitive — fills books, magazines, the Internet, TV, and virtually every other medium of communication. We will leave that to others for our purposes here.

Instead, five areas are worth examining that *are* within our ability to explore and that could be considered goals to be achieved that will help us shape a good "third age."

1. The engine that drives other tasks is a decision *consciously* to *choose* how we are going to age. We can ignore necessary changes in lifestyles that affect our health, we can refuse to surmount disabilities and surrender to them, we can withdraw from activities because we no longer can do them as speedily as before, and we can shut down our sexual dreams, desires, and fantasies as inappropriate. Older men and women can also choose to do the opposite of all those, and there is little doubt that these decisions will affect how one actually does age.

2. Create a plan for generativity, for passing on knowledge and skills to the next generation and beyond.

3. Map a vital involvement in the world; this will fight stagnation and keep one engaged.
4. Begin a search for wisdom. It does not come automatically with age — not at all — but wisdom has specific attributes that age seems to encourage and that can be developed to the end of life.
5. Try to develop a better understanding of solitude and aloneness, which is not the same thing as being lonely. Women, particularly, are so programmed to think about others, that a solitude that *could* denote freedom, self-actualization, and growth, appears terrifying to many, even for relatively short periods of time.

We can look both within and without to see which of these five treasures we might be able to keep before we run out of time.

Conscious Living: Reinventing Our Choices

What do men and women past sixty think of when they think of getting ever older and envision gains and losses in love, health, and happiness. What do they most wish for, what do they most fear? Some answers to these questions can be found in a division of human development psychology research known as "life span" studies. In these studies, the concept of a person's basic *self* is seen as the core repository of all experience, motivation, and action plans. This "self" is seen as capable of change all the way through life and it is held that by imagining the possible selves that we might become, we are motivated to take steps to achieve that later self, or steps can be taken to avoid becoming a self that we fear.

Two researchers, Professor Susan Cross of the Iowa State University Psychology Department and Professor Hazel Markus of the Stanford University Psychology Department, asked 173 people in four age groups — ranging from eighteen to eighty-six — to list selves they hoped to become and selves that they feared to become. Six respondents were nonwhite, the rest were white. The whole sample was screened for similar educational levels.

The oldest age group — sixty to eighty-six — said they would like, in the future, to be an older person who is reasonably healthy in mind and body, content with life, had enough money to live worry-free, is close to his or her family, and is able to enjoy some leisure activities like travel, sports, music, and lifelong personal interests.

What were their fears?

This group of past-sixties feared serious health problems that would take the ability to control their lives out of their hands, outliving family and close friends and being alone, losing the respect and love of their children in very old age (The idea being that very old people are essentially unlovable? This was not clear in the study), and being forced into a nursing home.

When the researchers came to evaluate these responses from the oldest age group they studied (the others were grouped into eighteen to twenty-four, twenty-five to thirty-nine, and forty to fifty-nine years), they found a number of inspiring realities.

1. *The idea of continued growth and development is very real and important to older people.* At least in this survey, they were very far from viewing life as over or diminished; they had clear ideas of how they wanted to age, and the researchers assumed they would be motivated to try to meet those new "selves" in the future. Though most of them, according to the Cross-Markus study, were retired from formal work, they did not give signs that they were withdrawing from other relationships or involvements.

    Since people between sixty and eighty-six have already achieved some of the goals that younger respondents mentioned — marrying and completing whatever work experience they were going to accomplish — the older group indicated that what they wanted their future selves to do was more and better of what they were doing now, indicating some satisfaction with current "givens" in their lives. For example, many mentioned wanting to be even better grandparents or, in some way, to cement family relations even more; they wanted to see themselves as loved and wanted by their families. They were motivated by this vision of their future selves to work hard at what was needed to reach that goal.

In a calm, professional tone, the researchers stated quietly that "one might construe many of these possible selves as personal attempts to combat negative social stereotypes ... Such stereotypes of the aging person can result in capitulation to expectations that the person will be dependent, frail, or antisocial, resulting in actual decrements and loss of functioning." To cheer us on, the Cross-Markus team continued, "the elaboration of positive images of the self, with the attendant steps and strategies for realizing these selves, may be instrumental in helping the older person successfully avoid the self-fulfilling nature of such stereotypes."

Leaving the scholarly framework in which these findings are presented, we see that people *can* affect their own aging to some degree. While external factors like national economic disasters, accidents, and just plain bad luck cannot be controlled, there are lots of things on the road to old age that are within one's control and elders seem quite ready to deal with those.

2. *Older people continue to be concerned with significant others.* While the selves the participants feared they would become mostly revolved around health and dependency issues, they were not seen by the interviewers as totally self-absorbed (another stereotype

about older folks), but as being worried about becoming burdens to their love partners or others around them or becoming, as a result of health problems, "disagreeable individuals."

3. *Future fears are less threatening to older adults because they have learned which elements of love can be controlled and which cannot.* On the question of how to handle things over which one has no control — becoming suddenly widowed was a big concern — it was fascinating to see that while elders know there are many things they are not going to be able to change, they mean to take vigorous and preemptive steps on the things that they can control, such as improving their health through giving up smoking, more exercise, and better attention to nutrition.

These notions that people can, to some extent, affect their own aging are being addressed not only by academics and medical specialists, but also by artists, writers, and philosophers, as well as by ordinary folks. Most want to figure out how they are going to meet this new phase of their lives (for which most of us are woefully unprepared by society, our parents, or our doctors) and how to become citizens of this new country of the old. How does love happen in that country, not only with partners, but with all the loved people still in our lives?

The idea of developing a positive approach to aging and to elder love is derided and scorned by many, who take the position that it is all loss, all simply increasing bad health and eventual humiliating dependency, and that nothing can compensate for the body's decline. At the other end of the spectrum we find folks who believe that their aging bodies can be disregarded, that "the best is yet to be," although poet Ogden Nash thought those words "could, certes, emanate only from a youngster in his thirties." Somewhere between the sentimental slush about how wonderful getting older is and the desperate sadness of those who are willing to let today go in fear of tomorrow, most people are struggling to craft a conscious aging that will maximize the good and help them cope with the hard parts.

How do some people arrive at a measured sense of wanting to continue; to heed what is, in many, a strong life force, and yet not flinch from the sorrows, losses, and indignities that age can bring?

The answer is: They try all kinds of routes to get to a place where they can see the glass half full. Some try common sense; some try experiments in living (different housing arrangements, becoming closer to family and friends, undertaking new volunteer activities); some consciously sharpen their senses to enjoy nature, people, the world, in a way they had not before, and some turn to introspection and study. Here are six who tried a variety of paths and what they say about conscious aging.

Six Views of the Path That Crosses to Safety

Two voices that perhaps embody the common sense approach to coping with getting older are those of the late M. F. K. Fisher, the noted writer who, among other things, took writing about food to new heights of art and philosophy, and Peg Bracken, another food writer, who reached the souls of her readers by heading in exactly the opposite direction from Fisher.

Fisher convinced her readers that caviar on toast, with candlelight and wine, was a symbol of affirming life through all the senses. Forty years ago, Bracken, by writing the *I Hate to Cook Book* and specializing in such delicacies as "Hurry Curry" and "Spuds O'Grotten," convinced *her* readers to get out of the kitchen with all deliberate speed.

Perhaps it is a coincidence that these two witty, grounded women, who offer us common sense as we age, both worked in the kitchen, but here is what they say:

Fisher, who died in 1992 at age eighty-three, wrote in her book *Sister Age*: "[S]ome of us who seem meant to survive, [don't] need to do it blindly. I think we must use what wits we have to admit things like the fact that it is harder to get up off the floor at seventy than at forty...We must accept and agree with and then attend to with dispassion all the boring physical symptoms...but what is important, though, is that our dispassionate acceptance of attrition be matched by a *full use of everything that has ever happened in all the long wonderful-ghastly years.*" She goes on to say, "[What is important] is to use the experience...so that physical annoyances are surmountable in an alert and even mirthful appreciation of life itself."

Still writing cookbooks at eighty-one, Bracken is equally grounded as she abandons cooking for the moment to do a book called *Getting Older for the First Time.* In an interview with Susan Crowley in "The AARP Bulletin," Bracken dismisses attempts to glorify old age as "nincompoopery," but says there is "lots of good stuff, too." In her seventies, she married for the fourth time and says she "finally got it right" (not a bad achievement, however late) and finds that this is the time to enjoy a "spacious leisure" so that one can "do as you please when you please."

This mixture of the bad tasting with the spicy "good stuff" is an apt symbol of how love and aging can be served up as a palatable dish.

Three other figures from the literary world have dug deeply into themselves to show us some of the gold still to be mined.

Poet-writer May Sarton, who died in 1995 at eighty-three, wrote many journals and memoirs in addition to her novels and poems, and commented often about what she was learning as she aged.

She kept a daily journal of her seventieth year (*At Seventy*) and recounted how, at a poetry reading she gave at a Connecticut college, she mentioned that "This is the best time of my life. I love being old." When a voice from the audience asked loudly "Why is it good to be old?" Sarton, sensing the questioner's incredulity, answered "Because I am more myself than I have ever been. There is less conflict. I am happier, more balanced and...more powerful...or better able to use my powers."

For women, who, more than men, worry about their aging bodies and about a changed appearance when they are older, Sarton had an honest and bittersweet statement: "Why do we worry about lines in our faces as we grow old? A face without lines that shows no mark of what has been lived through in a long life suggests something unlived, empty...still, one mourns one's young face sometimes. It has to be admitted...at the same time, I feel my face is better now [at seventy] and I like it better. That is because I am a far more complete and richer person than I was at twenty-five...in some ways, I am younger now because I can admit vulnerability and more innocent because I do not have to pretend."

Maurice Goudeket (1889–1997), a French businessman and man of letters, who was married to the celebrated author, Colette, for twenty years, wrote a book about aging when he was seventy-five. This was after he remarried, following the trauma of Colette's death, and fathered a son at the age of seventy-one.

In his book *The Delights of Growing Old,* Goudeket wrote, "[Let me] tell you a secret: it is not really a fact that you grow old at all. And you seventy-five-year-olds...has the 'me' of your first adult years changed in any way? There is shortness of breath, a slowness of movement, a back that will not bend so easily, to be sure, but these are things for our bodies to cope with. The immaterial being that gives our threatened building all its life does not show a single wrinkle, nor will it ever do so."

Young Americans who value the wrinkle-free body perhaps more than they value the "immaterial being" find this hard to accept, but Goudeket continues: "[N]ow every fresh day finds me more filled with wonder and better qualified to draw the last drop of delight from it.... [I]s it indeed *this* that they call growing old, this continual surge of memories that comes breaking in on my inner silence, this contained and sober joy, this lighthearted music that bears me up, this wider window on the world, this spreading kindly feeling and this gentleness?"

Another outstanding American writer, Doris Grumbach, struggled hard and sometimes painfully to find her way to this "contained and sober joy" of aging. She thoughtfully considered and wrote about the process in four books of memoirs that began in her seventieth year and continued through her seventy-seventh.

In 1991, Grumbach published *Coming into the End Zone*, a book in which she candidly detailed the physical declines she noted and abhorred; confessed to a fear and a repugnance at what city life had become, especially for older people (at that time she lived in Washington, D.C.); and listed a number of losses and sorrows that seem to accompany late years. The book is about as far from the "golden years" theme as it is possible to get; one critic even called it "flinty." Yet throughout, she also listed many of her pleasures in work, in friendship, in books, in good food and wine, and in companionship and love with her partner.

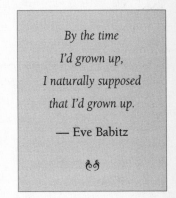

By the time
I'd grown up,
I naturally supposed
that I'd grown up.

— Eve Babitz

A few years later, in 1993, a glint of amusement appears in a new memoir, *Extra Innings*. While continuing to say how important it is to not be "dishonestly cheerful," she quotes the late comedian, George Burns, who said he liked living into his nineties because "I don't have to worry about peer pressure." She also enjoyed, she said, pioneer advocate for the aging and Gray Panther founder Maggie Kuhn, who chortled with delight in her late eighties that she had "outlived the opposition."

The next year, in 1994, Grumbach published a third memoir in the form of a meditation on fifty days of solitude she arranged to spend alone at her home in Maine. In this latest book, she once more reviewed the difficulties of aging, but concluded that "if I have learned anything... it is that the proper conditions for productive solitude are old age and the outside presence of a small portion of the beauty of the world" (she lives on a cove on a peninsula on the Maine coast).

Two years later, in her seventy-seventh year, Grumbach wrote a fourth book, *Life in a Day,* continuing the effort at shaping her own aging. The last line in the book on solitude is: "I have learned that, until death, it is all life."

The struggle to age in a conscious way with our partners or other loved figures is neatly summed up in an exchange between Mitch Albom, the well-known sports writer, and his old professor from college, Morris Schwartz. When Albom learned his much-loved old teacher was dying of Lou Gehrig's disease, he arranged to visit with him weekly, just as he had so many years ago in college, to learn what his old professor might be able to teach him in his last months about living, loving, and dying. The result was a book titled *Tuesdays with Morrie* in which Professor Schwartz's guidance is reflected in this exchange:

"Have I told you about the tensions of opposites?" [Schwartz asks Albom.]

"The tension of opposites?"

"Life is a series of pulls back and forth. You want to do one thing, but you are bound to do something else. Something hurts, yet you know it shouldn't. You take certain things for granted, even when you know you should never take anything for granted. A tension of opposites, like a pull on a rubber band. And most of us live somewhere in the middle."

"Sounds like a wrestling match."

"A wrestling match," he laughs. "Yes, you could describe life that way."

"So, which side wins?"

He smiles at me, the crinkled eyes, the crooked teeth.

"Love wins," the old professor says. "Love always wins."

As our guides, Fisher, Grumbach, Professor Schwartz, and

the others, have shown us, conscious aging seems to require new angles of vision for living in a new country. These new ways of seeing include: a realistic acknowledgment of time's toll without pretense; a determination to use hard-won knowledge and experience to increase life's pleasures and rewards where possible; and a new appreciation of the sacredness of ordinary daily life, of nature, and of love.

Generativity: Links to the Future

Ever since Moses brought the Ten Commandments down from the mountain to his flock — and possibly before that in human history — caring elders have been holding out their hands to others to help them scale the steep mountains of their worlds. Sometimes those who might be helped push the elders aside; sometimes they take the help offered, but find they can't use it, for a variety of reasons, and sometimes the magic of "generativity" — of an older person displaying caring, creativity, and productivity toward family, friends, and community — brings radiant new life both to elders and to those in their orbits.

One of the big tasks of getting older is to learn how to offer care and help and to become comfortable, in turn, receiving it. Again, the great American emphasis on independence and self-sufficiency makes many people uncomfortable when someone tries to help them, especially when they have for so long played the parental and then grandparental role in which they are always *giving* caring and help.

One older Indiana woman, Dorothy T., was widowed at seventy-four, and since her own children had long since left the big family home and founded their own families, she was left with a large house to maintain. Since she lived near a college, she decided to take in students, several of them from foreign countries. She did not need the money and she did not even need new friends, having lived in that town all her married life. She enjoyed many long friendships as well as warm relations with her own children and grandchildren who, however, lived at considerable distance.

What she needed, as a stay against stagnation and despair at widowhood and aging, was to exhibit the caring and creativity that had always marked her life. She became "family" to the students, enjoyed their campus reports, found it fun to keep snacks and soft drinks around once more (she had four children of her own), and offered solace in times of trouble for the young ones. They, in turn, offered to help on house maintenance and took her to movies they thought she'd like, "movies not too violent," she explained, grinning at the generational differences.

Dorothy didn't realize until the shared life was well underway that their contributions to *her* were almost as great as hers to them in offering shelter and warmth. This linkage of generations is one of the most profound pleasures of aging, though of course many young and middle-aged people display these qualities as well, but are usually so tremendously involved in raising their own children or pursuing their own jobs and careers that grandparenting or surrogate grand-generativity must wait.

The enrichment that comes in older years from sharing all one has learned, helping others, and receiving much in return, is demonstrated clearly in the stories of Amelia and Frances.

Amelia N. is a seventy-five-year-old grandmother, long divorced, who, at the time of the interview, had just returned from taking two teenage grandchildren to Europe for their first trip out of the United States. They were troubled by bad weather in London and a heat wave in Paris, and this forced Grandma to invent new strategies beyond sitting in the sidewalk cafes and admiring monuments on long walks. She found indoor swimming pools she didn't know existed for her over-heated twosome in Paris and out-of-the-way movie houses and small museums in London that were in none of the guidebooks.

Exhausting? Amelia said she slept for two days straight when she got home. "Between jet lag and running around with two teenagers, I was beyond exhaustion," she says, laughing. "It was an experience I'll treasure forever. We got to be good friends in a way we never have time for at home, and seeing these places that were familiar to me through their eyes was so interesting, I can't tell you." Who was giving and who was receiving in this journey? It seems probable that we can't separate out an answer to that question, but rather can accept the picture Amelia draws as a fine moment of putting all one's resources of time, energy, and money in older years into the service of staying connected. It is important to stress, however, that these generative projects often are *not* connected to one's own family and friends, but move outward to strangers, too.

Frances B., sixty-eight, is long married to a physician about her age who has no intention of retiring or even slowing down his enormously busy medical life. Frances learned long ago, in the immemorial manner of doctor's wives, that she must make a life of her own, and this she did, taking a late college degree, maintaining a wide circle of friends, and working as a medical records administrator. Though her life was busy and contented, she looked forward to the day when her two daughters would marry and provide grandchildren. By the time she reached her late sixties, a few things about her family life became clear. One daughter had, indeed, married, but she and her husband let everyone know they did not intend to have children. The other daughter remained single and neared the point of no return, biologically speaking, as Frances turned sixty-five.

"I had what you might call 'grandmother lust,'" Frances recalls over coffee in her comfortable living room. "I really wanted the experience of tiny babies again and to watch their growth — briefly, of course! — and I had always heard that the great thing about grandparenting is that you can hand them back to their parents whenever you want. It always seemed like a wonderful way to enjoy little children without having the real responsibility for them, but it just wasn't going to happen for me and Elliot, I had to realize that."

The catch, she explained, was that while she and her husband seemed outwardly to have reached some level of acceptance, her "grandmother lust" continued and seemed to get worse as time passed and made more emphatic the fact that she would not have biological grandchildren of her own. This is not an uncommon predicament for thousands of older Americans as their children postpone marriage later and later and then find it isn't so easy to bear children, even with modern medical advances, in young midlife.

Frances solved the problem in a way that turned this sadness into a kind of contentment she had not anticipated. Overhearing nurses from the maternity floor talking in the hospital cafeteria one day, she learned that up in the hospital nursery were "boarder babies," tiny infants who had been abandoned by their parents for a whole variety of reasons — illness, drug addiction, poverty. No one came to see these babies; the nurses only had time to see that they were clean and fed, but volunteers were needed to rock and hold these babies. They were not thriving and not developing well without the normal consistent attention of a parent or caregiver. Until they could be given for adoption or placed in foster homes, they continued to languish in the hospital.

> *Don't be afraid*
> *your life will end — be*
> *afraid that it will*
> *never begin.*
>
> — Grace Hansen
>
> ☙

Frances spends two hours two afternoons a week, talking to the babies, holding them close, and taking over some of the feeding and diapering routines from the overburdened nurses. The nurses knew at once she was an experienced mother and could be trusted; she complied with hospital rules, wore sterile clothes, and did not move outside the nursery with the babies. They brought a rocking chair into the nursery for her, so that supervision was on hand all the time.

Frances was amazed at herself the first day she volunteered. "I remembered everything, even though it had been more than forty years since I diapered a baby," she says. "It's true, it really *is* like riding a bike — you never forget." Her rewards have been incalculable; seeing the children respond, learn to smile, gain weight and to hear them laugh at toys and other children. Her need to grandparent has been somewhat satisfied, and the fact that her surrogate grandparenting has resulted in the children being so much healthier that they are more likely candidates for adoption has given her great satisfaction. Insurance companies frown on this form of volunteerism, however, and it is unclear how many hospitals now permit it.

"Of course, I'd still love to have my own," Frances says, "but this is so satisfying that I am hoping to continue doing it for a long time." The ways in which creative giving, and balancing outward turning with inward learning, shapes older years and makes for more conscious aging is dramatically demonstrated in the real-life story of two clergymen, one quite old, one unusually young.

The Tale of Two Rabbis (A True Story)

The story unfolds in a homey, cluttered study on the second floor of a small synagogue on the east side of Manhattan on a beautiful summer day. It is the study of Rabbi Sidney Kleiman, eighty-six years old and recovering from a stroke. He sits at his desk, with his daytime health aide, a charming, warm young woman named Anna, who sits quietly doing paperwork at another desk nearby.

The rabbi is describing his long life, most of it spent with one Orthodox congregation, Talmud Torah Adereth El, and his decision, three years ago, to allow his board of trustees to hire an assistant for him. The young rabbi, just out of the seminary at Yeshiva University is Gideon Shloush; he was twenty-five when hired to be Rabbi Kleiman's assistant.

For sixty years the senior scholar has worked ten- and twelve-hour days, beginning with early morning services at 6:30 a.m. and often ending with pastoral counseling late into the night with members of his congregation. In addition, he is the senior chaplain, serving with Catholic priests and Protestant ministers, at a nearby medical center, one of the largest hospitals in the city.

Rabbi Kleiman confides he was loath to have help, but as his eighties advanced, he fought off retirement and compromised on the decision to have an assistant; the plan was settled and ready to go into operation. Before the older man could sit down with his very young helper to discuss how they would assign duties, he suffered a major heart attack that required quadruple bypass surgery.

The young Rabbi Shloush tells how shocked and stunned he felt to realize that this leader, who had reassured him he would not be expected to perform major duties right away, was hospitalized for an unknown amount of time, and how the leadership mantle had not just fallen on his shoulders, it had almost knocked him over.

And all this, both men tell with the obvious relish of survivors, one week before the High Holy Days, the most important time on the Jewish calendar when the New Year and the period of repentance that follows are observed!

With a sympathetic and understanding congregation, the younger man was able to conduct the necessary services, and before long, the man he describes as his guide, mentor, teacher, and surrogate grandfather was able to return to work. The bonding that ensued is both familial and generational; it is both father/son and teacher/ student, both caring for the wounds of the world and giving and receiving from each other.

The generativity image took yet another turn when Rabbi Kleiman had a stroke recently and once more had to turn duties over to the younger man. But now, with physical rehabilitation and a will of steel, the older rabbi is back in the harness.

What has each given and received in this caring for each other and for their congregation, in this generativity that stresses creativity and productivity, as well as caring? The comparison with fathers and sons is clear, but almost too easy. (Rabbi Kleiman discouraged his own two sons from the rabbinate; he told them the work was too hard!) These two men are also partners in an enterprise sacred to both of them.

The older rabbi confessed that yes, it was hard to see

someone else taking over the helm of his ship, however briefly, but that it was comforting and reassuring to know his work of so many years would go on and go on well. He praises his helper's qualities of leadership and character and is eager to initiate him in all that a leader must know and do.

The younger man says he is "so honored" to have the senior rabbi's confidence and so impressed with his colleague's courage and never-give-up stance. "What a role model!" says the younger man. He and Rabbi Kleiman now alternate conducting Sabbath services each week. (The congregation, once faltering as neighborhoods changed, has now doubled its membership and has outreach programs of all kinds going forward in the community.)

When asked the secret of his strong will and his continuing creativity and drive, Rabbi Kleiman, a round, chubby, Buddha-looking gentleman, pokes his fingers upward toward the ceiling — in an evocation of God — but then he smiles, as his stroke-limited left arm rests immobile on his chair, and with his still working right hand, he makes a fist, saying "and I'm a fighter."

His parting words are "You have to know what's going on in the world; you have to stay involved." His own involvement in the affairs of the world from the dawn of his career to its near sunset is demonstrated by the fact that one of the very first sermons he preached, as a very young rabbi just settling in to his new congregation, was an anti-isolationist speech in the late 1930s. He told his congregants that, despite English Prime Minister Neville Chamberlain's statement that there would be "peace in our time," there would be no peace while Adolph Hitler threatened Europe. It wasn't a popular position then and he has taken many unpopular positions in the long sixty years since, but he sees his role as not only staying alert and involved himself, but as persuading the members of the congregation to take similar roles.

From the privacy of his study to the bright sunlight of the street, Rabbi Kleiman's words — "you have to stay involved" —

resonate with the experience of many elders. There is a tremendous range of interests and activities that older people have developed in their long lives and it seems so important, looking toward old age, to have such active interests.

The physically battered figure in his study saying "I'm a fighter" was forged in the actions and passions of his time. There are many strong elders who show us the threads that tie them to life, and their interests are various and multifaceted.

Vital Involvement: Bread and Roses

Edna T., eighty-seven, is a demon gardener, a grower of prize roses, and the source of gardening wisdom for everyone lucky enough to cross her path. She has help these days with some of the more strenuous chores, but is, in every way, the master planner and supervisor of her kingdom, despite a variety of physical problems.

Bernard F., seventy-nine, used to be a fiery political activist and union organizer. He doesn't mount many barricades these days, since two arthritic knees and a replaced hip have slowed him down; however, he's a venerated member of a local political club and attends most meetings, and, as he puts it "I write checks for all the causes I believe in…modest checks nowadays, but I know what candidates and what programs should be supported."

Serena T., eighty, always thought she had a good ear for music and could often pick out tunes on the piano that she had only heard once or twice; her singing voice seemed pleasant, but she did not pay any attention to it in the busy years of family raising and working. She was sixty-four when her first grandchild was born and she found herself singing lullabies to the baby so effectively that everyone marveled at how he would stop crying, smile, and obediently fall asleep if she sang to him at bedtime. A neighbor heard her singing to the baby on the back porch one summer day and invited her to join a neighborhood choir. Today, Serena is a key member of a respected thirty-five-voice choir that gives concerts all over the region in

Ohio where she lives. Her home is in a small community that has little access to the great concert halls and artists who can be heard in big urban centers. Her music, however, is as important to her as if she were playing Carnegie Hall every night. "It's a marvel," she says, "especially since I really didn't begin to think of myself as a singer at all until I was in my late sixties."

What do Edna, Bernard, and Serena have in common, though they do not know each other and live in widely separated cities and towns? They are all three connected to the world through things that they care about — Edna to her roses, Bernard to the political scene, and Serena to music. "Only connect," said novelist E. M. Forster, and most older people come to their aging process with a lifetime of caring behind them, most frequently beginning with their immediate circle of family and friends.

But the astonishing thing about aging is that with the freedom from mid-life cares and with the extra time increasing longevity has granted, the possibility for strengthening existing involvements — whether to one's immediate circle or to a larger circle of interests — and the possibility for new connections beckons on the horizon as yet another way to choose how one is going to age.

This involvement in something vital as we age does not necessarily mean frenetic activity; the gift of time can be used to explore one's inner life as well as the outer connection to family or community. In fact, psychologist Erik Erickson, the author of many life span studies, says that the balance to be sought is "integrating outward-looking care for others with inward-looking concern for self." Giving those around us a chance to return some care to us as we age is, again, a good thing for intergenerational interdependence and allows younger people to experience vital involvement themselves. Many wise family doctors and others who work with the aging population have told oldsters, "*Let* your daughter help you with that; she wants a chance to be a good daughter, let her have it." In independence-minded America, elders find it hard to believe that their adult children would *welcome* the chance to help with chores or give assistance in a wide variety of settings, but we can understand it better if we remember that in our own roles as adult children of our own aging parents, we wanted very much to conform to our own ideas of what a good son or daughter would do.

And just as staying connected to the larger world doesn't mean necessarily having a finger in a dozen pies at once, it also can mean caring for the world on a much less intensive basis by caring for individuals, one at a time, who may be outside our families, but who can strengthen our ability to participate in the world.

Driving an elderly neighbor who has limited vision to grocery shopping or to a doctor's appointment, just calling an old friend far away who has been battling illness, using a newfound skill at computers to help someone else learn — older people around America do these connecting and involving activities every day and so are designing the kind of aging they will have.

The activities of the elders described above show it is impossible to categorize or count the myriad ways that gardeners, clergymen, surrogate grandparents, and political activists — all people who have not had even fifteen minutes of fame — continue to participate, even if they no longer do the heavy lifting of maintaining the world.

The retired Canadian businessman with vision problems who has not surrendered his love of theater and manages to be in the front row at plays he's heard on tapes; the retired school teacher in Iowa who is hobbled by arthritis, but continues to create, even with gnarled fingers, the beautiful quilts she makes for every new baby in the family; the stroke-hampered former truck driver in Maine with the mellow baritone voice who continues to do readings for the blind from his wheelchair — all these friends and neighbors who might live next door to us are worthy of laurel wreaths for courage and stoic refusal to give in to despair; they keep it at bay by remaining vitally involved.

If asked, most such friends and neighbors probably see

their activities as second priority after the care of and connection with family and close friends.

But as ever-optimistic, ever-future-oriented Americans, we also have in front of us examples gathered from all over the world of intense late-life interests that have nothing to do with personal love objects, but that illustrate what older people still can give to the world and how much satisfaction they gain from pursuing passions — whether for roses or music.

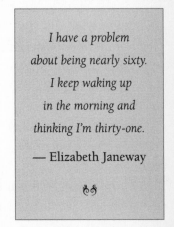

I have a problem about being nearly sixty. I keep waking up in the morning and thinking I'm thirty-one.

— Elizabeth Janeway

These role models are largely drawn from the arts — music, dance, theater, literature, among others — because they are well-known enough and have enough continuing attention paid to their lives that we learn when they have physical problems of aging, when they are suffused with getting-older sadness or anger, and when they are triumphant in continuing creativity. Those are the same aging experiences our neighbors and friends have, but their challenges and triumphs are largely hidden from us in the quiet circles of their own families or communities.

But famous people can show us aging in a bright spotlight; what can we learn from the larger-than-life images they project on the screens of our own minds and imaginations? One of the things we can learn is that no matter how large they may loom in the contemporary culture of stardom, they age as we do; they have the same struggles against adversity; and they occasionally have failures and, once in a while, glorious successes.

A larger-than-life figure who bestrides the contemporary music scene is Oscar Peterson, the legendary jazz pianist, now seventy-three, whose contributions to this seminal American music over half a century are known throughout the world.

In 1993, Peterson suffered a stroke that immobilized his left arm and hand. Short of death, what crueler fate could befall a pianist, especially one known for an inventive approach to his instrument and the most original lines of sound, created with both hardworking hands and a soul full of musicality?

The two hands no longer could work, but the musical soul refused to give up. Peterson credits four things with his amazing comeback to great critical acclaim five years after his stroke. Two are people — his wife and his physical therapist — and two are matters of deciding how he was going to age and battle his body: he chose perseverance and his love of music, despite having gone into a deep depression immediately following the stroke.

He now has quite restricted use of his left hand, but has developed a whole new approach to playing primarily with his right, once more demonstrating the ability of older people to select, optimize, and compensate (see chapter 2, "The Anatomy of Bravery") and not incidentally, lifting themselves from depression.

The truly stunning aspect of Peterson's story is not that he is performing in a less-than-top-notch style just to be performing at all (a sadness we sometimes see with athletes who cannot leave the field gracefully), but quite the reverse. He has developed an authentic new style that has critics raving, referring to his "unstoppable drive" to create new sounds. The *Chicago Tribune* says he "relearned the instrument without full use of his once powerful left hand;" the *Minneapolis Star Tribune* music critic finds his new style riveting; and the *New York Times* says Peterson "still delivers a singular pianistic sound: perfect in its rounded full-tone precision....[The] lyricism of his long cascading runs is enriched with blues filigree that finds a balance between contemplation and earthiness."

In his seventies, Peterson is far from alone in offering us a mark to shoot for. Others who managed to do the digging and come up with surprising strengths include:

- Dancer Merce Cunningham, who remains open to the most extreme forms of dance experimentation and change as he celebrates his eightieth birthday, usually not a happy milestone for a dancer. He uses the bodies of young dancers to express the most avant-garde choreographic ideas, since his own body is no longer the chosen instrument that it was at his debut a half century ago.

- Poet Maya Angelou, who at seventy undertook a sixth career as director of a new film about black life, *Down in the Delta*. Not content with merely reading her poems at President Clinton's first inaugural, she is also a college teacher, an actress, a bestselling author of both prose and poetry, a playwright, and a film producer. Adding yet another career to this list, she says, no matter how big a load it may seem, is the way to march steadily into her seventies with grace.

- Italian architect Ettore Sottsass, Jr., who critics say seems to grow younger with the years, though he is eighty-two now and was eighty when he designed the much-admired new airport interiors in Milan, Italy. He continues to travel a lot, but doesn't tear through airports with the speed of today's young technocrats because eighty-two is eighty-two. But even so, his airport is seen as a model of understanding for the kind of creature comforts and visual soothing that tired travelers really need. He is roundly blessed by international fliers when they sip coffee between flights amid the muted colors, earth tones, wood counters, and sound-deadening plaster walls of his sympathetic design.

More older adults could take counsel from dozens more famous elders such as Gloria Stuart, the oldest actress ever to be nominated for an Academy Award at age eighty-seven for her role in *Titanic*; or Gabe Pressman, the veteran NBC network newsman, who, at seventy-five, is still chasing politicians and accident victims with his in-your-face microphone; or seventy-five-year-old Charles Aznavour, whose cabaret songs about love and loss still make swooners out of respectable matrons at chic clubs in Paris and New York.

The lessons we can draw from Peterson's story and some of his famous counterparts are reasonably clear:

1. Allow yourself time to grieve over losses. Peterson did not deny his depression after the stroke and received treatment for it.
2. Let others help you explore how to adapt to both physical and emotional limitations. Without the consistent patience and knowledge of a skilled physical therapist, it would have been harder for Peterson to understand what skills could still be maintained, and, as it turned out, even changed into a set of new achievements. His musicality is so intense he probably could have learned these things on his own, but it would have taken much longer.
3. There has to be a digging deep into one's own resources to mount the kind of successful counterattack against adversity that we all would like to be able to replicate from Peterson's and other stories.

What all these folks demonstrate is that they have found that elusive ability to change with new circumstances where they can, to avoid the problems that can't be changed, and to know the difference. Sometimes it's called guts; sometimes it's called stubbornness — and sometimes it's called wisdom.

The Search for Wisdom

Many people over the age of sixty seem to have gained wisdom through the years, while others remain torn by conflict, bitterness, and anger, both about growing old and about the hand they were dealt in life, and are unable to feel life's joys on any level or to be supportive to others.

The worldview that leads to wisdom is expressed in many different venues by both old and young, from the biblical story of King Solomon's wisdom to the song lyrics of a modern wise woman, singer-composer Joni Mitchell, whose song, recorded in 1967, proclaiming that she can see life from "both sides now" certainly contains an element of wisdom.

History and different cultures identify certain figures as wise regardless of age — Buddha, Jesus (who was in his thirties when crucified), Abraham Lincoln, Mother Teresa, and many more. In our own lives, we might nominate a few people whom we know, either in our families or outside, as wise persons.

What are the common threads, the identifying attributes, that seem to mark people who are wise? What in ourselves do we need to develop in order to gain the kind of wisdom that could illuminate our later years with some measure of serenity?

Most of us don't observe the Ten Commandments the way we should, or any other golden rules laid down by a variety of religions; we are always struggling to do better, and so it is with our hopes to become wiser as we age.

It seems to become a journey, not a destination, and one of the steps on that journey is identified by the late Helen M. Luke, a counselor, follower of Carl Jung, and a writer and philosopher. Luke, who lived in Michigan and died in 1995 at the age of ninety-one, believed that, as she stated in her meditations, titled *Old Age,* that we need to be able to show a sense of discrimination about all of life's events.

"Now that the harvest is gathered and you stand in the autumn of your life... [there is] a spirit of discriminating wisdom," she wrote, "separating moment by moment the wheat of life from the chaff, so that you may know in both wheat and chaff their meaning, and their value in the pattern of the universe."

Luke was a senior sage herself, but examples of this "discriminating wisdom" are all around us and are ageless, found in the young as well as the old, and in matters of importance as well as in the most trivial.

> *The truth is never known until the future becomes the past.*
>
> — Delmore Schwartz

A beautiful young woman, not more than twenty, was overheard in a beauty salon to have discovered that the appointment she reserved in anticipation of an important social event could not happen at the required time because of the illness of the operator she so much wanted to work with. The manager of the salon was wildly apologetic. Possibly hoping to have the young woman so beautifully turned out that she would, in effect, become an advertisement for his shop, he went on and on about how terrible it was that she couldn't have the hairdo she wanted and offered many substitutes.

The young woman patted his arm consolingly and said, "It's all right — think about the fact that many children all over the world go to bed starving or sick every night — this is only hair, David, it's only hair." This impressive demonstration of "discriminating wisdom" in one so young can serve as inspiration for all of us to try to keep just such a firm grip on what is wheat and what is chaff.

Another element of wisdom seems to be humility in the face of all we don't know, beginning with all we don't know about ourselves. If, as novelist John Barth said, "self knowledge is always bad news," that might explain why it is so difficult for us to know ourselves well enough to develop the humility that is so often a component of wisdom.

Even the great psychologist-philosopher Carl Jung himself, at the end of his life, after a lifetime searching for self-knowledge, wrote: "The older I have become, the less I have understood or had insight into or known about myself...this is old age, and a limitation. Yet there is so much that fills me: plants, animals, clouds, day and night, and the eternal in man."

And not only is it hard to know about ourselves, it is also problematical to know about the external world around us.

Bertrand Russell, the great British philosopher-mathematician-social activist, on his eightieth birthday (he lived to be ninety-eight) wrote of his many failures, despite a Nobel Prize and international praise for his work. His humility caused him to confess that he had not accomplished what he wished in the field of social change — major and minor wars and social unrest dogged the last half of his life — nor had he accomplished what he wished in his chosen field of mathematics and philosophy, as much as his work is admired.

"But," Lord Russell wrote, "beneath all this load of failure, I am still conscious of something I feel to be victory... personal [victory]: to care for what is noble...beautiful... gentle; social: to see in imagination the society that is to be created, where individuals grow freely, and where hate and greed and envy die because there is nothing to nourish them. These things I believe, and the world, for all its horrors, have left me unshaken."

In addition to discrimination and humility about all we do *not* know about ourselves and the world around us, what other attributes should we be cultivating on the road to wisdom, a destination we might not reach, but toward which it is surely good to journey?

Another component of wisdom might be kindness, and an associated group of qualities, such as the ability to put ourselves in the other person's shoes and, as young people say, "understand where he or she is coming from." The North American Indian proverb, "never judge a man until you have walked three moons in his moccasins" puts it perhaps a bit more poetically, but expresses the same idea about how to develop a kinder understanding.

In a lecture on altruism, a noted psychiatrist put it succinctly: "Be kind to all whom you meet. They are having a hard time." When asked after the lecture how that could apply to people who obviously were *not* having a hard time, such as healthy, handsome, well-functioning young or middle-aged people, he reiterated, "They are having a hard time, you just can't see into it. You can't see into their hearts; you don't know what hurts or worries or troubles are there, some of them not too clearly identified even to themselves. But trust me, most of the people you meet, whatever facade they present, are having enough troubles to warrant your kindness."

Most of us trying to rate ourselves on a kindness scale might find we didn't score nearly as high as we would like to, and certainly that is true for people of all ages. Cruelty of the young to each other is legendary, but older people can dole out cruelty with a more practiced hand than anyone because we, metaphorically, "know where all the bodies are buried" and can hit vulnerabilities all too hard and with all too much ease.

However, psychologist James Hillman, author of *The Force of Character and the Lasting Life,* believes that overall, older people find that kindness to strangers plays a larger role in their lives as they age. He speculates this may be, at least, partially because the aging tend to shift focus from maintaining the health of the body to maintaining the health of what is variously called *character* or *soul* or *spirit.*

This spirit of empathy or kindness is part of yet another component of wisdom, and that is good judgment, which includes a sense of balance and the ability to, as songwriter Joni Mitchell says, see life "from both sides now."

We all know some people we would characterize as wise, and if we stop to think about their qualities, certainly we would note a dispassionate ability to withhold judgment and to try to understand all the elements in a difficult or painful situation.

One older interviewee who had been involved in an extremely unhappy divorce illustrated this detachment in his own life. He confided a few details, not many, but it seemed clear that his ex-wife had behaved very badly in the breakup and that he would be justified in being furiously angry at her. The way in which she participated in the divorce also injured their children.

But when Dale T., aged seventy-two, speaks about the

divorce, which took place twenty years earlier, he explains a few things about his ex-wife that show she, too, was suffering greatly from the divorce. "There was," Dale explains, "enough pain to go around and you have to understand that *everyone* thinks they have their reasons." Dale's second wife, Pauline, is still angry at the ex-wife, but, she says, "I recognized Dale's wisdom in the matter."

The elements of wisdom we have looked at — discrimination, humility, kindness, balanced judgment — are all qualities we know we should have, along with a number of others, such as self-control and the ability to be helpful without immersing ourselves too deeply in other people's troubles. Wisdom is a process, not a product.

The consoling reality — as we rate ourselves lower on these qualities than we would like — is that wisdom is a process of *becoming,* and those of us who have lived and loved for a long time have a good chance of learning from all that we have suffered and known in our lives.

Consolation for the way we fall short of wisdom is offered by Douglas H. Powell, Ph.D., a behavioral scientist at Harvard University, who, in his book, *Nine Myths of Aging,* points out that "being highly intelligent and older are advantages [in trying to gain wisdom] . . . but wisdom requires neither." It also, he says, is within the grasp of most ordinary people because what wisdom requires grows out of the experiences we all have. If we're alive, we suffer; if we're alive, we have a chance to live passionately and widely; if we're alive long enough to age, we can keep open minds and hearts and constantly learn more about the world and others, as well as about ourselves.

That last component of wisdom — learning about ourselves — often requires something most Americans shun like Satan himself, and that is solitude and time alone to think and to try to make sense out of our experiences and meaning out of our lives.

The value of solitude, which can promote insight, change, and creativity, is not much discussed in American life, where loneliness is the great terror and a person who is taking solitary time for himself or herself is seen as being crippled in some way, probably a failure in interpersonal relationships generally or intimacy specifically.

But solitude, for women particularly, offers great possibilities for re-creation and growth, especially in late years when the burdens of family life and work are lessened somewhat (though usually not completely). A return to the self can mean much in terms of growth, creativity, and enrichment for the rest of the journey.

The Gifts of Solitude

We will end as we began, with a special focus on women, for they make up the largest group of aging people in our society. The iron prison of demographics keeps many women in the role of woman alone — a widow — and another group in solitary women who are divorcées who did not remarry or women who never married.

Most of these older women have connections with family and friends, often very close and sustaining. Others who may not have had children, frequently have impressive friend networks and those who never married often reach old age better skilled than widows in constructing surrogate families, serving as beloved godmothers and aunts to nieces and nephews, and at working out rituals for holidays and other communal times that uphold them against loneliness.

However, given the superabundance of widows, it seems certain that some aged women will spend some portion of their late years living alone, either between marriages and new relationships or following successive losses of both partners and housemates. It would seem then that a brief foray into the "company of one" might yield some insights into the nature of solitude and its possible pleasures.

Americans are deeply ambivalent about the solitary person in our midst. On the one hand, the lone hero is much admired in national folklore — the cowboy alone on the ridge at sunset, the daring adventurer on the road (most often a man, but in contemporary life, women also, as seen in the wonderful 1991 film *Thelma and Louise)* — all free of bonds. There's been a kind of romantic admiration for the loner, sometimes with a pal, who strikes out, independent and self-reliant, roaming the backroads and having adventures that can only come to those who are unfettered and isolate.

On the other side of our ambivalence is the belief that to be alone, even temporarily, is to have been abandoned and to be sunk in a black misery of loneliness. This is understood to be particularly dreadful for women, many of whom have been, for most of their lives, so busy dealing with life on behalf of what feels sometimes like multitudes of people that to be alone must, it is argued, feel like a soul-shattering desertion by fate.

As many older women can wryly testify, a little alone time after lifetimes of juggling work and family is not quite the sentence to desperation that men, especially, have outlined for them. It is believed that it was a male physician who coined the term "empty nest" to refer to the time when a women's child care responsibilities had shifted (they never end) to adult children, and then, often, to grandchildren.

For many women, the period when there are no more children at home has poignant moments of nostalgia, to be sure, but most survive nicely, feeling more the emotion sung in the civil rights anthem, "free at last, free at last, thank God Almighty, free at last."

Moira Alone: A New Adventure

Moira V., sixty-seven, is the mother of six children and at the same time that her youngest left the homestead for school and marriage her seventy-year-old husband also took a six-month consulting job overseas. He retired as head of a Tacoma, Washington, engineering firm but still took occasional consulting assignments.

Suddenly, Moira was alone in the house for a longer period than she had ever been before since the birth of her first child, who now is in his late forties.

The first morning of the new solitude found Moira practicing to be a voluptuary. She first fixed herself a beautiful breakfast tray with all her favorite foods and a big thermos jug of fragrant coffee. She took the tray back into her bedroom with the morning paper, turned off the telephone, read, ate, and napped.

Describing it later, she says, "of course, it was especially sweet because I knew that Roger would be coming home eventually and I would be so glad to see him, I'm sure."

What Moira was doing, essentially, was playing at being alone, safe in the knowledge that her most intimate relationship would resume when her husband's temporary assignment was over.

What such women often cannot bear to think about is that should they be widowed there might be fairly long stretches, even after the late-life romances that we have chronicled here, when they will be truly alone, at least for a time, and must examine what remains after the family demands change and there are losses in their friends network.

One of the difficulties in carrying out this examination is that in the United States at least, and probably in many of the family-oriented cultures in Europe and the Far East, all our hopes and dreams are fastened to interpersonal relationships. That is where our most important life is assumed to be taking place — in marriage, in deep friendships, even in collegial structures at work. Everything, we are told, depends on how we interact with others, especially in our most intimate moments.

This emphasis on intimacy with another as the measure of our health and happiness is fairly recent, historians tell us, and probably comes from the fact that in earlier centuries the tribe and clan had so much to do to simply survive with enough food and shelter that this intense emphasis on close, intimate relationships probably did not exist.

Anthony Storr, M.D., a respected British psychiatrist and author of many books on psychoanalysis, has written an insightful book called *Solitude: A Return to the Self* in which he suggests that modern men and women pay a price for the freedom from the starvation and disease that burdened early societies.

That price includes the reality that modern industrialized societies are unstable and lack the structures of class and hierarchy of the past. In addition, because we have so many choices about where we live, what work we do, and how we are going to construct our lives, our relations with the other people who make up our world become, says Dr. Storr, "matters of increasing concern and anxiety." An example of this anxiety is the modern belief that marriage is supposed to meet all needs, satisfy all human desires. Maybe that unrealistic expectation is why our divorce rate is nearly 50 percent.

> One's life has value so long as one attributes value to the life of others by means of friendship, indignation, compassion.
>
> — Simone de Beauvoir
>
> ๑ฦ

Most of the women we have met in this book were raised to believe that to be without a daily link to intimacy with another is to live in misery, even though there have been times when they might have wished to be free of that daily link for a while.

The real question then — if women, through widowhood and the loss of friends, find themselves alone — is how to find the way back to the self.

How can women develop a capacity for solitude that will appear to them as more benign, as even a resource for growth?

Five Steps to Harvesting the Fruits of Solitude

Becoming friendly with ourselves alone is a gradual learning program that includes these steps:

1. *Move toward wholeness by grounding yourself in a basic idea:* all human beings need some kind of human connection that includes a degree of intimacy. No one can exist in health as a hermit or recluse, except perhaps the most productive of geniuses and even

they always seemed to know how to get a good dinner at a friend's house.

But given the probability that most older women will have someone — children, grandchildren, friends, colleagues — with whom some portion of their life can be shared, a certain comfort immediately appears because, in truth, one is *not* completely alone in the world. There are even many settings in which colleagues provide a great deal of needed human connection — the armed forces, company workplaces, offices, institutions, and organizations of all kinds.

2. *Take a fresh look at the phenomenon of solitude itself.* Of course, voluntary solitude is much to be desired, but given the circumstances of older women, involuntary solitude is more likely, and so the task of finding one's "self" is part of the process of exploring the benefits that developing a capacity for solitude might yield.

3. *Embrace the alone time, and consider it beneficial.* It might help you tap into the creativity that exists to some degree in everyone; it need not be as formally structured as picking up a brush to paint or sitting at the piano to compose. However, solitude can allow a return to creative, imaginative pursuits that have been abandoned since childhood. Women who always meant to learn a musical instrument, or make pottery, or keep a journal or a diary, or study languages are, sometimes quite suddenly, able to imagine a self that does those things in a pleasurable solitary pursuit.

4. *Maximize the possible gifts flowing from your burgeoning capacity for solitude,* gifts that include the chance to sort things out, especially after a loss. There is a certain amount of grief work, for widows and for all who have lost close intimates, that has to be done alone. It is wonderful to have the comfort of friends

and family, but, in the end, the widow must lie alone in the dark and begin to come to terms with loss, as must the newly-divorced or those separated in any way from a world they once knew. These slow approaches to healing cannot all be experienced in the company of others, no matter how much reassurance and help they provide. And the solitude necessary for sorting things out also applies to other important life decisions, notably moving away from home, changing jobs and careers, and dealing with disappointment and betrayal — all benefit from alone time, no matter how useful it is to talk to partner, friend, or therapist.

5. *Develop a true understanding of yourself and work on your ideas and deepest beliefs.* Getting to know one's deepest feelings, opinions, and attitudes is one of the hardest tasks of living — at any age — but it becomes more and more necessary as we age so that we can shape our "third age" in a way that gives us the most serenity and pleasure.

The ideal, of course, is to balance solitude and connection, but for American women, the need to always be in the company of others has been part of their socialization as women, as citizens, and as workers; so widowhood or not remarrying after divorce presents special challenges that might be enriched by the gifts of solitude.

Whether in solitude or in companionship, there exists a kind of pride in making do, in carrying on, in holding things together. Author Barbara Holland wrote a book called *One's Company* in which she looks at the need for connection and closely analyzes solitude. She writes: "It's important to stop waiting and settle down and make ourselves comfortable, at least temporarily, in this moonscape, and find some grace and pleasure in our condition...like a patient, enchanted princess in a tower, learning to wring honey from a stone...after all, here we are. It may not be where we expected to be, but for the time being, we might as well call it home."

As we seek the transforming power of love, as we seek deeper understanding of ourselves and those around us, we must summon all our courage to choose our old age and to believe that we can make it rich with meaning. Albert Camus, the French writer, said: "In the midst of winter, I finally learned that there was in me an invincible summer."

Those of us in the winter of our lives can find that summer, too, if we remain open to the wonders of the world.

TRAILBLAZER

Václav Havel

"I am not an optimist, because I am not sure that everything ends well. Nor am I a pessimist, because I am not sure that everything ends badly. I just carry hope in my heart."

This statement by Václav Havel, president of the Czech Republic and an international human rights leader, is only one of many sage observations that this noted playwright, ex-political prisoner and dissident anti-Communist revolutionary has offered the world since he helped to lead the Velvet Revolution in Czechoslovakia against Russian dominance in 1989.

Havel's own life experiences have been the stuff of intense drama, crossing literary, political, and cultural lines with bewildering speed and acumen. Born to wealthy parents in Prague, the Communist takeover in 1948 meant not only the loss of the family fortune, but exclusion for Havel from higher education. He managed to finish high school at night and took economics in a technical university. He found work as a stagehand in a Prague theater and before long he was writing plays with one hand and running underground political dissident activities with the other.

He wrote articles and essays in secret literary and theater magazines banned and denounced by the government and was offered opportunities to leave the country, but declined, saying "the solution of this human situation does not lie in leaving it."

He served time twice as a political prisoner in Czech prisons for his tireless work, both under and above ground, for democracy and human rights. When he received the Fulbright Prize for International Understanding from the United States in 1997, Secretary of State Madeleine

Albright, referring to his years in prison, said "we are the beneficiary of his wonderful 'crimes.' Because his nation and his neighbors are free, we too are free."

Havel, delivering the commencement address at Harvard University in 1995, made clear his vision of the future. He sees a new world order coming into being in which the proponents of globalization will recognize that, underneath the seeming one world technology has created, there are many cultures at many different levels of development that must be unified and brought together.

"While the world as a whole increasingly accepts the new habit of global civilization, another contradictory process is taking place: ancient traditions are reviving, different religions and cultures are awakening to new ways of being, seeking new room to exist."

"[This global civilization] is challenged to start understanding itself as a multicultural and multipolar civilization whose meaning lies not in undermining the individuality of different spheres but allowing them to be more completely themselves." The only way this can happen, says Havel, is if "we all accept a basic code of mutual coexistence, one that will enable us to go on living side by side."

Havel believes that while science has given us a hold on the objective world, mankind still faces a world of experience that seems chaotic, disconnected, and confusing. "In short," he says, "we live in the postmodern world where everything is possible and almost nothing is certain."

The Czech leader holds that the new global civilization must manage individual human transcendence beyond ordinary political and intellectual structures.

Even respect for human rights is not enough. That respect must, says Havel, "derive from the respect for the miracle of Being, the miracle of the universe, the miracle of nature, the miracle of our own existence." He says these ideas are found in all the great religions and cultures.

"Transcendence is the only real alternative to extinction," says this brave leader, who, now in failing health and looking back on many years on the barricades, still stands as a bulwark against cynicism and apathy.

He counsels us to look forward with hope for mankind. His summary words are these:

"Hope is a state of mind...it is the ability to work for something because it is good, not just because it stands a chance to succeed...it is hope above all which gives us the strength to live and try new things."

Works Cited

Preface

Jhabvala, Ruth Prawer. "The Man with the Dog." In *Love in Full Bloom*. New York: Ballantine Books, 1994.

Kuhn, Maggie. *Maggie Kuhn on Aging*. Philadelphia, Pa.: Westminster Press, 1977.

Le Guin, Ursula. "100 Visionaries." Interview by Jon Spayde. *The Utne Reader,* no. 67 (January/February 1995), 54-81.

Levenson, Robert W. "Emotion in the Elderly and in Late-Life Marriage." Faculty seminar paper, Berkeley, Calif.: University of California, 1997.

Rice, Susan. "Sexuality and Intimacy for Aging Women: A Changing Perspective." *Journal of Women and Aging* Vol. 1 (1989): 1–3, 245–264.

Introduction

Embree, John F. *Suye Mura: A Japanese Village*. Chicago: University of Chicago Press, 1939.

Trilling, Diana. *The Beginning of the Journey: The Marriage of Diana and Lionel Trilling.* New York: Harcourt Brace, 1993.

Chapter 1

Fisher, Helen. *The Anatomy of Love: The Natural History of Monogamy, Adultery, and Divorce.* New York: W.W. Norton, 1992.

Latham, Aaron. *The Ballad of Gussie and Clyde.* New York: Villard Books, 1997.

Proulx, E. Annie. "At Midlife, a Novelist Is Born." Interview by Sara Rimer. *New York Times,* 23 June 1994, sec. C10.

Schlesinger, Benjamin. "The Sexless Years or Sex Rediscovered." *Journal of Gerontological Social Work* 26 (1996): 117–131.

Chapter 2

Baltes, Paul B. "The Aging Mind: Potential and Limits." *The Gerontologist* 33 (1993): 580–594.

Brokaw, Tom. *The Greatest Generation.* New York: Random House, 1998.

Brubaker, Timothy H. *Later Life Families.* Newbury Park, Calif.: Sage Publications, 1985.

De Luca, Sara. *Dancing the Cows Home: A Wisconsin Girlhood.* St. Paul, Minn.: Minnesota Historical Society Press, 1996.

Heilbrun, Carolyn G. *The Last Gift of Time: Life beyond Sixty.* New York: Dial Press, 1997.

Moss, M. S. and S. Z. Moss. "The Image of the Deceased Spouse in Remarriage of Elderly Widow(er)s." *Journal of Gerontological Social Work* 3 (1980): 59–70.

O'Faolain, Nuala. *Are You Somebody? The Accidental Memoir of a Dublin Woman.* New York: Henry Holt and Co., 1996.

Seay, Elizabeth. "Elizabeth Seay Reports." *Wall Street Journal* 1 June 1998, sec. Encore.

Simpson, Eileen. *Late Love: A Celebration of Marriage after Fifty.* Boston and New York: Houghton Mifflin Co., 1994.

Chapter 3

Browder, Sue. "Too Good to Be True."*New Woman Magazine* (November 1994).

Goldsmith, Olivia. *First Wives Club*. Crofton, Md.: Poseidon Press, 1992; New York: Pocket Books, 1994.

Hite, Shere. *The Hite Report: A Nationwide Study of Female Sexuality*. New York: Dell, 1977.

Hoffman, Dustin. "At the Movies." Interview by Bernard Weinraub. *New York Times* 26 March 1999, sec. E.

Márquez, Gabriel Garcia. *Love in the Time of Cholera*. New York: Alfred A. Knopf, 1988.

Pickett, Keri. *Love in the Nineties*. New York: Warner Books, 1995.

Seabrook, Jeremy. "Mr. and Mrs. Cosgrove." In *Aging and Later Life*. Thousand Oaks, Calif.: Sage Publications, 1993.

Szwabo, Peggy A., and Kenneth Solomon. "The Work-Oriented Culture: Success and Power in Elderly Men." In *Older Men's Lives*. Thousand Oaks, Calif.: Sage, 1994.

Age-Related Variation in Sexual Activity and Interest in Normal Men: Results from the Massachusetts Male Aging Study. MacArthur Mid-Life Development Project, 1994.

Chapter 4

Bayley, John. *Elegy for Iris*. New York: St. Martin's Press, 1999.

Carter, Jimmy. *The Virtues of Aging*. New York: Ballantine Books, 1998.

Cavell, Stanley. *Pursuits of Happiness: The Hollywood Comedy of Remarriage*. Cambridge, Mass.: Harvard University Press, 1981.

Collier, David. *Living Happily Ever After*. San Francisco, Calif.: Chronicle Books, 1996.

Davis, Ossie, and Ruby Dee. *With Ossie and Ruby: In This Life Together*. New York: William Morrow and Co., 1998.

Kautz, Donald D. "The Maturing of Sexual Intimacy in Older Adult Couples." Unpublished Ph.D. thesis, University of Kentucky, 1995.

Kellett, J. H. "Sexuality of the Elderly." *Journal of Sexual and Marital Therapy* (St. George's Hospital, London) 6, no. 2 (1991): 147–155.

Lakritz, Kenneth R., and Thomas M. Knoblauch. *Elders on Love.* New York: Parabola Books, 1999.

Chapter 5

Adelman, Marcy. *Lesbian Passages.* Los Angeles, Calif.: Alyson Publications, 1986.

Berger, Raymond W. *Gay and Gray: The Older Homosexual Man.* New York and London: Haworth Press, 1996.

Holmlund, Mona, and Cyndy Warwick. *Women Together: Portraits of Love, Commitment, and Life.* Philadelphia and London: Running Press, 1999.

Jackson, Charles O. *The Other Americans: Sexual Variance in the National Past.* Westport, Conn.: Praeger, 1996.

Mackey, Richard A., Bernard A. O'Brien, and Eileen Mackey. *Gay and Lesbian Couples: Voices from Lasting Relationships.* Westport, Conn.: Praeger, 1997.

Slater, Suzanne. *The Lesbian Family Life Circle.* New York: Free Press, 1995; Urbana, Ill.: University of Illinois Press, 1999.

Sullivan, Andrew. *Virtually Normal: An Argument about Homosexuality.* New York: Alfred A. Knopf, 1995; New York: Random House/Vintage, 1996.

Chapter 6

Albom, Mitch. *Tuesdays with Morrie.* New York: Doubleday, 1997.

Cross, Susan, and Hazel Marcus. "Possible Selves across the Life Span." *Journal of Human Development* no. 34 (1991): 230–255.

Erikson, Erik. *Vital Involvement in Old Age.* New York: W.W. Norton, 1989.

Fisher, M. F. K. *Sister Age.* New York: Vintage Books, 1984.

Grumbach, Doris. *Coming into the End Zone: A Memoir.* New York: W.W. Norton, 1991.

————. *Extra Innings.* New York: W.W. Norton, 1993.

————. *Fifty Days of Solitude.* Boston, Mass.: Beacon Press, 1994.

————. *Life in a Day.* Boston, Mass.: Beacon Press, 1996.

Hillman, James. *The Force of Character and the Lasting Life.* New York: Random House, 1999.

Holland, Barbara. *One's Company.* Pleasantville, N.Y.: Akadine Press, 1996.

Luke, Helen M. *Old Age: A Journey into Simplicity.* New York: Parabola Books, 1987.

Powell, Douglas H. *Nine Myths of Aging.* New York: W. H. Freeman and Co., 1998.

Sarton, May. *At Seventy.* New York: W.W. Norton, 1984.

Storr, Anthony. *Solitude: A Return to the Self.* New York: Ballantine Books, 1988.

Resources

Further Reading

Alexander, Lydia Lewis, Marilyn Hill Harper, Otis Holloway Owens, and Mildred Lucas Patterson. *Wearing Purple: Letters of Four Old Friends*. New York: Harmony Books, 1996.

Banner, Lois W. *In Full Flower: Aging Women, Power, and Sexuality*. New York: Vintage Books, 1993.

Berman, Phillip L., ed. *The Courage to Grow Old*. New York: Ballantine Books, 1989.

Blythe, Ronald. *The View in Winter*. New York: Harcourt Brace Jovanovich, 1979.

Facio, Elisa. *Understanding Older Chicanas: Sociological and Policy Perspectives*. Thousand Oaks, Calif.: Sage Publications, 1996.

Jackson, James S. *Aging in Black America*. Newbury Park, Calif.: Sage Publications, 1993.

Janeway, Elizabeth. *Between Myth and Morning: Women Awakening*. New York: William Morrow and Co., 1974.

Keith, Jennie. *The Aging Experience: Diversity and Commonality across Cultures.* Thousand Oaks, Calif.: Sage Publications, 1994.

Macdonald, Barbara, with Cynthia Rich. *Look Me in the Eye: Old Women, Aging, and Ageism.* Minneapolis, Minn.: Spinsters Ink Press, 1983. Reprint, 1991.

Markides, Kyriakos S., and Charles H. Mindel. *Aging and Ethnicity.* Newbury Park, Calif.; London; and New Delhi, India: Sage Publications, 1987.

Nelson, Jill. *Straight, No Chaser: How I Became a Grown-Up Black Woman.* New York: G. P. Putnam's Sons, 1997.

Pogrebin, Letty Cottin. *Getting Over Getting Older: An Intimate Journey.* New York: Little Brown, 1996.

Rowe, John W., and Robert L. Kahn. *Successful Aging.* New York: Dell Publishing, 1998 (The final report of the ten-year MacArthur Foundation Study of Aging in America.)

Trujillo, Carla. *Living Chicana Theory.* Berkeley, Calif.: Third Woman Press, 1998.

Vaz, Kim Marie. *Black Women in America.* Thousand Oaks, Calif.: Sage Publications, 1993.

Wolf, Naomi. *The Beauty Myth.* New York: William Morrow and Co., 1991.

Senior Web Resources

AARP at http://www.aarp.org

The AARP Guide to Internet Resources Related to Aging can be found on-line at http://www.aarp.org/cyber/guide1.htm The guide lists and describes Internet sites of interest to older people and those concerned with aging-related issues, including researchers, policy makers, service providers, caregivers, and students.

Age of Reason at http://www.ageofreason.com/

A Seniors Internet Resource Center "Wherever You Want to Go Today, You Can Get There from Here!"

ElderWeb at http://www.elderweb.com

This award-winning site is the oldest and largest eldercare sourcebook on the Web. It is a research site for professionals and family members, with more than forty-five hundred links to eldercare and long-term care information on legal, financial, medical, and housing issues, as well as policy, research, and statistics.

Medicare Web Site at http://www.medicare.gov

The official U.S. Government site for Medicare information.

American Medical Association Physician Select at http://www.ama-assn.org/aps/amahg.htm

AMA Physician Select provides information on virtually every licensed physician in the United States and its possessions, including more than 650,000 doctors of medicine (M.D.) and doctors of osteopathy or osteopathic medicine (D.O.). All physician credential data have been verified for accuracy and authenticated by accrediting agencies, medical schools, residency training programs, licensing and certifying boards, and other data sources. Visitors are invited to search for a physician

Grand Times at http://www.grandtimes.com/mags

Serving savvy seniors since 1995, this is a unique weekly Internet magazine for seniors. Controversial, entertaining, and informative, *Grand Times* celebrates life's opportunities and examines life's challenges.

National Aging Information Center at http://www.aoa.dhhs.gov/naic

Part of the U.S. Administration on Aging, this Web site features programs that help older people and their caregivers enhance and support their independence.

National Senior Citizens Law Center at http://www.nsclc.org

The National Senior Citizens Law Center advocates nationwide to promote the independence and well-being of low-income elderly individuals, as well as persons with disabilities, with particular emphasis on women and racial and ethnic minorities. As a national support center, NSCLC advocates through litigation, legislative and agency representation, and assistance to attorneys and paralegals in field programs. NSCLC's functions vary with the needs of its clients. NSCLC maintains a national reputation for professional quality and successful advocacy.

Cyndi's Genealogy Links at http://www.cyndislist.com
A very comprehensive site, with more than thirty thousand links, that provides a great deal of information for anyone interested in genealogy. This site is frequently updated and is ideal for beginners and experts alike.

Pharminfonet at http://pharminfo.com
Devoted to delivering pharmaceutical information to pharmacists, physicians, and patients, it includes frequently asked questions about drugs with answers from pharmaceutical manufacturers and other sources, and a moderated archive of drug-related discussion threads. The site is sponsored by VirSci Corporation in cooperation with Pharmaceutical Information Associates, Ltd. (USA)

Seniors Search at http://www.seniorssearch.com
The only search directory exclusively for the over-fifty age group.

Social Security Administration at
http://www.ssa.gov/SSA_Home.html
The official Web site of the Social Security Administration.

Third Age at http://www.thirdage.com
ThirdAge.com is the on-line home of a vibrant on-line society filled with ideas and interactions generated, hosted, and

reflected by the views of its citizens — the ThirdAgers themselves. It is a Web-based community started by ThirdAge Media, Inc. where ThirdAgers can voice their opinions, recount experiences, and share advice with new friends through interactive technologies such as chat rooms and discussion boards. It presents the best the Web has to offer for active older adults. ThirdAge.com offers rich advice and helpful information on topics critical to the ThirdAge community, such as retirement housing and estate management — areas typically ignored or glossed over by traditional media. T. S. Eliot said, "The job of older men [and women] is to be explorers." ThirdAge.com is the place to explore and discover the people, activities, and resources important to the third age of life.

Virtual Reference

Senior's Issues at http://www.dreamscape.com/frankvad/reference-seniors.html
This site contains links to more than twenty-five hundred of the most popular information reference locations and tools on the Web.

WidowNet at http://www.fortnet.org/WidowNet
An information and self-help resource for, and by, widows and widowers. Topics covered include grief, bereavement, recovery, and other information helpful to people, of all ages, religious backgrounds, and sexual orientations, who have suffered the death of a spouse or life partner.

YAHOO: A Guide to WWW at http://www.yahoo.com
YAHOO! (Yet Another Hierarchically Organized Oracle) is an easy-to-use hierarchical subject-oriented catalog for searching the World Wide Web on words or phrases contained in a URL, a title, and/or description of a WWW home page. YAHOO! is especially useful for making a fairly quick search through major Web resources and produces good search results

that are not overly exhaustive or comprehensive. There's also a link to the YAHOO Seniors' Guide (http://seniors.yahoo.com/) that includes news, community message boards, and links to numerous topics of interest to seniors.

CapWeb at http://www.capweb.net

A guide to the U.S. Congress that provides a mailing address, telephone and fax numbers, and an E-mail address for every member of the House and Senate. It also provides committee assignments. It has links to the separate home pages of both the House and the Senate, as well as to home pages within the executive and judicial branches of the U.S. government.

Health: Diseases and Conditions at http://dir.yahoo.com/health/diseases_and_conditions/

This site contains an alphabetical listing of numerous links to sites with information on particular diseases and conditions located at the YAHOO Web site.

Books and Book Collecting at http://www.trussel.com/f_books.htm

This site enables searching for used, out-of-print, hard-to-find, rare, and collectible books on the Web from on-line booksellers. Search by individual booksellers or use forms that will search multiple booksellers at once.

Mapquest at http://www.mapquest.com

Looking for an address, town, or zip code? Get and print maps worldwide! This site provides driving directions from starting address to destination address shown as maps and text.

Dogpile at http://www.dogpile.com

Search for information on the Web using multiple search engines at once.

infospace.com at http://www.infospace.com
This site offers a white pages directory for phone, E-mail, and address searches and includes reverse home or business phone lookup and reverse address lookup services.

US Postal Service Zip+4 Code Lookup at
http://www.usps.gov/ncsc/lookups/lookup_zip+4.html
Don't have a zip code? Simply enter an address. If found, the standardized address and ZIP+4 Code will be displayed.

Telephone Directories on the Web at http://www.teldir.com
Telephone Directories on the Web is the Internet's original and most detailed index of on-line phone books with links to yellow pages, white pages, business directories, E-mail addresses, and fax listings from more than 150 countries.

Non Profit and Service Organizations for Seniors

SAGE — Senior Action in a Gay Environment
305 Seventh Avenue, 16th Floor
New York, NY 10001
(212) 741-2247
http://sageusa.org
Located in New York City, SAGE is the nation's oldest and largest community-based intergenerational social service agency dedicated to honoring, caring for, and celebrating the lesbian and gay community's senior members. With a membership base of more than three thousand, the agency runs a Senior Drop-In Center, is a licensed mental health clinic, and provides complete case management and social services to more than one thousand clients each month. Through its outreach and education efforts, SAGE combats the dual discrimination of ageism and antigay bigotry faced by senior lesbians and gay men.

AARP
60 E Street, NW
Washington, DC 20049
Phone: (800) 424-3410 or (202) 434-2277
www.aarp.org

AARP promotes and supports senior advocacy, education, and community service activities in states and communities. AARP works in both private and public sectors to improve the quality of life for its members and for all Americans as they grow older. There are offices in every state. Consult the AARP office directory at http://www.aarp.org/statepages for state offices.

NCOA — The National Council on the Aging, Inc.
409 Third Street, SW
Washington, DC 20004
(202) 479-1200
Fax: (202) 479-0735
E-mail: info@ncoa.org
http://www.ncoa.org

NCOA is a private, nonprofit association committed to promoting the dignity, self-determination, well-being, and contributions of older persons.

Corporation for National Service
1201 New York Avenue, NW
Washington, DC 20525
(202) 606-5000
E-mail: webmaster@cns.gov
http://www.fostergrandparents.org

Through the CNS's National Senior Service Corps, nearly half a million Americans age fifty-five and older share their time and talents to help their communities.

Elderhostel, Inc.
75 Federal Street
Boston, MA 02110-1941
(877) 426-8056
(Toll free Monday through Friday, 9:00 A.M. to 9:00 P.M.)
http://www.elderhostel.org
Elderhostel, Inc. is a not-for-profit organization with twenty-five years of experience providing high-quality, affordable, educational adventures for adults fifty-five and older. These short-term educational programs are a fun and exciting way to share new ideas, explore new places, and make new friends.

SeniorNet
121 Second Street, 7th Floor
San Francisco, CA 94105
(415) 495-4990
Fax: (415) 495-3999
http://www.seniornet.org
The nonprofit SeniorNet provides adults age fifty and older with education for and access to computer technology to enhance their lives and enable them to share their knowledge and wisdom.

Federal Agencies (Selections from the Government Organization Manual On-line)

Department of Health and Human Services
200 Independence Avenue SW, Washington, DC 20201
(202) 619-0257 http://www.dhhs.gov

Administration on Aging
330 Independence Avenue SW, Washington, DC 20201
(202) 401-4541 http://www.aoa.dhhs.gov

State Resources of the Administration on Aging:
State Agencies on Aging at
http://www.aoa.dhhs.gov/aoa/pages/state.html

Resource Directory for Older People at
http://www.aoa.dhhs.gov/aoa/dir/toc.html

State Index of Aging Agencies and Programs at
http://www.aoa.dhhs.gov/aoa/webres/index.htm

Listing of Area Agencies on Aging by state at
http://www.aoa.dhhs.gov/aoa/webres/area-agn.htm

Listing of State Agencies on Aging at
http://www.aoa.dhhs.gov/aoa/webres/state-ag.htm

Health Care Financing Administration
200 Independence Avenue SW, Washington, DC 20201
(202) 690-6726 http://www.hcfa.gov

National Institutes of Health
9000 Rockville Pike, Bethesda, MD 20892
(301) 496-4000 http://www.nih.gov

U.S. Department of Labor
200 Constitution Avenue NW, Washington, DC 20210
(202) 219-5000 http://www.dol.gov

U.S. Department of Veterans Affairs
810 Vermont Avenue NW, Washington, DC 20420
(202) 273-4900 http://www.va.gov

Social Security Administration
6401 Security Boulevard, Baltimore, MD 21235
(410) 965-1234 http://www.ssa.gov

Smithsonian Institution
1000 Jefferson Drive SW, Washington, DC 20560
(202) 357-1300 or Smithsonian Information Center at
(202) 357-2700 http://www.si.edu

U.S. Government Printing Office
732 North Capitol Street NW, Washington, DC 20401
(202) 512-0000 http://www.access.gpo.gov

Library of Congress
101 Independence Avenue SE, Washington, DC 20540
(202) 707-5000 http://www.loc.gov

For a list of government search engines (U.S. and foreign)
go to http://www.internets.com/govt.htm

LA-2001-17-7

Permissions
Acknowledgments

Grateful acknowledgment is made to the following publishers and authors for permission to reprint selected materials:

"General Review of the Sex Situation," © 1926, renewed © 1954 by Dorothy Parker, from *The Portable Dorothy Parker*, by Dorothy Parker. Used by permission of Viking Penguin, a division of Penguin Putnam, Inc.

"Both Sides Now," by Joni Mitchell, © 1967 Siquomb Publishing Corp., © renewed, assigned to Crazy Crow Music. All rights reserved. Used by permission of Warner Bros. Publications U.S., Inc., Miami, FL 33014.

From *The Last Gift of Time* by Carolyn G. Heilbrun. © 1997 by Carolyn G. Heilbrun. Used by permission of the Dial Press/Dell Publishing, a division of Random House, Inc.

265

Left Out: The Politics of Exclusion/Essays 1964-1999 © 1999 Martin Duberman. Reprinted by permission of the author and Basic Books, a member of the Perseus Books Group.

One's Company by Barbara Holland. © 1992 by Barbara Holland. A Common Reader edition published 1996 by The Akadine Press, Inc. Excerpt reprinted by permission of author.

"Senior Citizen On an Uptown Bus" by Irwin Hasen; © 1999 by the New York Times Co.; reprinted by permission of the New York Times Co. and the author.

Dancing The Cows Home, © 1996 by Sara De Luca; reprinted by permission of the Minnesota Historical Society Press, St.Paul, MN.

"Old Is for Books" from *Verses from 1929 On* by Ogden Nash; © 1954 by Ogden Nash; first appeared in The New Yorker. By permission of Little, Brown & Co.

"I'm In Love Again," by Cole Porter, © 1925. Renewed, Warner Bros. Inc. (ASCAP). All rights reserved; used by permission Warner Bros. Publications, U.S., Inc., Miami, FL 33014.

Acknowledgments

My first thanks must go to the many men and women who shared their personal stories with me over the many hours and days that stretched into years. They were inspiring examples of love and aging. Though I have carefully disguised their identities as they wished, I hope my admiration of, respect for, and gratitude to each elder is clear.

In the preparation of this book, a feminist collective emerged, spiced with assistance from men who understood and supported the venture.

The path to publication began with advice and suggestions from my colleague and friend, Linda Nelson. Next in our network was Joyce Engelson, my editor on an earlier book, and now a guiding member of an independent editors' group. Joyce's skills and experience, developed during her distinguished publishing career, were invaluable in getting the work moving.

My agent, Roslyn Targ, has a fund of wise experience in the care and feeding of authors, the pursuit of publishers, and the generation of triumphant sales of virtually every genre. The road to publication is often torturous and misery laden, but Roz offered not only her professionalism but also made that path almost enjoyable with her competence and her sparkle (a cross between Auntie Mame and Susan Sontag). Her early support of the central idea was crucial.

The manuscript could not have developed and come to fruition without the dedicated work of these three women:

Gina Misiroglu, my editor at New World Library, who is, in every way, an author's dream of an editor. Her indefatigable devotion to helping me shape a book that would inspire readers with thoughtful philosophy combined with accurate reporting was a gift that graced the work at every step.

Mary Greene, research assistant and computer consultant, whose unusual abilities as an empathetic reader of the text made her able to provide help almost before I knew where it might be needed. Her sense of humor was, as always, a key prop for sanity. Her outstanding research abilities contributed so much that the collaboration has solidified a twenty-five-year friendship that grows deeper and dearer as we survive more near shipwrecks together.

Roberta Livingstone, production chief, who early and late, took mountains of messy copy into her skillful hands and made all into seamlessly handsome, correct digital text. Her patience and cheerfulness in the face of many revisions, numerous drafts, sudden new requirements, and shifting deadlines have become legendary. She made the task of writing the book in New York in cooperation with an editor in California seem uncomplicated, and her warm, witty kindness — with supportive faxes at midnight — brought comfort and connection to the isolating task of writing. Her computer fix-it skills verge on the surreal.

Additional expertise, help, insights, and support were given by Richard J. Cross, M.D.; Mildred Byrum, Ph.D.; William

Segal; Marielle Bancou; Steve Crohn; Carolyn Altman and Phillip Piro of SAGE; Rabbis Sidney Kleiman and Gideon Shloush; Adele Holman, Ph.D.; and Janice Sorkow.

A blessed circle of close friends gave hospitality on fact-finding trips, made dinner when even Chinese takeout seemed too hard to arrange, and listened patiently to endless discussions of late life love. These are the same friends who have been by my side through joys and sorrows of every kind and are cherished always. Two more women — Toni Lemoine in Block Island and Irene Caceres in New York — helped keep domestic life going while I was incommunicado.

Profound love and gratitude goes, of course, to my partner, Bud Nye, who was cheerleader-in-chief from the beginning, always believing our story and others like it would be helpful to older people if we could get these stories told in a hopeful way. His unwavering belief was a great antidote to doubt and discouragement.

And crowning all such gifts were the love and support from my family: my three children and their mates and my grandchildren. They have enriched my knowledge of love in the later years. They sustain, educate, and delight me.

— Zenith Henkin Gross

About the Author

Zenith Henkin Gross has been a journalist for nearly five decades, beginning as a copy girl on an Ohio daily while still in high school. In college, she was a "stringer" for nearby metropolitan newspapers, and then worked for the Associated Press and several Midwestern papers. She became a researcher-writer on public affairs for the RCA Corporation and was the first woman executive at RCA's corporate headquarters in the l960s and 1970s. She is the author of the bestselling book on family relations, *And You Thought It Was All Over: Mothers and Their Adult Children*. Her second book, *Seasons of the Heart,* was written from the heart — from both her personal experience with late-life love and the testimony of countless others. She lives and works in New York City.

If you enjoyed *Seasons of the Heart,* we recommend the following books from New World Library and H J Kramer.:

Creative Visualization by Shakti Gawain. The classic work (in print for more than twenty years, three million copies sold) that shows us how to use the power of our imagination to create what we want in life. Available on audio as well, in two formats: the complete book on tape and selected meditations from the book.

Embracing Each Other by Hal Stone, Ph.D., and Sidra Stone, Ph.D. This highly acclaimed, groundbreaking work describes the Psychology of Selves and the Voice Dialogue method, one of the most effective techniques in psychology today. Internationally renowned psychologists Hal and Sidra Stone introduce the reader to the Pusher, Critic, Protector/ Controller, and all the other members of your inner family.

Living in the Light: A Guide to Personal and Planetary Transformation (Revised) by Shakti Gawain, with Laurel King. A newly updated edition of the recognized classic on developing intuition and using it as a guide in living your life.

The Path of Transformation: How Healing Ourselves Can Change the World (Revised) by Shakti Gawain. Shakti gave us *Creative Visualization* in the '70s, *Living in the Light* in the '80s, and now *The Path of Transformation* for the new millennium. This book delivers an inspiring and provocative message for the path of transformation.

Partnering by Hal Stone, Ph.D., and Sidra Stone, Ph.D. This practical and inspiring guide shows readers how to keep the magic in relationships alive and how to embrace the lessons that relationship has to teach.

The Power of Now by Eckhart Tolle. In *The Power of Now* Tolle shows readers how to recognize themselves as the creators of their own pain, and how to have a pain-free existence by living fully in the present. Accessing the deepest self — the true self — can be learned, he says, by freeing ourselves from the conflicting, unreasonable demands of the mind and living "present, fully, and intensely in the Now." A brilliant work.

Soulmates by Carolyn Godschild Miller. In her lively conversational style, Dr. Carolyn Miller, author of *Creating Miracles*, takes an in-depth look at a topic of perennial fascination. Sharing her own quest and that of dozens of other couples for a meant-to-be relationship, she uses true and extraordinary stories to illustrate what she means by inner guidance. Contrary to popular belief, soulmate couples do not usually recognize each other at first glance.

20 Communication Tips for Couples by Doyle Barnett. This is a readily accessible guide aimed at any person interested in improving communications with his or her partner. If you spend just five minutes with this little book, you'll find yourself picking up tips that help make every relationship you have a better one.

20 Communication Tips for Families by Eric Maisel. This book is aimed at busy parents who want to improve their relationships with their spouse and children but don't have time to wade through a thick self-help guide. *20 Communication Tips for Families* takes about 30 minutes to read and offers specific ways for family members to communicate better and, in the process, grow closer.

New World Library is dedicated to publishing
books and audio and video projects
that inspire and challenge us
to improve the quality of our lives
and the world.

New World Library
14 Pamaron Way
Novato, CA 94949

Phone: (415) 884-2100
Fax: (415) 884-2199
Or call toll-free (800) 972-6657
Catalog Requests: Ext. 50
Ordering: Ext. 52

E-mail: escort@nwlib.com
www.nwlib.com
www.newworldlibrary.com